COLSTON'S GIRLS' SCHOOL

Colston's Girls' School
The First Hundred Years

Sarah Dunn

with additional material
contributed by

Margaret Swindale
Jill Clough

REDCLIFFE
Bristol

First published in 1991
by Redcliffe Press Ltd.,
49 Park St., Bristol

ISBN 1 872971 31 8

Typeset by Selectmove Ltd
and printed by The Longdunn Press Ltd., Bristol

CONTENTS

Beginnings	1
Miss Smith	27
Miss Hughes	43
Miss Sparks	83
Miss Drew	115
Miss Morgan	122
Miss Green	150
Miss Dunn	170
Miss Parkin	193
Mrs Franklin	217
Head Mistresses and Chairmen of Governors	223
Governing Body 1990-91	224
Staff on Centenary Day, 1991	225
Contributors	229
Acknowledgements	230
Index	231

BEGINNINGS

Each year on the first Friday in November, Colston's Girls' School meets in Bristol Cathedral for a Commemoration Service. Within the framework of the service of Matins the Chairman of the Governors reads an extract from the Colston Settlement:

> To all Christian people to whom these Presents shall come, I Edward Colston, of Mortlake in the County of Surrey, Esquire, send greeting. Whereas I have by indenture, bearing date 24th and 25th November in the seventh year of the Reign of our late Sovereign Lady Queen Anne, Annoque Domini 1708, granted and conveyed several Manors, Messuages, Fees, Farm Rents, Lands, Tenements and Heridataments therein particularly mentioned, in trust . . . that the Master, Wardens, Assistants and Commonalty of Merchant Adventurers in the City of Bristol and their successors for ever, hold and enjoy the said Manors and Premises and apply the Rents and Profits thereof for the Maintenance, Schooling, Education and binding Apprentice of One hundred poor boys.
>
> Now know ye further by these Presents that I the said Edward Colston do make several Orders Rules and Directions to the end that all such Children as shall be admitted to the Hospital may be educated and brought up in the true faith and belief of the Church of England and may not swerve, stray or fall off from the same.

Even allowing for this being a short quotation from a long document, it is puzzling, and successive Chairmen have added explanations:

> The use of the expression 'Hospital' to describe a boys' school sounds strange to our ears, but we must remember that at that date the word did not only denote an Infirmary, but could mean any institution in which anyone received free board and lodging or hospitality.
>
> In 1875 the terms of Mr Colston's Hospital Trust were drastically reformed by the Endowed Schools Commissioners. By their scheme a portion of the endowment was to be set aside to provide a Day School for Girls. The scheme could not however be fulfilled until 1885 when the Merchant Venturers relieved the Trust of the whole expense of the Bristol Trade School (afterwards known as the Merchant Venturers' Technical College) by making their own Society directly responsible for it. By this action they set free sufficient money to enable the Colston Hospital Trust to build and establish the Girls' School in the Cheltenham Road. The School was opened in January 1891.

Questions remain. What was the Endowed Schools Commission and why did it make 'drastic reforms'? How does the Bristol Trade School come into the picture? And why, if a Girls' School was decreed in 1875, did it not open until 1891?

Edward Colston was a Bristolian who made an immense fortune in the City of London. He never married and had no direct heirs, although he came of a numerous family. During the latter part of his life he gave away great sums of money but it was a feature of his benefactions that he laid down very strict rules as to the administration of the charities he founded and the conduct and way of life of those who benefited from them. High Anglican and high Tory, he would feel it was his duty to do so.

He thought that poverty could be relieved and crime reduced if poor boys were given shelter and the means eventually to earn an honest living. His first idea was an institution in which fifty boys would be housed, fed and clothed, taught the Church Catechism, reading, writing and elementary arithmetic and, as soon as practicable, apprenticed. No boy was ever to be apprenticed to a Dissenter and the Master of the School and his few assistants were all to be members of the Established Church. Staff and boys were to attend church services regularly, not only on Sundays but also on Saints' Days. His requirements for the organisation and inspection of his Hospital were as stringent. He proposed to endow it in perpetuity and needed some corporate body to agree to be its Trustees. He is said to have first thought of offering it to a London borough, and did open negotiations with Bristol Corporation but could not reach agreement on his terms. The Society of Merchant Venturers in Bristol was thus not his first choice, but he had already had dealings with the Society when in 1696 he endowed the Colston's Almshouses on St Michael's Hill, and the Merchant Venturers had accepted the responsibility of administering the endowment and, after Colston's death, of choosing the people who should live there. At Merchants' Hall there would be sympathy for Colston's views and intentions. The Society already gave substantial sums of money to charities in Bristol and the surrounding area, with much the same aims.

In 1706 the Merchant Venturers agreed to be the Trustees of Colston's Hospital. The early stages of the negotiations must have met with Colston's approval, for he increased the number of boys who were to be in residence at any one time from fifty to a hundred. He had spent £18,000 on estates which he reckoned would yield the £850 a year needed for the original fifty and now added to this purchases which would provide a further £600 a year. The Hospital did not admit the first scholars until 1710. Much of the time since 1706 had been spent in negotiation over the exact terms of the settlement.

In spite of the length of these discussions, in practice there were difficulties from the very beginning. The first Schoolmaster was dismissed in 1717. The Society, whose duty it was to choose the next incumbent, passed over the candidate Colston suggested and appointed their own Beadle who in future would combine work for the Society, such as rent collecting, with being the Master of the Hospital. Colston was incensed. He also disapproved of the quality of the supervision the Society gave to the work of the Hospital, reminding the Merchants that it was their duty to inspect it at least four times a year. He proposed a grievance procedure which was agreed to by the

Society. The Society must have felt that their whole conduct of the Hospital was being watched and critically commented on only too readily.

The Society's problems did not end with Colston's death in 1721. It took nearly fifty years and an action in Chancery to make his executors produce money which was due to the Society under the Colston's Hospital Settlement. Worse still, an unresolved ambiguity as to the management of the Hospital's financial affairs led in 1842 to an action being brought by the Attorney General against the Society. Put very simply, the case against the Society depended on the view that all the income from the Colston's Hospital endowment should be devoted to the Hospital and that any property acquired with that income should belong to the Colston's Hospital Trust. The Society, on the other hand, believed that its responsibility was to make provision for up to 100 boys (the number had dropped at the end of the eighteenth century) in the way that Colston had required them to, and that their obligation ended there. They were able to show that for most of the first hundred years the Hospital had been in debt to the Society and that the Society had not demanded payment of these debts when times for the Trust were better. They argued that when there was a surplus after the boys and staff of the Hospital had been provided for they could use the money for other purposes. Their interpretation of the matter was shared by other Trustees at the time and they believed sincerely and indeed passionately in the rightness of their past conduct. The case was heard by the Master of the Rolls, who found against the Society. The Society decided to appeal to the Lord Chancellor. Eventually in 1848, he upheld the previous decision and the Society had to repay the Colston's Hospital Trust the money it had used for other purposes; it was not, however, able to reclaim the sums it had spent on the Hospital in times of need. The Merchants could have been pardoned for regretting that their predecessors had ever taken on the Colston's Hospital Trust. In fact, they continued to discharge what they saw as their duty both faithfully and generously. There was a worse upheaval to come in the affairs of the Hospital than the Attorney General's suit.

The Committee of Inquiry into Charities began its work in 1818 and continued for the next twenty years. Its purpose was a review of existing endowed charities and an investigation into records and accounts which would reveal the conduct of trustees. Abuses which had long been suspected were shown to exist and where necessary, legal steps were taken to put right financial irregularities. Then and later, people's attention was drawn to a feature of endowed charities: it is extremely difficult to devise a charity which will continue for a long period of time to be useful, or even to comply with the benefactor's intentions. A charity is set up to meet a particular need which exists at the time of its institution. In future the need may disappear, or be met in some other way. An example of this is to be found in the many charities set up in the late nineteenth and early twentieth centuries to enable poor students to take up university places. When local education authority grants became available to everyone who secured a university place and whose parents could not pay the full cost of the student's maintenance during the course, the usefulness of these charities for undergraduates declined. At the same time, the effect of inflation has been that an endowment designed to provide a fixed sum each year may have also declined in real value. The Inquiry into Charities, by making people aware of the impossibility of forecasting future needs, led to a re-appraisal of the inviolability of a benefactor's wishes. The re-examination of ends and means had particularly far reaching results in the field of education.

It is hard for us near the end of the twentieth century to imagine a time when not only not every child went to school but there were not enough school places if all parents had wished to send their children to school. This was the case in the mid-nineteenth century. There was a great variety of schools, from the great public schools such as Eton and Winchester, which were boarding schools for the sons of the wealthy, to dame schools like the one in Dickens's *Great Expectations*, presided over by Mr Wopsle's sleeping great aunt and actually being taught by Biddy, an untidy girl with her pitifully few tattered books. Between these two extremes there were the endowed schools, the denominational schools and schools set up as private ventures of different kinds. Those who were capable of judging considered that English education as a whole compared unfavourably with that of many Continental countries, both in the standards achieved and the proportion of the population being taught. It was accepted that the better educated a soldier or a craftsman was, the more effective he was when plying his trade and it was feared that in competition for trade and commerce the country would lag behind those whose workforce was better instructed generally as well as vocationally. There was widespread interest in the matter and in the Eighteen Sixties national initiatives, as distinct from individual enterprises, were taken.

One of these culminated in the Elementary Education Act of 1870 which was intended to give every child, however poor his parents might be, the opportunity to attend school. It did not sweep away the variety of schools which already existed, but added to the number of available school places. Local school boards were to be elected. They were to discover how many additional school places were needed in their locality and with the help of the government were to provide them. Parents were to be charged no more than 9d a week; many boards charged much less than this. Children went to school at five and could remain until they were thirteen; for those already in employment under that age there existed regulations as to the number of hours of instruction they were to receive each day. By 1880 it was compulsory for parents to send their children to school, although the rate of attendance was low by modern standards. After 1891 school boards were not required to charge a weekly fee.

This system of elementary schooling was designed for the children of the 'labouring classes'. What upper and middle class parents wanted was better provision of what we now think of as secondary schools. A commission set up in 1861 under the chairmanship of Lord Clarendon investigated nine public schools and found much to commend in them. They were encouraged to widen their curricula; in particular, to include the elements of natural science. The commissioners, noting that some schools were being limited as to the subjects they could teach by the terms of their original endowments, took steps to remove these barriers to a wider education.

A second commission in 1864, chaired by Lord Taunton, looked into the rest of secondary education, the schools of the middle classes. The commissioners did not report for four years and had not been idle during that time. They found standards low, aims mistaken and the provision unequal when one district was compared with another, a serious defect as most of these schools were day schools. They were particularly scathing about the girls' schools they visited, where the emphasis was on accomplishments, which could be paraded socially, at the expense of thorough learning and the training of the mind. So gloomy a picture could not but alarm those concerned with the education of the nation, but nothing was done immediately about the entirety of these schools. Instead, parliament turned its attention to an important group among them. The Taunton report had highlighted the great range in the effectiveness of the endowed grammar schools. A few were flourishing, many were still pursuing antiquated curricula with little relevance to contemporary needs, and some had an endowment and a headmaster but few or no pupils. The government by the Endowed Schools Act of 1869 set up another Commission, but this time with powers to act. Its brief was to examine the income each school received from its endowment to decide whether it could be put to better use, both in respect to the number of pupils and to what they were being taught. Where the commissioners found schools were being hampered by out of date and inappropriate rules laid down by long dead benefactors, they could alter or abolish them. In particular, they were to bear in mind the great need for better schools for girls which the Taunton report had revealed. They would draw up new Articles of Government which would regulate the Governing Body, the appointment of staff, the admission of pupils and all the other matters involved in the conduct of each school. They had very wide powers and a complex task ahead of them, for each foundation was different and as they were usually local day schools, the local situation had to be considered as well.

It is perhaps not surprising that the government chose to concentrate on the endowed schools. By definition, they had money, and this might be used more rationally to produce more school places. If, however, the hope was that some national system of secondary education could be produced by a redeployment of endowed schools' funds, the idea was doomed from the beginning. The schools were scattered very irregularly over the country, in the places where their founders had chosen to put them, and although some were generously endowed, demand for secondary education would by the end of the century far outstrip anything this piecemeal provision could achieve.

The Endowed Schools Commission started work in January 1870. There were three commissioners: Lord Lyttleton, who was connected by marriage to the Prime Minister, Mr Gladstone; Arthur Hobhouse, a lawyer; and Canon Hugh Robinson, the Principal of St John's College, York, an elementary teachers' training college. The Secretary was Henry Roby, and both he and Arthur Hobhouse had worked on the Taunton report and so came to the work with a great deal of knowledge of the state of affairs in secondary schools. They appointed Assistant Commissioners to negotiate with the trustees of the schools and to draw up the new schemes for their management. Amongst these was Joshua Fitch who had been an assistant to the Taunton Commission and had inspected schools in a large part of the north of England. At 46 he was the oldest of the assistant commissioners and he had a long experience of several kinds of teaching. He had been an elementary school teacher, had taken a degree at London University, taught on the staff of a teacher training college and then become its Principal. He was a recognised authority on secondary education. Fitch was sharp tongued and immensely hardworking, and was relentless in his advocacy of the highest possible standards. He was not a member of the Establishment; if he had been he would probably have been a Commissioner instead of an Assistant. He was not afraid of innovation, and infinitely preferred genuine reform to the status quo. One of his particular interests was the education of girls, and he was a helpful friend to several of the leading women educationalists of the time, among them Emily Davies, the founder of Girton College, Cambridge. Unlike the vast majority of his contemporaries he believed that the mental powers of men and women were the same. There were some clever women and some not so clever, just as there were clever men. 'Intellect', he said, 'has no sex.'

The Commissioners knew that Bristol was going to be a hard nut to crack. Before the Commission had even started, a deputation from Bristol had asked that the 'Hospital Schools' – Queen Elizabeth's Hospital, the Red Maids' and Colston's – should be exempt from the provisions of the new Bill. This had of course been refused. When the Commissioners chose Fitch to deal with the Bristol schools they were selecting someone equal to the task.

Before the end of January 1870, Fitch was in Bristol. A local paper refers to him as 'Inspector Fitch' and although this was not his proper title he certainly was inspecting the Bristol schools: their curricula and methods, their standards of achievement, their staffing, the social class of their pupils, and most importantly of all, their finances. In the years of negotiation which lay ahead this was his greatest strength. He could always support his assertions with the evidence he had gathered during this exhaustive investigation. His irredeemable faults in the eyes of the city of Bristol were that he was not a Bristolian, and that he was criticising Bristolian institutions.

He said several times in public and probably even more frequently in private conversation that he wished to listen to the suggestions for reform of local people, and that he did not intend to take any step without the fullest consultation with the trustees of the schools. There is however a difficult stage at the beginning of any negotiation when proposals are as yet so broad and general that it is scarcely useful for anyone to comment on them. People are reluctant to produce counter suggestions without knowing what is not negotiable and what is merely one of several possibilities. Before much progress can be made someone has to produce a plan which can serve as a basis for discussion. Fitch was the one to do this. Even before arriving in Bristol he had become familiar with the requirements of the Endowed Schools Act and he had some ideas on how these might be met in Bristol. His first problem was that he was dealing with people who had little knowledge of the detailed provisions of the Bill. He set about explaining these at public meetings and private discussions. He wrote:

> The general aim of the Commissioners is to provide for boys, wherever the funds of the endowment suffice, a graduated system of schools, receiving scholars above the rank of those of (the elementary schools), and arranged in three classes. It may be well to keep the distinction of the three grades of school clearly in view, in order to understand how far analogous institutions would be desirable for the instruction of girls.
>
> By a first grade school the Commissioners understand one of the highest rank, namely, one designed to prepare boys for the universities. The course of instruction in such a school can not be completed unless the pupil stays until he is 18 years of age. The fees are necessarily high, corresponding to the probable means of the parents who will use the school, and to the qualifications required in the teaching staff. They vary from £10 to £20 per annum for day scholars, and from £60 upwards for boarders. There is an unquestionable demand for such schools for boys, and this demand is already supplied, as you know, in Bristol and elsewhere.
>
> But the Commissioners, as at present advised, do not contemplate the establishment of a school of this class for girls. One may hope that the need of a girls' school of the first rank on a public basis may soon be felt and that an institution similar to the ladies' colleges in London and Cheltenham would be useful and popular in Clifton. But the persons who would first be conscious of such need can easily afford to supply it; and it may well be doubted whether the alienation of any funds now devoted to the educational charities of Bristol, in favour of such an object, would be equitable or expedient.
>
> By a school of the second grade, the Commissioners mean one designed for boys who are not intended for the university, but who will leave school for professions and the higher branches of business at 16 or 17. The course of instruction of such a school would not include Greek; but Latin, French and

German would be taught, mathematics and physical science would receive special attention, and the whole aim would be to give a practical, but yet liberal and high-toned English education, of a modern rather than an exclusively classical type. The fees in such a school would range from £6 to £12 per annum for tuition only; and from £35 to £60 for board and instruction together.

The corresponding schools for girls can hardly be said to exist at all as public institutions. Yet it is the strong opinion of the Commissioners that they are much needed; and all experience and testimony combine to prove that the girls of this class are at present very unsoundly and superficially taught. The course of instruction in such a second grade school as the Commissioners would desire to see established in Bristol would comprehend:

Latin
French and one other foreign language
Arithmetic and the elements of algebra and geometry
History and geography
English language, composition and literature
Drawing
Vocal music
Needlework and the elements of economic science

Instrumental music would also be desired by the parents of the class for whom these schools are designed; but it is doubtful whether it could be advantageously made part of the regular school course, except in the case of boarders.

The head of such a school should be a lady of superior acquirements and proved teaching power. I should look forward to an arrangement whereby the greater part, if not the whole, of the teaching would eventually be entrusted to women. But at present it is hard to find a sufficient supply of governesses possessing the needful qualifications; and some at least of the lessons might with advantage be given by men of the same standing, for example, as the assistant masters in a grammar school. This is a matter, however, which might be left to the governing body.

There should be no extra subjects for instruction at separate charges. The whole teaching resource of the school should be accessible to every pupil, at a fixed rate, or one graduated by age or class only. The fees ought not to be less than £6 or £35, nor more than £10 or £60 a year for day scholars and boarders respectively.

The third grade day school for boys receives, as a rule, the children of those who do not like to use the elementary school, and can afford to dispense with their children's wages until they reach the age of 14 or 15. The course of instruction includes all that is taught in a good primary school, besides French and the rudiments of mathematics, drawing and physical science. It is found that such schools, when on a sufficiently large scale, may be well equipped with good teachers and school requisites, and be practically self supporting at a charge of £4 to £6 per head for day scholars and £18 to £25 per head per annum for boarders, provided that good buildings can once be secured.

Girls' schools of a similar type, and adapted for the same class of scholars, could probably be sustained at less average cost than those for boys; and in them the fees need not rise much higher than the lower of the estimates I have just given for boys. The course of instruction would not be materially different from that for boys. It should aim at a thorough knowledge of English, much sounder discipline in arithmetic than is usually contemplated in even the best

> ladies' schools, and at the same time would not exclude French, drawing and vocal music. Needlework and simple lessons on economics should be taught to all the pupils; while for the boarders – who would, as a rule, be the daughters of farmers and country tradesmen – some practical instruction in household economy would also be necessary.
>
> The mistress and teachers of such a school would best be found among the élite of the certificated mistresses in the elementary schools. It is well known that the governesses of this class have been specially trained in the art of teaching and of school management; and among them are many who have also acquired superior knowledge and cultivation, and are well qualified for higher and more lucrative posts than they now fill.

This summary of a detailed and complicated Bill needs a little further explanation. Greek was required for admission to Oxford or Cambridge and so was taught in the Grade 1 schools. The difference in the tuition fees charged by the three different grades of schools reflects the difference in the salaries paid to the teachers, the more highly qualified being paid more. But it will be noticed that the boarding element in the fees paid by boarders is also different in the three types of school and this reflects the means of the parents using the schools. The parents of a boy in the Grade 1 school were expected to pay more for their son's board and lodging than those with a child in a Grade 3 school; and of course the former expected more for their money than the latter.

Fitch draws attention to two important matters which determined whether fees could be kept down to a level within the means of the parents of the children for whom the lower grade schools were designed: the provision of buildings and the size of the schools. If good and appropriate school buildings could be provided from some source other than the fees charged to parents and the numbers in the schools were large enough, it would be possible to offer a good education at a moderate price. The endowments of the Bristol schools were an obvious resource for school building.

In the letter from which the foregoing quotation is taken, he sketches a system of free or partly free places involving either tuition alone or tuition and boarding which would be competed for by children in the elementary schools. Furthermore, pupils in the lower grade schools who showed exceptional promise could by means of scholarships be transferred to the higher grades and the way opened to them to higher education generally. For girls, he particularly mentions Hitchin where Emily Davies was in charge of the small group of young women which was before long to become Girton. This is a very early statement of the idea of an educational ladder which would enable the most able poor boys and girls to reach the universities and the opportunities which study there would open to them.

He admits that there was some small problem over what these new schools should be called. 'Grade 3' might be misunderstood as meaning inferior in quality, but this could be overcome by not using this designation in the title of the school – the name of a place or of some famous person could be used instead. But of the potential value of these schools he had no doubts. A properly run Grade 3 school would be superior to any of 'the expensive seminaries for young ladies' available at the time. The new school would aim to train the pupil's mind through learning and logical thought rather than teaching superficial accomplishments. The teachers would be broadly educated and well trained. Parents and pupils would be encouraged to value a rigorous but none the less enjoyable and invigorating schooling.

Fitch's own enthusiasm for the new 'graduated system of schools' is obvious, but how was it to be applied in Bristol? His first idea was that Clifton College should be the Grade 1 school, Bristol Grammar School the Grade 2 and schools funded by the three hospital trusts should be Grade 3. His examination of the endowments revealed a combined annual income of £18,500. Allowing £4,500 for management expenses this still left £14,000: sufficient, he estimated, to provide nine schools, five for boys and four for girls. It was a plan that appealed to no one except the Revd Dr John Percival, Headmaster of Clifton College. Walking on the Downs and listening to the sounds of city life rising from Bristol he had had the same idea. The person who particularly disliked it was, of course, the Headmaster of the Grammar School. Fitch realised then, if he had not already done so, that there was no simple, obvious answer to the problem of the reorganisation of Bristol schools and that he must enter into careful negotiations with each of the three separate bodies of trustees.

On March 7, 1870, the writer of the second leader in the Bristol Times and Mirror reported a meeting between Mr Fitch and the Charity Trustees (the forerunner of the Bristol Municipal Charities), and the trustees for the endowments of Queen Elizabeth's Hospital (variously known as Carr's or the City School), the Red Maids' School and the Grammar School. The journalist has only a vague notion of the proposal, but does not like what he has heard.

> . . . the charities left entirely for the instruction of poor children will be made to subsidise the educational machinery for the upper and middle classes, which was certainly not what the founders intended. If the intention is carried out, there will be no more Colston's, or Carr's or Red Maids' Schools: all will be merged, and the names of the very founders lost, in the new and generalising system.

Fitch was to meet Colston's Hospital trustees a few days after this, but neither this meeting nor its result was reported in the local papers. It looks as though the Society of Merchant Venturers had even at this early stage decided that nothing was to be gained by public debate. Those Merchants who were concerned with Colston's Hospital school saved their energies for direct negotiations with Fitch and the Endowed Schools Commissioners. One imagines that their first reaction was one of incredulity that the Colston Settlement which had been tested and enforced in the courts less than 25 years earlier could now so easily be set aside. Convinced of the reality of the threat to the status quo, they fought back. Their main arguments were that Colston had intended his charity to benefit poor boys and not any other group of people, and that he had insisted that the boys be instructed in the doctrines of the Church of England by teachers who were practising Anglicans: it was in effect a denominational school.

If the Colston Trustees presented a low profile, representatives of the other endowed schools went into the attack. Early in April two correspondents to the Bristol Times and Mirror signing themselves 'J.C. and H.M.' wrote long joint letters arguing against what they took to be Fitch's proposals. They produced figures very different from his to show that the money from the endowments was being used most economically if the amount spent on each pupil was calculated. They do not go into the question of the quality of the education received. They turn instead to Bristol's educational requirements. The city certainly does not need another large, middle class, 3rd grade school. There are plenty of school places already. Here they seem to be supported by the evidence of the newspaper itself. There are a great many schools advertising for pupils, although a closer look at the advertisements suggests a number of very small schools of doubtful standard and few facilities. Fitch's exhaustive enquiries for the Taunton Commission had revealed the unsatisfactory nature of such establishments.

'J.C. and H.M.' then go on to propose their own plan for the Bristol endowed schools. The custom of giving apprenticeships to boys and dowries to girls should be discontinued and the money thus saved should be devoted to the funding of scholarships to 2nd and 1st grade schools for the outstandingly talented. Instead of giving pupils four years at the schools, the age of admission should be raised from ten to twelve, and twice as many children should each be given two years at school. Admission should be by competitive examination. The most radical suggestion was that the Colston endowment should be divided into two. One part of it should go to enlarge the school on Brandon Hill so that it could take 300 boys and the other part should go to the Red Maids who would move to the Stapleton building and increase their numbers to 200.

Fitch had asked for suggestions from the trustees of the endowments. He can not have expected this public advice from writers who do not reveal what their standing in the matter is and who seem to have little idea of what is needed or what is possible. He took to debate by newspaper and the next day an open letter from him to the Chairman of the Charity Trustees appeared. He deplored the sensational disclosure of draft plans as though they were the final proposals. He pointed out that the trustees had had plenty of opportunity to comment and to make other proposals both before and after his visit in January and this they had not done. The Endowed Schools Act was specific in opposing the principle of 'hospital schools'.

'May I remind you', he wrote, 'of the one cardinal point on which I sought to insist so strongly at our meeting: that a rich endowment can be far more advantageously used, if instead of giving a gratuitous education to a few – and those not necessarily the poorest or the most deserving – it is made the means of cheapening and ennobling the education of ten times that number.

'Indeed, those who allege "the spoliation of the poor" will do well to forecast how the principle of the Act could work for Bristol. According to the returns now before us, the three great Hospital Schools have between them a gross income of £14,000 per annum, out of which they educate no more than 436 children, in a population of 180,000. The quality of the education at Queen Elizabeth's is undoubtedly excellent: that at Colston's Hospital and Red Maids' School does not profess to be higher than is usually attained in good charity schools. But at none of them does it appear that arrangements are made for the more promising pupils to attain a further reach of education and to rise to the position for which their gifts may qualify them.'

He goes on to describe the effect of these proposals. There would be large day and boarding schools run on the best models, and the most promising pupils could proceed to higher grade schools and even to university. All these benefits would be 'conferred in such a way as to stimulate industry and good conduct'. Like most liberal thinkers of his time he was convinced that free or 'gratuitous' education impaired the dignity and discouraged the efforts of both parent and child. He assured the trustees that the aim was not to alienate funds from Bristol, but to benefit the citizens more widely.

He repeated his allegation that even at present the benefits of the Bristol hospital schools were not confined to the poorest classes and this seems to be the one matter on which all the parties to the dispute were agreed: that the method of recruiting pupils for the Schools must be changed.

In the case of Colston's Hospital, admissions to the school were in the gift of two separate bodies, the Society of Merchant Venturers and the Colston Nominees. The latter had been originally chosen by Colston himself and they perpetuated themselves by co-options. Each body had fifty places to give in the school. When, for instance, a boy nominated by the Society left the school, his place was to be filled by another chosen by the Society. Long before Fitch appeared on the scene, the procedure had not been working smoothly. At different times, each of the two groups presenting scholars complained that the other had more places. This can only have come about when a vacancy was not filled by the appropriate body: in other words, there was difficulty in finding sufficient poor boys. In 1870, the protagonists of the other endowed schools gibed that Colston's would never be touched by the Commissioners because it already was a school filled with middle class boys. Fitch's investigation into the trades of the boys' parents went some way towards substantiating this. It was a system of patronage which was not being effective and its abolition was the one concession which the Society of Merchant Venturers made voluntarily.

The negotiations between the Society and the Endowed Schools Commission were protracted. Fitch's proposal was that Colston's Hospital should become a feepaying boarding school for boys, with up to a hundred free places. The money thus made available would be used to found two Church of England Day Schools, one for girls in Redcliffe and the other for boys in Bedminster. In both cases there would be a conscience clause for parents. This was a provision which had been the saving of the 1870 Elementary Education Act, which all but foundered on the question of sectarian religious instruction. It gave parents the right to withdraw their children from instruction in a religious denomination to which they did not subscribe.

The Society did not object to day schools but wanted the money to go to schools already in existence. The Commissioners wanted new schools, so that the maximum number of new places could be created. The Merchants would accept the conscience clause but without enthusiasm and would not agree that it would apply to the holders of free places: that far at least Colston's wishes must be respected.

Correspondence with the Commissioners, and there was a great deal of it, continued into 1872. The tone became increasingly sharp, with arguments as to the precise meaning of certain paragraphs and complaints of a three months 'suspension of negotiation' – the Commissioners' term – or 'refusal to negotiate' – the Society's description. In February 1872, the Society produced an Alternative Scheme which retained the free education of poor boys, in accordance with the aim of the Founder, the requirement that religious instruction should follow the doctrines of the Church of England, that the Headmaster must be an Anglican and that the Society should continue to be the Governing Body. Patronage was to be abolished, in the case of both the Society and the Colston Nominees, a concession which as we have seen was considerable but not inconvenient. Finally, any money saved by putting this Scheme into practice should be applied to the continuation and extension of the Bristol Diocesan Trade and Mining School.

This was new thinking in an argument which had become repetitious. It represented a longstanding interest of the Merchant Venturers. Since the seventeenth century they had run a school for the sons of poor mariners and early in the eighteenth century had used two legacies to set up a Navigation School. Later they combined the two. Some of the most interesting and beautiful treasures possessed by the Society are the manuscript books from which the boys were taught. In 1863 this school had been merged with the recently established Bristol Diocesan Trade and Mining School but the Society continued to contribute financially to the new venture and to receive reports on its progress. It had day and evening classes for both boys and adults and was a pioneer in scientific and technological education. It was later known as the Merchant Venturers Technical College and though it no longer survives today in that form various departments of the college gave rise to, among other institutions, the Engineering Faculty of Bristol University, Cotham Grammar School, and the Bristol College of Advanced Technology which became the

University of Bath. The Merchants of 1872 could not foresee the whole of the splendid future of the Diocesan Trade School, but it was a project dear to their hearts.

There were more letters and delays. The Commissioners produced an Amended Scheme which met the Society's objection to the extent of substituting the Trade School for the Boys' Day School. There was much discussion of detail and half way through 1873 three Merchants were invited to the Commissioners' office in London at fairly short notice – 'any of the last three days of next week' – to discuss the Society's latest objections to the Scheme for the reorganisation of Mr Colston's School. At the Merchants' Standing Committee meeting on June 17, the Master reported:

> The Colston's Girls' School is to be erected on a scale and site in Bristol to be determined by the Governors, the religious instruction to be in accordance with the principles of the Church of England, subject to the conscience clause, and the general education to be of the type of a third grade school. It will be managed by a committee of 13, eight members of which are to be chosen by the Governors (of the Boys' School) from their body and five ladies to be chosen by such eight Governors.

So the Scheme took something like its final shape. The Society had not wanted change in the beginning, but after nearly four years of a hard fought battle the Merchants felt that this was something they could live with. It was less than the Commissioners had hoped for but it represented to them a notable improvement on the status quo. They had many other battles on their hands in other places, and the fact that the Society of Merchant Venturers was willing to give the Colston Trust £10,000 must have gone some way towards modifying their disappointment.

The Society had not in any way lost its suspicious antipathy to the Commission and to Fitch. At first the Merchants had queried the Commissioners' powers and had been dismayed to discover that the agreement of the trustees was not needed to change the Settlement in almost every respect. Now, having reached a sort of agreement, they took Counsel's opinion as to whether the Commission could change the Scheme unilaterally, without reference to the Society, at any time in the future. They can not at this stage have been surprised to learn that the Commission had such powers. They were told that it was unlikely to exercise them if the Society kept to the present terms of the Scheme.

In fact, alterations were made fairly frequently over the next thirty years. They were agreed without difficulty or delay between the Trustees and the Commissioners, and the interesting point is that they were initiated by the Trustees. Once over the first discomforts of change it was Merchants who made the running, not the Commissioners. But this is to anticipate events.

On October 31, 1873, the Society passed a resolution formally agreeing to the Scheme, although it did not receive the Queen's signature until February 1875. By then several things had happened. The Merchants had begun to think that it was unwise to put a limit on the size of either the Boys' School or the Trade School. Fitch had already said that feepaying schools must be large if they were to make ends meet and at the same time keep down the size of the fee paid by parents. The Colston Trustees had hitherto seen the size of the Boys' School as regulated either by Colston's idea of a hundred poor boys, although this at various times in the past had not been regarded as a precise number, or by the actual income of the endowment. The transition to feepaying changed this. The more feepayers, the bigger the income, and the more scope there was for development. After all the emotional arguments about 'benefiting the rich by the plunder of the poor' and the natural resentment felt by the Merchants at the implied criticism of their stewardship, they were beginning to look to the future in a positive way.

If there were changes in the thinking at Merchants' Hall, these were as nothing compared with the changes in the fortunes of the Endowed Schools Commission. Originally it had been appointed for five years. By 1873 it was generally unpopular. Liberals thought it was not making fast enough progress: few people appreciated the complexity of the work the Commissioners were attempting. Conservatives thought it was 'communistic' and Anglicans thought it was 'robbing the Church'. A Select Committee was appointed to investigate the Commission. The Committee on the whole approved of the Commission's efforts and recommended that its life should be extended by three years. Parliament cut this to one year. Then in 1874 Gladstone's government fell and the Conservatives returned to power. Social reform was not as high on Disraeli's list of priorities as it had been on Gladstone's.

By June it had been decided to transfer the Commission's powers to the Charity Commission at the end of the year. Two of the three original Commissioners and the Secretary resigned, leaving only Canon Robinson of the original team. Such Assistant Commissioners as remained were transferred to an Endowed Schools department of the Charity Commission. Vacancies were filled by newcomers with no experience of the work. The momentum of the first four years was lost, and from this point until the work of the Endowed Schools department was transferred to the newly formed Board of Education in 1903, progress was slow and the coercive powers of the original Commission rarely exercised.

The Colston's Hospital Trust Scheme became law on February 4, 1875. It included a section on Colston's Girls' Day School:

> Within three years from the date of this Scheme, the Governors (of Colston's Boys' Boarding School), with the sanction of the Endowed Schools Commissioners, if then acting, or, if not, of the Charity Commissioners, shall provide, on

> some convenient site, or sites, in Bristol, School buildings and accommodation, whereof the sites, plans, estimates shall be subject to the same sanction, sufficient and suitable for a Day School for about 200 girls . . .

It will have been noticed that this passage contains, in addition to a gross overuse of the comma, a veiled threat. If the Governors did not build a Girls' School within three years, the Commission would use Colston's Hospital Trust money to do it for them. And when the Governors came to build the site, plans and estimates of cost had all to be approved by whichever Commission was then in charge.

In 1875, however, there was a task the Society of Merchant Venturers had to perform immediately. A Governing Body for Colston's Boarding School had to be set up. It would have twenty one members, thirteen of whom would be Merchant Venturers and the remaining eight representatives of other institutions, so that the Society could, if it wished, exercise a controlling influence on the affairs of the School. The Society was to continue to manage all the property belonging to the Colston Trust and to produce annual accounts which were to be made public. Nevertheless, the effect of the new legislation was to make the Society, the Colston Trust, the Boys' Boarding School and the Trade School separate entities.

The new School Governors met frequently in the succeeding months. Technically, Colston's Hospital had to be closed and the Colston's Boarding School opened. A prospectus was published. The education it offered was 'adapted to the wants of sons of Farmers, Tradesmen, Clerks and others'. The annual fee was £31, which the prospectus said was heavily subsidised. In addition parents paid £5 a year clothing fee; the uniform was new and was provided by the School. At once there were applications that this fee should be w ived. In this respect the Governors were thinking as though they were still the managers of a charity school. Very soon they changed this rule and parents themselves bought their sons' clothes including the uniform. There were perhaps other false starts like this, but the Governors can not be accused of delay. The entrance examination for feepayers was held on July 22 and the first feepaying pupils were admitted soon afterwards. The boys already in the School retained their free places. In the future, 'Foundationers', as they were known, won their free places in competitive examination, a condition being that they had attended a public elementary school for at least a year.

The problems facing the Governors were great. In 1966 the Girls' School changed from being a wholly non-feepaying school and took in some feepayers. These feepayers were joining a school of pupils who were there because they had done exceptionally well in an examination they had taken at the age of eleven. In 1875 the Boarding School feepayers were joining a school of pupils who were there because their parents were poor. Their claim to their places was their parents' financial circumstances, not their academic merit: and in the past the avowed policy of the School had been that it would not 'interfere' with the social class of the boys. We should not be too much surprised at this determination to keep the children of the poor within the class into which they had been born. Exactly the same argument was advanced against the grammar schools in the Nineteen Sixties. The even more rigid view of social class of the Eighteen Seventies was a powerful obstacle to the recruitment of pupils from middle class families. Fortunately for the new School there were other forces at work. Not even Fitch foresaw all the results of the 1870 Education Act which made elementary education to the age of thirteen available to every child. Parents who aspired to something more than this basic education were looking for places in secondary schools.

By July 1877, two years later, it was clear to the Governors that they would not be able to meet the deadline set by the Charity Commissioners for the opening of the Girls' School. They wrote to the Secretary of the Commission a long letter, twelve handwritten pages of foolscap, setting out the financial affairs of both the Boarding School and the Trade School and describing what still had to be done before either school could be said 'in any sense of the word' to be fully developed.

The Boarding School now had 50 feepayers in addition to the 100 Foundationers. This had increased the number of boys in the School but it had also created another problem. By the introduction of this 'new class of boys, . . . paying scholars, the moral tone of the School has been greatly raised.' But this minority of boys in the School 'can not altogether hold its own against the jealousy of the Foundationers.' The solution was to increase the number of feepayers to parity with the Foundationers: that is, take in 50 more feepayers. But the accommodation, the former Bishop's Palace in Stapleton, where the Colston's Hospital School had moved in 1861, was already overstretched, and no more could be housed in acceptable living conditions. Considerable extensions and modifications were necessary even to carry on with the present numbers. For instance, the water supply to the lavatories in the basement, two floors away from the dormitories on the first and second floors, was inadequate; the kitchen was the same as when the house was occupied by a single household; and the boys had nowhere to play in bad weather except the teaching rooms.

The estimated cost of the improvements was £2,500 to £3,000; but there would be more revenue from the larger number of feepayers who could be admitted.

When the letter goes on to describe progress at the Trade School, it is evident where the greater interest of the Governors lay. The School will become 'the most important place of technical and scientific education in the West of England for the operative class of the population.' It was not however limited to the 'operative class'. One former student won the Chemical Scholarship by his performance in the most recent London B.Sc. Intermediate examination. Two others had now received their doctorates in science.

The School needed a new building. The Governors had done what they could with the present one but it was now completely overcrowded. They would like the new building to be in a 'more open and salubrious part of Bristol.' They have able and efficient teachers 'who give promise of distinguished careers' but they were not going to be able to keep them unless they could increase their salaries. The cost of all the necessary improvements would be £6,000 to £7,000. If this were not forthcoming they would have to close some departments. They listed the ones in danger: Commerce, Practical Chemistry, Mining and Engineering. (The list is interesting, particularly in that it included Commerce. This department would not be one of the big spenders and does not make extravagant demands on teaching space.)

If they were to provide a Girls' School, the site and a building for 200 girls would cost at least £4,000. After it was opened they would have to contribute £300 a year. At present they had neither the capital sum for the building, nor could they afford the £300 a year.

Would it not be better, they asked, to get the two existing institutions into good working order first? They were hopeful that if they could attract and accommodate more feepayers in the Boarding School, it would more nearly pay its way. They thought that if they could consolidate the success of the Trade School, they might get some outside help with its finances because of its particular interest to 'the people of this city.'

As set out in this way, the request to postpone the setting up of the Girls' School is a reasonable one. The letter indicates no opposition to the idea of a girls' school. It merely puts it in third place to the other two schools, the position it occupies in the Scheme, and, indeed, occupied in all the discussions preceding the Scheme.

Three weeks later the Charity Commissioners' Secretary wrote agreeing to the postponement of the establishment of a Girls' School for not more than 5 years from January 1, 1873; that is, it must be open by January, 1888. The Secretary added a warning:

> (The Commissioners) would feel great difficulty in giving their sanction to any expenditure on these Schools (the Boys' Boarding, the Trade) which would interfere with the establishment of the Colston's Girls' School at the expiration of the extended period.

So the Colston Governors had their breathing space. Their minute books of the next eight years contain no mention of a Girls' School. That is not to say that the subject did not crop up in conversation, possibly when some urgent need of the Boys' School or the Trade School was being discussed with gloom . . . 'and don't forget, we shall have to do something soon about the Girls' School . . .'

Were the Governors being exceptionally dilatory? Other girls' schools were opening in Bristol, Clifton High School in 1878 and Redland High

School in 1882. These were 'proprietary' schools, founded by parents and philanthropists for the benefit of their own and other people's middle class daughters and funded in the manner of joint-stock companies. The record of the Colston Trustees should be compared with those of other endowed schools. The Scheme for St Paul's School in London was signed in April, 1876. The St Paul's Trustees had the same relationship with the Mercers' Company as the Colston Trustees had, and have, with the Society of Merchant Venturers and were similarly required to establish a Girls' School, from a much larger endowment. The St Paul's Girls' School was not opened until 1904. In 1878 the Scheme for Louth Boys' Grammar School was signed. It contained a requirement that a girls' school should be opened 'within three years'. When nothing was done, the local County Council tried to make the Charity Commissioners act 'to secure the observance of the Scheme made by them.' By 1899, it seems that the Commissioners were reluctant to use the only sanction left to them, that of sequestrating the Louth endowment and building the girls' school themselves. Louth never did open a girls' school. After 1902, the County Council established one.

There is a persistent rumour, although I have found no documentary proof, that in 1886 someone from Bristol complained to the Parliamentary Select Committee on Education that neither the Red Maids' School nor the Colston Trustees had opened the new girls' schools they were required to. Whether the complaint was made or not, the Society of Merchant Venturers had not forgotten the matter.

The Merchants' interest in the Trade School had grown with the years and they agreed with the Trustees that the provision of better and more spacious premises was essential to its development. In 1879 a site on St Michael's Hill was considered as a possible place for both the Trade School and the Girls' School. It evidently turned out to be unsuitable, for the next year they were thinking about the disused Grammar School premises in Unity Street. The asking price then was £8,000, far too high for the Trustees who knew that the building would need alteration and expansion after it had been acquired. A small group of Merchants, presumably offering ready money, bought the premises for £5,500, and then persuaded the Society to endorse the purchase.

At that stage, they proposed to offer the building to the Trustees at a nominal rent, but it needed a great deal of replanning and refurbishment before it could be used by the Trade School. Coincidentally, the Trust income had shrunk because the estates in Somerset were producing so little return, and the Trustees could not undertake the necessary alterations. Once more the Society stepped in and by 1885 a very good new building was ready in Unity Street. The Society was by now so much involved with the Trade School that the Merchants decided to take it over from the Colston Trustees and make themselves responsible for its future. There was a suggestion that they should be answerable to the Charity Commissioners, as the Trust had been.

Past experience did not make this an attractive option. The Merchants were able to convince the Commission that they could settle funds on the School sufficient to secure its future. It passed from the Colston Trust to the Society and became the Merchant Venturers' School, later the Merchant Venturers' Technical College.

Without the responsibility for the Trade School, the Colston Trustees could turn their attention to the Girls' School. The first need was to find a site, and to do this they enlisted the help of Mr Josiah Thomas, the City Valuer. It is interesting that they never considered beginning in a converted dwelling house as most other girls' schools had done, and would do for many years to come. The Merchant members of the Trust had recently had the pleasure of opening the new building in Unity Street and also knew all about the problems of the Boys' Boarding School buildings at Stapleton, which had not been purpose built. Mr Thomas inspected a site in Arley Hill, but reported that the price was exorbitant. In July 1886 he sent the Trustees particulars of 'a site in the Cheltenham Road which might serve for Colston's Girls' School.'

The Trustees thought it promising. It was a piece of ground largely uncovered, with little more than a couple of very small cottages and a stable on it. The land had been bought by a Mr Samuel Robertson who proposed to build eight houses fronting on to Cheltenham Road and fourteen fronting on to a new street behind. The Clerk, Mr George H. Pope, wrote at once to the Charity Commissioners, without whose permission no move could be made. He received a reply dated August 24 saying that the Commissioners 'had separated for the usual autumnal recess' and nothing more was heard from them. Even if the Trustees had been prepared to wait indefinitely, Mr Robinson was not. On April 27, 1887, Mr Pope wrote again to the Commissioners to tell them that the owner wanted a decision by May 6. He enclosed a copy of Mr Thomas's report and added a comment that for the Trustees' purpose 'the position of this ground could not be improved.' On May 3, Mr William Proctor Baker, the Chairman of the Trust, went to London to argue with the Commissioners in person. A note made by a Commissioner records that Mr Proctor Baker based his case on the ease of access to all parts of Bristol by road, tram and railway, and said it was 'surrounded by villas of a class likely to provide girls for the School.' The Commissioners gave their consent and agreement was reached with Mr Robertson. Mr Pope set about getting the Commission's approval, which he had asked for eleven months earlier, to selling investments to raise the purchase price and the cost of building. Before he could get very far with this, another difficulty had arisen. Preliminary investigations into the title of the land revealed a ground rent of £10 agreed in 1727, only part of which – £5 – seemed to have been brought to an end. The Commissioners, perhaps not so familiar with ground rents as Bristolians are, would have none of this and withdrew their consent. By December 13 Mr Robertson was becoming extremely restive and his solicitors threatened proceedings in the Chancery Division if the purchase was not concluded within 14 days. In the end, the Society's lawyer, Mr Jere Osborne, was able to show that whatever had happened to the balance of £5 of the ground rent, it had never been successfully claimed, and on February 3, 1888, the Commissioners' agent signed an Order permitting the Trustees to buy the land with Trust Fund money. The Order was accompanied by a description of the purchase:

> A piece of land, situate in the District of the parishes of St James and St Paul, in the City of Bristol, which piece of land contains . . . 5,210 square yards or thereabouts, and had a frontage of 190 feet on the Cheltenham Road, and is bounded on the west by the said Cheltenham Road, and partly by the gardens of houses fronting Cheltenham Road, on the south by land attached to Rennison's Baths, on the east by the Clifton Extension Railway and on the north partly by a house and shop fronting Cheltenham Road, partly by a back road, and partly by bicycle works entered therefrom, together with two cottages, and a stable and coachhouse and other buildings standing thereon.

It will have been noticed that little of this delay was the fault of the Trustees. In fact, as soon as they had decided that the site was suitable and were sure that Mr Robertson would sell, they set to work on their preparations without waiting for the Charity Commissioners' assent. They first considered the market. Their necessarily informal enquiries convinced them that there would be a sufficient number of girls whose parents would want to send them to the kind of school they had in mind. They thought the location of the School could be in its favour: there were more houses to be built in the developing suburb of St Andrews as well as the 'villas' Mr Proctor Baker talked about. Public transport was improving and they could expect girls to come from other parts of Bristol. They decided to increase the number of pupils from 200 to 300. 'No school of the kind proposed already exists in Bristol. The Governors do not doubt that this larger number of girls will always be easily obtained,' Mr Pope told the Commissioners.

But what kind of building should they provide? It was not only that the Trustees had no experience of purpose built girls' day schools: there were very few of them in existence. As they looked for help and advice it did not occur to them to apply to the endowed schools department of the Charity Commission. Instead, Mr Pope got into touch with Joshua Fitch, who had left the Commission ten years earlier. Fitch provided him with a list of girls' schools to visit in London and elsewhere and he set off on his travels, asking questions and making notes. The result was a Memorandum which he laid before the Trustees at an Extraordinary Meeting held three weeks after permission had been received to purchase the ground.

They decided that the building should cost about £6,000, and should contain the following accommodation:

A large assembly Hall capable of seating 400 persons
A Drill Room, with gymnastic appliances, for 100 girls
A Lecture Room to hold 100
7 Classrooms to hold on average 40 girls, each seated at single desks
A Head Mistress's private sitting room
A Common Room for the Assistant Mistresses
A Waiting Room
Abundant Cloakroom accommodation
Lavatories etc etc
A Dining room to seat 50
A small kitchen, with offices
Store rooms of various kinds

Living rooms for a caretaker and his wife and in case it was finally decided to teach instrumental music – sound proof cells.

This list is as interesting for what it omits as for what it includes. There is no provision for teaching practical science; in this respect it would not be different from most schools, boys' as well as girls'. There are no specialist rooms at all. For a long time both drawing and needlework were taught at ordinary desks. The several classrooms will not hold all the 300 girls. Wherever the extra 20 girls are to go, there are no desks for them. Most striking of all, there is no office. All the administration and most of the correspondence was to be done at Merchants' Hall.

Four Bristol architects would be invited to submit plans based on this schedule, and letters were dispatched. There was an almost immediate and unanimous reaction from the architects. £6,000 was not enough to provide all this accommodation.

The Governors met again quickly and issued some modified instructions, resolving

> That the classrooms may be reduced to 13 feet high.
>
> That the limit of expenditure be withdrawn, and that the Architects be informed that if any of the designs be accepted, it will be that which appears best to fulfil the requirements of the Governors in the most economical manner.
>
> That each competitor should give a basis of his estimate, by means of statement of the total number of cubic feet in the building, distinguishing the more from the less costly parts and assigning a price or prices per cubic foot, at which he estimates that the work can be executed.

The phrase 'in the most economical manner' sounds a depressing note, but it represents more than the determination of successful businessmen to get value for money. Once depleted, the endowment would be difficult to build up again. The Boys' Boarding School had continuing problems of both finance and recruitment, and these could not be solved by increasing the fees charged to parents, for the level of fee was fixed by the Scheme. Besides all this, every letter from the Charity Commissioners, on whatever subject, included questions about the Trust's capacity to provide a second school. Apart from Joshua Fitch's encouragement, all the Governors had to support them was their research into the probable demand for this kind of education for girls and their instinct that a 300 girl school was a more viable proposition than a 200 girl one. They were going to have to look closely at every penny.

On April 20, 1888, the Governors met to consider the designs submitted by the four architects and chose that of W.V. Gough. He had estimated the cost as £9,820. By using the additional information they had requested in their revised instructions, they could see that by omitting the gymnasium and the lecture theatre the cost might be reduced to £7,984. Gough was invited to attend the next meeting in ten days' time, bringing with him plans of a building reduced in this way and some indication of how the whole of the ground might be utilised. He was told that the approval of the Charity Commissioners was needed before work could actually start, but there was some confusion as to the precise stage in the development of the plans at which they had to be submitted to the Commissioners. Gough naturally wanted this as early as possible, so that he did not waste time on proposals which were never likely to gain acceptance. The Commissioners seem to have been interested in seeing the plans in as much detail as possible. The Governors' concern was that they should approve the plans before the Commissioners saw them. The result was that the Commissioners' conditional approval did not reach the Governors until February 1, 1889.

Very little, if any, of the blame for this delay can be laid at the door of the Governors. They met regularly and took decisions promptly. They busied themselves with matters which would become urgent when permission to start building eventually did arrive. They drew up a list of 12 builders who might be asked to tender for the work: Gough wanted one of the names removed, and the Governors had second thoughts about another, so they were left with 10, a very sizeable list. Gough thought the plumbing should go out to tender separately. The Governors suggested three names and Gough supplied a fourth.

There were other matters which received their attention. By July of 1888 they had the Commissioners' approval to enlarge the School to 'not more than 300 girls' and one of the important modifications of the 1875 Scheme had been agreed. There were two others. Before the School opened in January 1891 the Governors had permission to raise the school leaving age to 17 and the annual fee from £4 to £5. Both were important. It will be remembered that in 1870 different 'Grades' of school had been proposed. Pupils at a Grade 2 school could stay until they were 17; Grade 3 schoolchildren left at 15. The use of the term 'Grade' had proved unpopular, as Fitch feared it would, but schools were still classified according to the length of the pupils' school life. Boys could now stay on at the Boarding School until they were 16, and if they wished to continue their education the Governors could assist them to take up places at, for instance, Bristol Grammar School or, in another case, Wells Grammar School. The extra year in the Girls' School may reflect the shortage of schools in which girls could continue their education, but it is also likely that the later school leaving age was suggested by Fitch who had been disappointed that there seemed to be no opportunity to open a Grade 2 school in Bristol. The increase in the modest school fee was justified partly by inflation and partly by the experience of the Governors of an insufficient income from feepayers in the Boys' School.

While waiting for permission from the Commissioners to go ahead, they gave much thought to the finances of the new school. They had already spent £2,700 to acquire the Cheltenham Road site and, persuaded by the four Bristol architects, they now thought they needed £10,000 to build and 'fit up' the school. They could use £2,000 from Trust income and would sell Stock to raise the other £8,000. They went on to consider the running expenses of the school when it was in operation. They thought these would be:

Headmistress's salary	£300
Salaries of assistant mistresses	£700
Rates and Taxes	£80
Water	£25
Caretaker's and other 2 servants' wages	£150
Care of garden and playground	£25
Stationery, etc.	£50
Advertising	£25
Examination expenses and prizes	£50
Repairs	£100
Leaving exhibitions	£100
Sundries	£50
	£1,755

They expected that 30 of the 300 places in the School would be awarded to pupils who had their education free. This left 270 girls who would pay the £4 annual fee, bringing in £1,080. The balance of £675 would have to be defrayed by the Trust.

It is an extremely tight budget. As well as being Governors of the Boys' School, those who drew it up were also Trustees of the Colston's Hospital Fund from which, according to the Scheme, 'not less than £200' was to be paid to the Girls' School each year. They were here counting on more than three times this amount. Raising the school fee from £4 to £5 would bring in another £270, but time would tell whether the Fund could be relied on for this annual subsidy.

The estimate of expenditure is interesting. Pupils would pay for their own books. The leaving exhibitions would not be needed for the first two years and although this provision is in keeping with the Scheme, it proved not to be necessary to earmark so large a sum for this purpose. There is no mention of administrative expenses and after the first year this omission was noticed and £100 was paid each year to the Society of Merchant Venturers for the services of the Clerk. Today the difference between the salary of the Headmistress and the Assistants looks strange. It harks back to a time when the Master of a school had full responsibility for running it. His assistants, usually few in number and of much lower social status, did his bidding. The difference in salaries went on well into the Twentieth Century.

The last modification required by the Charity Commissioners in February, 1889 was the removal of a turret from the design. One of the early drawings of the school building still retains this feature, an elaborate confection perched on the roof and with no imaginable function. However sad Gough may have been to see this go, he must have been much relieved to be able to make a start. In the days before planning permission had even been thought of, delays such as those caused by repeated referrals to the Charity Commissioners must have been unusual. The builders and plumbers were written to and the tenders examined on March 4. The lowest priced builders were Stephens and Bastow at £7,911.10.0d and the plumber was G.F. Tuckey at £758.10.0d. As soon as the Charity Commissioners had given their consent to these tenders, Mr Jere Osborne was to prepare 'proper contracts'. These were signed by April 11, but by then Gough had to report that by an arithmetical mistake Stephen and Bastow's tender had been £100 lower than they intended. However, Stephen and Bastow's tender had been much more than £100 less than any other firm, so the Governors decided not to change horses now. They would allow Stephen and Bastow to add £100 to the final sum, making it £8,011.10.0d 'provided that the work was carried out to the entire satisfaction of the Architect'. William Tanner, of Bridge Street, Barton Hill, was appointed Clerk of the Works at a salary of three guineas a week.

By the middle of July the foundations were complete. The work was already behind schedule. The contractors promised that the delay caused by 'difficulties in connexion with the supply of Pennant Stone' would be made up by working overtime. Gough's plan for the building had been so thoroughly considered by the Governors and by the Charity Commissioners that there was little need for modification after building started. The sound proof cells for instrumental music had gone and the architect's ingenious arrangements for drying wet clothes – coat stands which could be moved along rails in the floor of the lower cloakroom to a position over the boiler room – had been included. He could now turn his attention to less controversial matters, such as 'door furniture' and the design of the stained glass windows of the assembly hall. In spite of the need for economy both Gough and the Governors resisted any suggestion from the contractors that cheaper materials would do.

If work was proceeding smoothly, albeit a little slowly, on the building, the same could not be said of the playground. The Governors' reasons for thinking the site a good one for a school, ease of access and the proximity of a probable catchment area for pupils, did not take into account the nature of the terrain. The whole plot of land was much smaller than that now occupied by the School and did not include Pugsley's yard to the north, on which the Dolphin Building now stands, or the Pleasaunce. It sloped in two different directions and Gough's solution to the problem this presented was to build massive retaining walls and level the ground between, tarpaving part of this and having grass and flower beds in the other part. The Governors would have none of this. They wanted good boundary walls wherever these were feasible, although the steep slope upward of the railway land made it almost impossible to build a wall on the east which would keep out intruders. Grass and flower beds could wait to some later date and they were very firmly against any tarpaving. Their attitude seems strange today. It has to be remembered that organised games did not form any part of the curriculum and that when it was found necessary to reduce the cost of the building, the 'drill hall' was jettisoned along with the 'lecture room'.

On April 11, 1890, the Boys' School Governors discussed the Girls' School for the last time, and took the decision not to open it until January, 1891. They may have been influenced in this by the fact that the academic year ran from January to December, but it seems a long time ahead. Their last task was to set up the Governing Body of the new school. This was to consist of eight Boys' School governors who were to invite five women to join them, making thirteen Governors in all. Then they all trooped off to the building in Cheltenham Road. They seem to have been reasonably satisfied with what they saw, the result of so much thought and discussion. They may have been confirmed in their decision not to try to open before January: the windows in the assembly hall, for instance, were not yet in place.

MISS SMITH

The Governing Body of the Girls' School met for the first time on July 23, 1890. Except for the presence of women members, its composition was very similar to that of the group of Boys' School Governors which had seen to the erection of the building. The same people took on the responsibility for the Girls' School and now met on different occasions to consider the affairs of the two schools separately.

The Chairman was Mr William Proctor Baker, already Chairman of the Trust and of the Boys' School. He had retired a few years earlier from the corn business which his father had founded and which became Spillers of Cardiff. Even before his retirement he had been active in public service. He was an Alderman, a magistrate, a member of the Bristol School Board and the President of Bristol General Hospital. He had been Mayor in 1873, and during his mayoralty he and his wife had climbed the spire of St Mary Redcliffe's church to lay the capstone and complete the spire. He was a good speaker; a linguistic purist. He objected to the term 'Free Library', which he said ought to be 'Public Library'. To someone who objected on grounds of economy to works of fiction being stocked at branch libraries, he retorted that no one could understand or appreciate English literature who was not well acquainted with the English novel. He was a good musician and played the 'cello. He had been a founder member of the Bristol Philharmonic Society and had promoted the first Musical Festival in Bristol. It was said that he had played in an orchestra at the first Handel Festival at the Crystal Palace. His views on education were liberal. Through his involvement with the Merchant Venturers Trade School he had seen the advantages of giving young people as long an education as could be afforded. He thought children benefited from being brought up in beautiful surroundings.

He and his brother Arthur Baker, another of the Girls' School Governors, had been educated at Bristol Grammar School. Arthur had been a member of the family firm as well as having other business interests and was a City Councillor, sitting for Redcliffe ward, for twenty eight years. His tastes were literary and when the school acquired a library he contributed to it frequently and generously. Both brothers were wealthy men, living in considerable style. When Proctor Baker became Chairman in 1890 he was 56 years old and he retained the office until a few weeks before he died in 1907.

Four other Governors were, like the Baker brothers, members of the Society of Merchant Venturers as well as Governors of the Boys' School. They were William Wilberforce Jose, Mervyn Kersteman King, Colonel John Henry Woodward and John Noble Coleman Pope. The remaining two Governors, the Revd J.G. Alford and Revd C.E. Cornish, were Boys' School Governors but could not, because of their profession, be Merchant Venturers. They were Anglican clergymen of a kind not uncommon at the time, scholarly men who took an active interest in education. Mr Alford became a Canon of Bristol Cathedral and Chaplain to the Bishop. Charles Cornish became a Bishop. The Clerk, George Henry Pope, was the Society's Treasurer. It was a very strong team, and reflected the Society's interest in their latest educational project, for all the Merchants were men of standing in the Society.

They then had to co-opt five women. They chose Mrs H.M. Abbot, Mrs Proctor Baker, Mrs G.H. Pope and Lady Wathen, all wives of Merchants. The fifth was Miss M.E. Wait, an educationalist involved in teacher training. In this, the Scheme was well ahead of its time, for many girls' schools were managed by exclusively male governors. These women had the full status of governors and were in practice very active. With the Chairman, Mr Proctor Baker, they formed a Visiting Committee which met at the School regularly and gave the Head Mistress a great deal of support.

On July 23 the first task was to appoint a Head Mistress and they drew up an advertisement which was to appear in the Times, the Athenaeum, the Spectator, the Guardian, the Saturday Review, the Journal of Education and the three Bristol newspapers. They were looking for an unmarried woman between 25 and 35 years of age who could give proof of the ability to organise and administer a large school. Other things being equal, preference would be given to a lady who had obtained Honours in University or other Examinations. She would be responsible for providing religious instruction in accordance with the doctrines of the Church of England as by law established. The secular curriculum was a somewhat expanded version of that outlined by Fitch twenty years before for a Grade 2 school:

Reading and Spelling
Writing
Arithmetic and Elementary Mathematics
English Grammar, Composition and Literature
Latin or French, or both
The Outlines of History
Geography, Political and Physical
Drawing and Vocal Music
Household Management
The Laws of Health, and Needlework

The long delay in opening the School had had at least two positive results. It now offered a broader course of study which included the possibility of Latin, at that time essential for admission to a university course in either arts or sciences. The Governors were also able to advertise for a university trained

Head Mistress with some confidence that applicants would be qualified in that way. There had been very few university educated women in the Eighteen Seventies when, it will be remembered, Fitch had thought that it would be necessary to employ male teachers in academic girls' schools.

Applications had to reach Merchants' Hall by September 15. There were 69 of them although one of them was subsequently withdrawn. Fourteen of the candidates did not fulfil the conditions laid down by the Governors. An appointing body today would not be discouraged by a field of 54 runners. The Governors met on September 25 and made a short list of five, whom they invited to attend for interview at one o'clock on the afternoon of Wednesday, October 1, at Merchants' Hall.

All except one of the Governors turned up, and four of the five candidates. The difficulty the Governors encountered evidently took them by surprise. After prolonged discussion they could not decide on any of the candidates. Eventually Mr Alford proposed that they should not 'proceed to election' that day, but should invite four more candidates for interview. It was more difficult to get the Governors together again for this second set of interviews, and they met at two o'clock in the afternoon of Saturday, October 11, in the Library of the Merchant Venturers' School. In the end they offered the post by letter to one of the first four candidates, Miss Georgina Amy Smith. When she returned to Bristol on October 20 for her first Governors' meeting she signed the declaration that she should always discharge her duties to the best of her abilities with her usual signature of 'G. Amy Smith'.

What was the problem? It is of course true that none of the Governors had been involved in the appointment of a Head Mistress before, and were anxious not to make a mistake. In the much longer history of the Boys' School they had not always seen eye to eye with the Headmaster. At the same time it is clear that Miss Smith did not make an instant, overwhelming impression at her interview. Her qualification – the examination of the University of Cambridge – must have made her a serious contender for the job from the beginning, but then and for years afterwards the word most frequently used about her is 'quiet'. In the photograph of the Colston's Girls' School staff she looks small, neat, composed and a little remote.

The meeting on October 20 was in the new school building, now complete but still unfurnished. It was decided to have tarpaving from the side entrance in Cheltenham Road to the boundary wall of the railway land, and to have grass and flowerbeds elsewhere. As the last time the Governors discussed tarpaving they had been decidedly against it, it is tempting to think that the change of mind was on the advice of the person new to the party, Miss Smith. She doubtless disliked the prospect of a playground which did not contain a hard surface area. In addition, the Clerk was asked to write to the railway authorities suggesting that they grass over the embankment facing the back of the school and plant trees on their side of the boundary wall. It is as though the presence of a newcomer had persuaded the Governors to take another, more critical look at the surroundings of their bright new school.

The next day at Merchants' Hall they got down to serious business at a meeting which must have been very long. Furniture for classrooms, cloak rooms, the dining room and the school hall had to be ordered and Miss Smith's advice about sizes of desks was followed. She was asked to draw up a list of the furniture needs for her room and the staff common room, and to give thought to the design of the teaching desks for the staff.

Advertisements had to be placed in the local papers inviting parents to apply for admission for their daughters, but before this could be done a number of matters had to be settled. They were already in the process of getting the school fee raised to £5 a year. In accordance with the Scheme there would be a registration fee of 2 shillings and 6 pence payable on each application and an Entrance fee of 5 shillings. There would be a Stationery fee to cover all the books and stationery provided by the School, and all these fees would have to be paid in advance at the office in Merchants' Hall. In addition each pupil would need books and music for her own personal use and these would have to be bought at the school at cost price, usually during the first two weeks of each term.

There would be three terms in each year and three vacations: a fortnight in the spring, six weeks in the summer and four weeks at Christmas. School hours would be from 9.30 a.m. to 12.50 p.m., and from 2 p.m. to 4 p.m. Saturday would be a whole holiday.

There was, however, a matter even more pressing than these: the appointment of assistant mistresses. The urgency lay in the length of notice which school teachers have customarily been required to give before leaving a post. By now they were at most nine weeks away from the end of the autumn term, and the Governors would be fortunate to get advertisements into daily papers and weekly journals, receive applications, interview candidates and offer posts in anything less than a month. In fact, the first three assistant posts were offered and accepted on December 2. It seems probable that most of those applying were either teachers who were not in a post at the time for some reason or students who would complete an academic or professional course of study at Christmas. It seems strange that the Governors should have run this risk. It arose partly over the delay in the appointment of the Head Mistress, who was to advise on the appointment of assistants, and perhaps partly because they wished to see how many pupils they were likely to have in January before making appointments. So many applications for admission had been received by the beginning of December that they decided to limit the numbers in the first term to 200 pupils, and to appoint two more members of staff.

Miss Smith had drawn up what would now be called job descriptions. They reveal some of her thoughts on how she wanted to organise the School. It was then the custom in most secondary schools of whatever kind that the form master, or mistress, should teach his or her form for most of the time and be responsible for most or even all of the curriculum. Her first idea had been to have four assistant mistresses; perhaps she too was doubtful whether the full complement of pupils would present themselves.

The duties of the four are listed:

> 1. One specially qualified to teach Latin, French, Class-singing and ordinary English subjects, and competent to take the direction of the School in the absence of the Head Mistress. The salary of this lady will begin at £120, and may rise to £150 a year.
> 2. One specially qualified to teach Mathematics, Natural Science subjects, and French; her salary beginning at £100 a year, and being capable of rising to £120.
> 3. and 4. Two who are competent to teach ordinary English subjects, French, Drawing or Class-singing (but not both) and Needlework. In the case of these Mistresses it will be a recommendation if they are able to teach the Swedish system of Drill. The salaries offered will begin at £80 a year, and may rise to £100. (In the event, five teachers were appointed.)

It will be seen that she hopes to introduce a certain amount of specialist teaching. Only number 2 is required to teach Mathematics, while all are able to teach French. The curriculum which had been published as part of the advertisement for the Head Mistress has now been added to: neither a Natural Science subject nor the Swedish Drill appeared in that. It demands quite a complicated school timetable compared with each form being wholly or mainly taught by one teacher. Fourteen years later, inspectors appointed by the Board of Education commented: 'The School is thoroughly up to date in teaching methods, and the system by which a Form Mistress teaches her special subject to other Forms than her own is worthy of note and commendation.' With very many fewer staff, quiet Miss Smith was starting this system.

What was the quality of these Assistant Mistresses whom the Governors were belatedly appointing? Not until after the Board of Education was set up in 1899 were schools required to keep a record of the qualifications and experience of the staff they employed. It is by chance that we know anything more than the names of two of the women appointed in December, 1890. Miss Andrews, the Senior Assistant or, as the post was soon to be called, the Second Mistress, lasted just four terms. In March 1892 she was asked to resign and she left at the end of the Spring Term although she was entitled to a term's notice. The reason given was her behaviour, not her teaching ability. It is perhaps significant that the member of staff promoted to the post of Second Mistress, Miss Edith Brierley, had been appointed with greater deliberation after the School had opened. In 1895 she left to become the Head Mistress of Leek High School for Girls.

We know a great deal more about another of the December 1890 appointees. She was Edith Mary Openshaw and she was 21 years of age. Her father was the Revd Thomas W. Openshaw, the Second Master at the Grammar School, a mathematician and a stern disciplinarian who never lost his Lancashire accent. His pupils did well in University admission examinations and afterwards. Edith was one of the first pupils to enter Clifton High School when that School opened in 1878. She was nine, and stayed until she was twenty, the last two years as a 'Student Mistress', at the time one of the best ways of training as a teacher. She took the Higher Certificates of both the Oxford and Cambridge Joint Board and the Cambridge Board. Neither was a 'subject' examination in the modern manner, where the candidate has a free choice of as many or as few separate subjects as he pleases. Every successful candidate had to satisfy the examiners in the same range of obligatory subjects and then could choose to specialise in one or more groups of subjects. Edith chose to specialise in Mathematics. She left Clifton at the end of 1889 and for a year did not seek paid employment. Idleness, however, would not be encouraged in a household presided over by Mr Openshaw, and she probably made good use of her time.

The whole Openshaw family took an interest in her work and the new School. Her parents visited the School and her architect brother John later prepared plans for the drainage of some land which the School had just acquired. When Mr Openshaw retired from the Grammar School in 1892, and accepted a living near Banbury in Oxfordshire, he took with him his 'teaching chair' in which he had sat in the Great Hall with his class on benches round him. After his death in 1910, the family gave this wooden swivel chair to Colston's Girls' School and from then on it has been part of the furniture in the Head Mistress's room.

During the months of November and December, 1890, the Governors and the Head Mistress were seeing in great detail to the furnishing of the School. The design of the desks which had been ordered was modified so that the lids did not flop forward when lifted, and they were fitted with india rubber blocks so that they could not be closed otherwise than quietly. The room allotted to the Head Mistress on the ground floor, with windows overlooking Cheltenham Road (the present Secretary's room), had no dressing room attached to it. One was made by cutting off a strip of the Stationery storeroom next door and making another door into the corridor. It was a makeshift arrangement and the dressing room had no lavatory facilities. Messrs James Fawn and Son had applied to become Booksellers and Stationers to the School. They offered 25% off the published price of all the books they sold and they were allocated what remained of the Stationery storeroom, which was fitted out with shelves and cupboards for the use of their salesman.

A piano and a harmonium, or American Organ, was provided and a table to go on the dais for the Head Mistress's use in the Hall. The Clerk undertook to buy reading books suitable for the Entrance Examination. As late as two days before the first day of term in January, 1891, the Head Mistress was asked for a list of reference books which would be needed, and directed to order '8 easels and as many maps as may be required for School use, as well as the necessary materials for needlework, and dusters, table cloths, knives, forks, crockery and tumblers.'

The Chairman himself took charge of two further appointments, a man and his wife to be Caretaker and Housekeeper. The man was to look after the heating and lighting, the water supply, the condition of the roof and drains, the cleaning of the windows and the sweeping and cleaning of the approaches to the School and playground. He was also required to 'attend to the doors' and generally to be responsible for the security for the building and the premises. He would be given a livery and would answer the front door bell. The Housekeeper was required to receive the girls on their arrival at School each morning and superintend their change of clothes, to cook dinners and make all arrangements in respect of them, and to be responsible for cleaning the interior of the School.

Once again, the Governors' experience of a boarding school seems to have influenced the list of duties they drew up. There was accommodation for the couple and for one other servant within the building. They were to have thirty five shillings a week, and their coal and gas. The Housemaid would be paid £15 a year. As she too lived in, the Housekeeper would be paid seven shillings and sixpence for providing the Housemaid's food, and a shilling a week for doing her washing. The rest of the domestic staff consisted of two – later three – scrubbing women who were paid six shillings a week for cleaning from 6.00 a.m. to 9.30 a.m. five days a week.

The Chairman interviewed a couple who had been recommended to him by the Chief Constable, but it turned out that they had a family, and there was no accommodation for children. The two posts had to be advertised and on December 22 Mr Proctor Baker appointed Walter and Mary Fancourt 'subject to their references being found satisfactory'. They were to move in on January 1. Their joint wages meant that their income was higher than all except two of the rest of the staff. Those two were the Head Mistress and the Second Mistress and neither of the two women had accommodation with lighting and heating added to her salary. The Fancourts and their successors were important people in the life of the School, easily recognised in their uniforms by all the girls.

The Fancourts stayed for ten years, but their tenure was not without incident. Towards the end of that time Walter seems to have been developing other interests. In 1898 it was found that he had built a henhouse on ground belonging to the Trust beside the playground. He was told he could keep it there, but that if the Governors needed the ground it must be dismantled at once. On several occasions he was warned that he must not take any employment other than his work for the School, without first obtaining the permission of the Governors. Unfortunately for him, his moonlighting consisted of singing in public and his performances were reported in the local papers. The Governors insisted that this activity should be restricted to Places of Worship, and never during the working day. Eventually he bought himself a business which required his urgent attention, and which could perhaps be combined with his singing. Mr and Mrs Fancourt left abruptly and their place was taken by the much loved Mr and Mrs Stokes and their dog.

Back in December 1890 Miss Smith left Bristol for Christmas but not before writing to the Governors to say that she thought that they must advertise after the holiday for a sixth assistant member of staff, generally qualified to teach English subjects and Class-singing and to play the harmonium. She probably did this after having had a preview of the ages of the pupils who would be entering the School in January. Her dismay can be imagined when looking at the following table of the numbers and ages of pupils:

Numbers of pupils	Age in years
1	6
4	7
15	8
11	9
18	10
31	11
49	12
40	13
26	14
10	15
205	

It was of course gratifying that so many parents at once wanted to send their daughters to the School but even if Miss Smith taught full time, and she probably did, she and the five members of staff already appointed would have great difficulty in making six viable classes of these girls. If she put all the six, seven, eight and nine year olds together in one class of 31 girls with one teacher, she was probably recreating the conditions from which parents were trying to rescue their daughters. The remaining 174 girls, aged ten upwards, do not easily fall into five groups.

It must be remembered that at the time it was not thought important that all the pupils in a class should be of the same age. There was no general automatic promotion at the end of the academic year and a few pupils would be promoted to the class above at the end of each term. They entered the School with a variety of academic experiences. They had not all come from the elementary or 'Board' schools where a 'Standard' appropriate to each year of a schoolchild's age had by now been agreed on. Some came from private schools and some had been taught at home. This increased the problems and made the holding of the 'Entrance Examination' even more necessary.

When, before the School opened, the Clerk reported that 202 girls had 'passed the Entrance Examination' he did not mean what we mean by this today. The Prospectus says that the School is open to 'all girls who are of good character and of sufficient bodily health'; nothing about academic achievement. The Scheme says that the examination for admission must be graduated according to age and the standard must not fall below that required for admission to the Boys' Boarding School. This was minimal.

At ten the boys had to be able to read easy narrative, write on lines half an inch apart, add and subtract, and know 'the multiplication table'. This had been put in because, as Fitch had repeatedly alleged without contradiction, some of the Foundationers had been admitted before having learnt to read. So the Entrance Examination was in no way competitive. It was conducted by the Head Mistress to determine which class the girl should be placed in and probably took the form of a short interview in which the Head Mistress could begin to get to know her pupils. That this was so for at least the next twenty years is shown by the date of the Entrance Examinations, the day before the beginning of each term, when it would have been far too late to make the decision whether or not to admit the child to the School.

On Monday, January 19, 1891, Walter Fancourt opened the door on the Cheltenham Road to the girls. They were met by Mrs Mary Fancourt, who directed each girl to her numbered cloakroom peg, her book box and her umbrella stand. Then the teaching staff took over. School had begun.

Who were they, these first new girls, and where did they come from? We know the occupation of their fathers and, as it happens, this information forms part of the reports of the General Inspections of 1905 and 1914. The following table shows percentages of pupils in terms of their fathers' livelihoods.

	P	M	R	F	C	T	A	D
1891	15	10	17	–	28	7	14	9
1905	15	9	24	1	35	4	4	8
1914	19	11	25	4	25		14	2

Column 'P' shows the professionals. In 1914 teachers were not shown separately under 'T' but were included among these. 'M' stands for merchants and the

Board of Education civil servants included in this group anyone who worked in a bank as well as wholesalers. Those who owned or worked in retail shops appear under 'R'. 'F' are the farmers. 'C' are clerks, who worked in offices and did not make or sell anything. 'T', as mentioned before, are teachers. 'A' are artisans and 'D' means that the father is either dead or his occupation unknown. Of course, people do not always describe their trade or profession very precisely on application forms, which is where this information comes from, but the figures show a remarkably consistent pattern over the first twenty three years in the life of the School. In 1875 the Boys' Boarding School offered an education 'adapted to the wants of sons of Farmers, Tradesmen, Clerks and others.' The relatively few farmers' daughters in the Girls' School was probably because it was a day and not a boarding school.

Many girls did come, as the Governors had thought they would, from the residential districts nearest to the School, but some came quite long distances. There was a contingent from the east of the city, from Fishponds and Downend.

Although the additional post on the staff had been advertised after Christmas, Miss Smith thought none of the applicants suitable. The Governors had heard that a teacher employed by the Bristol Schools Board would like to transfer to the School staff and one of the women Governors, Mrs Abbot, and Miss Smith interviewed her but could not recommend her appointment. Eventually the Head Mistress suggested her own sister, Miss Annie Smith, who was qualified and free to come. The Governors agreed and the number of assistant staff increased to six for over 200 pupils. During this first term nearly a hundred more girls were accepted for the summer term and Miss Smith very reasonably asked for three more teachers. She only got two, possibly because there were no more suitably qualified staff available, and it was not until January 1892 that the additional teacher started work. Even so, nine teachers for 300 girls aged from 7 to 17 was scarcely adequate. In March, 1892, the first pupil teacher was appointed. She was Eva Saint Hill and it will be seen from the list of the ages of pupils when the School opened that she must at most have just turned eighteen. Her parents still paid her fees, but she was told that at the end of a year she might be paid a gratuity. She was. It was £3–6s–8d, less than the £5 school fees. The experiment was evidently a success, for from then on there were never fewer than two pupil teachers on the staff. They were not paid anything, but Eva Saint Hill's successors did not pay school fees, and did receive some tuition.

In 1894 a part time appointment was made which turned out to be very important to the School. This was Mrs Alice Mary Wensley Bunce who taught four hours of class singing a week for a salary of £30 a year. She was a singer well known locally and had a great reputation for being able to train choirs. She began a tradition of good choral singing in the School and she stayed until 1921. Her husband wrote songs for the School to sing.

When she was first appointed she helped the staffing situation by being able to teach two or more forms at a time and so allowed other members of staff to teach small specialist groups in other forms. There were still only seven classrooms, but Mrs Bunce would use the Hall and free classrooms for other teaching. The waiting room at the top of the main stairs, opposite the Cheltenham Road door, would hold 12 girls and was regularly used for teaching. Even in the mid-Nineties the building was beginning to feel small.

The other staff probably did not know that at £30 a year for a four hour week Mrs Bunce was being paid at a higher rate than the second mistress, Miss Brierley, whose salary was £120 a year. They did not need to know to be dissatisfied with their lot. Since the School opened they had worked and were working extremely hard, and no one seemed to be recognising this. The Governors had originally intended to increase salaries annually by modest amounts – £10 or £5 a year. They had at the last moment, after the job descriptions had been printed, come down on the side of caution and withdrawn the promise, so that every rise in salary had to be asked for and, as often as not, refused. During this decade the Bristol School Board was setting up post-elementary schools and the word was that the salary scales were better. Dedicated as people like Miss Openshaw were, and there must have been others like her, the mood in the staffroom was not always one of contentment. Nor was Miss Smith's task of appointing staff an easy one. Resignations too near the end of term, or during a term with no notice at all, meant that her choice was limited to teachers who happened not to be in work at the time.

Such problems are the symptoms of a system not fully worked out or imperfectly understood by employer and employee. There were also pupil and parent problems. At the end of the second term, the Clerk had to send out a circular letter to all parents reminding them that their daughters must come to school regularly and punctually. For many years voluntary attendance at day schools had been poor, with anything from paid occasional employment, such as hop picking, to sheer disinclination being seen as a sufficient reason to stay away. Even though by 1890 school attendance was compulsory, old habits of thought and old priorities remained. Miss Smith instituted Attendance Prizes, which could be won by being never absent and never late.

The habit of consistently hard work also had to be acquired. Punishments were by modern standards Draconian. In 1892 a girl was expelled for being 'persistently disobedient and idle and a bad influence in the School' and the next year another was expelled for theft. Perhaps these early measures had their effect, for there were no more expulsions until the Great Pornography Scandal of 1898. There was, however, a group of girls who literally could not afford to be idle. These were the Exhibitioners.

The number of Exhibitions was not increased. When the number of Exhibitioners left in School had fallen to five, five more Exhibitions were offered for competition. This happened at the end of 1895 and the opportunity was taken to modify the 1891 rules. Now two of the Exhibitions could be won by girls of the right age already in the School, and three could go to girls in schools other than Elementary. This change seems to have been made not because of any shortage of Elementary School candidates but because it was being recognised that some parents were finding it hard to continue to pay the Colston fee.

The scheme also required another kind of examination, the School Examination. This really was an examination of the School, not of individual candidates, and it took place over a number of days in December. The examiner, in the case of many schools a clergyman, set written papers, examined pupils orally, read syllabuses and watched lessons. He wrote a report which he sent to the Chairman of the Governors. It is a pity that none of these reports survive from Miss Smith's time, but it is certain that while they may have contained helpful advice they were not adverse. Only one criticism was sufficiently serious to require action. A recently appointed member of staff was told that her work must improve. She left two terms later. This custom of annual School Examinations was well established and went on for some time after the Eighteen Nineties. It came to an end when the new Board of Education made regular General Inspections and when public external examinations were taken by most pupils.

The School started to use public examinations quite soon. The Governors, who had been converted to the idea of these examinations by the Headmaster of the Boys' School, stipulated only that the girls should pay their own examination fees. In March 1892 Miss Brierley, who became Second Mistress and specialised in Art, entered candidates for the examination in Drawing set by the Department of Science and Art, the humbler forerunner of the Board of Education. At the end of the same year 31 girls were entered for the examinations set by the College of Preceptors and 28 passed. After this the School began using the examinations of the Cambridge Local Board and whole holidays were regularly given for outstanding successes. In December 1898 a Colston girl was placed 3rd out of 309 candidates in Botany in the Cambridge Senior division and in the Junior division one was 1st in English out of 8,470 candidates and another 1st in Botany out of 760 candidates. The next year 26 girls were entered for the Cambridge Local. No one failed and 8 achieved Honours over all the subjects they took. By now girls were being admitted to Universities, to University Colleges such as Bristol and to the Merchant Venturers' Technical College which prepared students both for admission to Universities and for the external degrees of the University of London. In less than ten years this was a remarkable achievement.

This went on against a background of financial stringency which had not been foreseen. The Governors had budgeted for a shortfall in the School's income and had been confident that this could be covered by Trust funds.

The school had cost more than they expected to build and this had reduced the income from investments. Even more serious was the effect of the agricultural recession in the early Eighteen Nineties, when the income from the tenant farmers on the great estates, purchased by Edward Colston as the basis of his endowment, virtually dried up. At the end of 1892 the Clerk warned the Head Mistress that expenditure had greatly outrun income. This was certainly the case. In the past year they had spent £1,886 and although the School was full, the fees only amounted to £1,450, leaving £436 to be found elsewhere. The position of the Boys' School was as bad. There the number of feepayers, which had never been high, was falling. A master who resigned was not replaced. The Girls' School made pathetic attempts to economise. The telephone – rental, £10 a year – was disconnected. The amount spent on prizes was reduced from £20 to £15. More importantly, the salaries of the teaching staff were kept as low as possible, to the point where a teacher left to earn more in a Board School. On the positive side, classes were proposed which would be paid for as extras. There were not enough takers to make a cookery class an economic proposition, but dancing classes in the Hall were popular and made a profit. Needlework was made part of the curriculum of every girl in the School. It was an important skill at a time when readymade clothes were not widely available, but the articles the girls made were not for themselves. In 1895 a Sale of Needlework was held and a profit of £16–13s–0d was made. Permission was given for half of this to be spent on tables for model drawing. This was a useful provision, for there was no artroom and drawing had to be done at ordinary desks. It is difficult to imagine where the tables were kept or, indeed, used. At another Sale two years later £18–17s–0d was raised. £10 of this was spent on 'three long desks'.

The saddest retrenchment was the removal of Latin from the general curriculum. It went to make way for the universal needlework and was offered as an extra. That some girls did learn Latin is shown by the University admissions.

The solution to these financial problems lay in raising the School fee, but this could not be done without the permission of the Charity Commissioners. The Clerk asked the Commissioners for the authorisation of a £6 annual fee in 1893. In reply, they enquired 'whether it was anticipated that the contemplated increase in the fee would tend to diminish the number of scholars and also whether the class of parents whose girls attend the School were able to pay the increased fee.' The first of these two questions is the only relevant one: if a school can not pay its staff's salaries, the rates, the fuel bills and the maintenance of buildings and equipment, it will in the long run have to close, and no pupil at all will benefit. Perhaps the Commissioners' preoccupation with social class found an echo in the Merchants' charitable feelings. They struggled on without, it seems, even attempting to find out what the effect of a higher fee would be on recruitment.

These financial anxieties made the Head Mistress's task of directing a new school even more onerous than it would have been in any case. The effect on the teaching staff was also felt. Their formal request for an all round increase in salaries was turned down by the Governors in 1893. Two years later they complained to a Governor, Mr W. W. Jose, interestingly enough not the Chairman, that they were 'overpressured.' The complaint was taken seriously and examined by a subcommittee of three Governors. They recommended that more help should be given by 'student mistresses', and the teaching platforms in the classrooms should be raised to double their present height so that the staff could sit, and still be able to see the face of every girl in the room.

Until 1898 there had never been any anxiety about the number of girls in the School. It had its full complement of 300 pupils and the Clerk usually reported that he had a short waiting list of girls whose parents wished them to be admitted. Quite early on in the School's history it had been possible to encourage younger girls to apply for admission and the good effect that a longer time in the School had on the results of public examinations at sixteen and seventeen has been seen. At the usual Governors' meeting at the end of 1898, however, the Clerk reported that at the end of the term there would be 57 vacancies and he had only received 10 applications for admission. He thought the reason was that the Bristol School Board had opened a coeducational Higher Grade School in Fairfield Road, Montpelier. But by the time the January term began the 10 applications had become 47 and by the end of the year the numbers in the School had returned to normal.

Alarming as this surprising drop in applications had been, worse was to come before the end of term. On Thursday, December 22, the day on which the Bishop of Bristol was due to visit the School to distribute the prizes, the Governors held an emergency meeting in response to a letter from Miss Smith. She had suspended 17 girls from school for having 'copied or circulated an immoral paper'. The Governors needed no convincing of the rightness of this action. They confirmed the suspension until the beginning of the January term in the case of 14 of the girls, and expelled the other three. Two of the fourteen were Exhibitioners, and their Exhibitions were to be terminated. The whole School was sent home a day early and the Prizegiving postponed. Presumably word was sent to the Bishop.

The Chairman, Mr Proctor Baker, took over. He wrote a personal letter to parents of the fourteen and signed each copy himself. It ran:

> Dear Sir,
>
> I am directed by the Governors of Colston's Girls' School to inform you that your daughter . . . (full name) . . . was concerned in the copying or circulation of an immoral paper in the Colston's Girls' Day School during the past term.
>
> While the Governors have refrained from taking the measure of expelling the girl from the School and are willing to restore her to her place, I am instructed

to say that your daughter can be received at the School next Term only on the condition that she is to be liable to immediate suspension should any misconduct on her part in or out of the School come to the knowledge of the Head Mistress.

Yours truly,
William Proctor Baker
Chairman of the Governors
Colston's Girls' Day School

The Governors recorded their confidence in Miss Smith: 'The Governors desire to place on record the expression of their sympathy for the Head Mistress, Miss Smith, in the very trying circumstances which she has reported, and their opinion that she has omitted nothing in the conduct and management of the School that could have prevented the occurrences – They also desire to record their high appreciation of the vigour, courage and intelligence which Miss Smith has displayed in the investigation of the matter and their approval of every step which she has taken.'

The affair did not go away for the whole of the next term. At Easter the father of one of the expelled girls was still pleading for her re-instatement, but the Governors remained adamant. It was discovered that the parents of one of the Exhibitioners had been told she would lose her Scholarship and 'through inadvertence at Merchants' Hall' the parents of the other had not. Being intelligent girls, they had both behaved so well during the Spring term that Miss Smith was able to recommend that they both retained their Exhibitions.

It is inconceivable today that the 'immoral paper' would have been taken so seriously, but Miss Smith and the Governors knew the public attitudes of their time and could not run the risk that the School became known as a place where explicit descriptions of sexual activity were passed freely from hand to hand without stern action from the authorities. Those who deplore the freedom of speech about such matters today should consider whether the furtiveness with which intelligent young people tried to inform themselves of their own sexuality, and the guilt they were made to feel when they were found out, were not worse.

In April 1899, the Governors asked the Head Mistress whether she wished to be included in a contributary pension scheme but she declined. In December her sister Annie resigned and the Governors penned the most glowing tribute to her of any of the leaving staff. The next year Miss Smith herself resigned.

She left no personal records of herself or her stewardship, and all we have from her pen are a few short letters she wrote on special occasions after she went back to London. All the reports she wrote for the Governors have disappeared. No reason for her going was given, but it was certainly not to another headship, which would have been recorded. Years afterwards, Miss Openshaw recalled that she retained her interest in scholastic matters, as she did in the School. She visited Bristol from London, sometimes staying for a few nights. She had not reached retirement age, which at the time was fifty.

Many years later she was to say that the ten years she had spent in Bristol were the happiest of her life but at this time, when the nineteenth century was changing into the twentieth, one can not help feeling that in December, 1900, she had just had enough.

MISS HUGHES

The headship was advertised rather more succinctly than on the previous occasion. Candidates were to be women between 24 and 35 years of age, unmarried and members of the Church of England. Other things being equal, preference would be given to a Lady who had attained Honours in some University or other public examination. The Clerk reported that 50 out of the 60 applicants fulfilled these conditions and four young women were interviewed on 26 November. This time the Governors had no hesitation. They offered the post to Miss Evangeline Margaret Hughes and she accepted. She signed her name in the minute book, the three initial letters more than twice the size of the rest.

It is as though a black and white silent film had flickered to a moment's blankness and then the screen had come alive in full colour with stereophonic sound. It is not only that co-incidentally the new Board of Education was requiring factual records to be kept by schools. It was also that Miss Hughes had a feeling for history which included safeguarding the present for posterity, and was surrounded by people, like Edith Openshaw, who wanted to preserve every scrap of paper, every formal note. So we know more about Miss Hughes from the moment she entered the School than we learn about Miss Smith in her ten years' sojourn.

Eva Hughes was the daughter of the Revd Williams Hughes, M.A., Rector of Llanfechell on Anglesey, and his wife Margaret. She was educated at a boarding school in Warwick until she was fourteen and then went to the North London Collegiate School for four years. From there she went to Bedford College in the University of London, where she took her degree in 1902. She taught at the Central Foundation School for Girls until she was appointed Head Mistress of Colston's Girls' School at the age of 28. Her father had died when she was sixteen, and she had at least three brothers, not all of whom survived to manhood. It seems likely that her mother was dead by the time she came to Bristol, for we do not hear anything of her. We do hear of a number of cousins and other relatives, some titled and others holding important posts in the Church. Her education had been expensive and she could afford to go on foreign holidays: for instance, to Greece and Norway with her cousin, Essylt Williams.

She was above average height and her erect carriage and graceful movement made her appear even taller. Her features were well marked and her lively changes of mood could be seen even in as large a room as the Assembly Hall. Wherever she went or whatever she was doing, she made an immediate impression.

At her first Governors' meeting the question of raising the school fee came up again. Besides being a way of relieving the chronic insufficiency of the School's income, it was necessary if the staff salaries were to be improved. The Governors repeated the question put to them by the Charity Commissioners six years earlier: would the number of pupils in the School be reduced? The Head Mistress was asked to find out and report at the next meeting. What enquiries she made we do not know but there is an art in asking the right question if you want a particular answer. She assured the next Governors' meeting that parents would be quite happy to pay the increased fee. The matter was put to the Charity Commissioners and permission to increase the annual school fee to £6 was given before the end of the year. There was another factor in the school income sum. It had proved possible to put up the fee. Why not increase the number of pupils? Miss Smith's answer to that would have been that the Scheme said 300 pupils and any admission over that number would be unauthorised. Miss Hughes simply went ahead. When two years later the Governors in consternation complained that she really ought not to go above 350 – at that point she had in mind 360 – she replied with earnest fervour that she really did not approve of having more than 40 girls in a class. The numbers rose steadily, like the tide coming in. In 1912, for instance, there were 523 girls in the School. Whilst it was all very well to admit pupils, she still had to find somewhere to put them. By the end of her first year in the School, she had had one good and one very good idea about this.

The opportunity to implement the good idea appeared to arise by chance, but luck favours people like Miss Hughes. The singing caretaker, Fancourt, gave in his notice at the end of her first term. What differences, musical or otherwise, which prompted this were not rehearsed. He said he had bought a business which required more of his time. She interviewed a Mrs Stokes for the post of Housekeeper and having satisfied herself that this lady was suitable, interviewed her husband. There was a circumstance which might have caused difficulty. The Stokeses did not want to live in the School building. Miss Hughes did not think a resident caretaker was necessary in a day school. Mr Stokes must have lived near enough to let in the scrubbing women at six o'clock in the morning and to lock up at night. Mr and Mrs Stokes were appointed and lived in their own home. It was an excellent appointment. Miss Hughes had her first empty space and the next time the Governors had occasion to use the services of Mr Gough, the architect, 'three small rooms in the basements' were 'thrown into one' and a new classroom was gained.

Mr Gough's reappearance was in connection with a more ambitious building scheme than this. The first addition to the ten year old building was to be a wing which included two science laboratories and a lecture theatre. Like several other proposals which came to fruition under Miss Hughes's guidance, this idea had been considered, but not acted upon, before her arrival.

MISS HUGHES

In July, 1990, the Bristol Technical Instruction Committee under the chairmanship of Mr Jose had asked the Governors whether they would equip a laboratory for the teaching of science in the School and offered £1,000 towards new buildings and £100 a year towards the cost of additional staffing. The Governors replied that not only had they no funds for capital outlay but their income was quite insufficient for existing needs. The next year the Technical Instruction Committee renewed the offer of government money to make possible the teaching of the sciences as practical subjects, asking only that the school should give three scholarships to encourage an interest in science. This time the Governors' response was different. The Clerk was instructed both to ask the Committee to increase the initial payment from £1,000 to £1,500 and also to write to the Charity Commissioners for permission to sell Consols (fixed interest government securities) to raise the extra money needed for the new building, the total cost of which was estimated at £3,000. The Committee refused to increase its offer, but the Charity Commissioners gave permission for the funds to be realised to cover the cost of the building.

The Governors decided to go ahead, and in doing so they were taking a step even more important than enlarging the school building or widening the curriculum. They were accepting public – that is, government – money for the first time. They had been advised to seek such assistance by a School Examiner, Mr C.A. Buckmaster, as early as 1895. At the time a sub-committee of the Governors, Mrs Abbot, Mr Arthur Brown and Mr Jose, was asked to look into the matter. No action was taken. The idea of accepting financial assistance from the government, national or local, was counter to most of nineteenth century thinking, in spite of the establishment of public elementary schools in 1870. The argument went thus: those that paid the piper called the tune: with denominational schools parents knew what the bias of the teaching was to be, but who could guess the bias of an education provided if only partially by the government set up by a political party? Six years later Mr Jose as the Chairman of the Bristol Technical Instruction Committee could play his part in reassuring Governors that their philosophical independence would not be compromised by accepting a government grant.

His was not the only voice encouraging his fellow Governors to take this course of action. Miss Hughes had her own opinion and her own methods, which appear very ordinary to us now and must have been most extraordinary then. The Board of Education pamphlet setting out the conditions for the award of grants and the recognition of a school as either an 'Organised Science School' or a 'Secondary Day School' is a complex document. She reduced these rules and their meaning for the School to what, in her florid but surprisingly legible handwriting (no typewriter in School yet), would go on to one side of a piece of foolscap. If the School became an Organised Science School, known as Division A, it would qualify for a grant of £490 a year. If it became a Secondary Day School, in Division B, it would have at least £410 and might have as much as £510. The difference between the curricula of the two kinds of schools was that those in Division A provided 13 hours of Mathematics, Science and Drawing out of a 25 hour teaching week for three years, and those in Division B, 9 hours of Mathematics and Science for five years. Miss Hughes preferred the second curriculum with its earlier start to science, and gave her numbered reasons for this on the reverse side of this remarkable document. Then she took to the school copier, provided years before by Miss Smith but not, it seems, used by her to publish her views so widely, and rolled off a sufficient number of copies to send one to each of the Governors. There were doubtless a number of spares for use wherever they could do good, but the copy we have has been folded to go into an envelope with the Board of Education pamphlet. Reason number 5 on the reverse side is an example of her style and her thinking:

> I do *not* think we shall be able to give our girls sufficient English and French under *Division A* nor to make time for Prayers, Assembly and Recreation and all that goes to make up the *corporate life* and to make the *difference* between *School* and a mere assembly of grant earning classes. I can not help thinking that the larger grant would be too dearly bought at the expense of losing for our girls a *well-balanced education*.

It will be observed that she is not arguing in favour of teaching science in laboratories built for the purpose but is pressing the claims of one scientific curriculum as compared with another. This was a tactic she frequently employed. Before most people had grasped the outline of the overall plan she was involving them in the enthusiastic discussion of detail.

In March 1902 Mr Gough was instructed to draw up plans for a new building adjoining the original building and taking up some of the playground. Later that month Miss E.L. Walter, B.Sc., a Board of Education inspector, was invited to School to give a preliminary course of lessons in physical science and Gough took the opportunity to consult her about current thinking on teaching laboratories. His plans were approved in April and the work went out to tender at once. The builder chosen in May was C.A. Hayes and a Clerk of Works to supervise both the work at the Girls' School and new buildings at the Boys' School was appointed. Building began on July 21. It took much longer than had been hoped and it was not opened officially until May of the next year. In the meantime Miss Hughes ensured that interest in Science did not abate among the girls. Physics was at once introduced into the curriculum of the upper forms. A science graduate, Miss Ison, and an assistant, Miss James, were appointed and began teaching in September 1902, and in the following January a Senior Science Mistress, Miss Blake, with a salary greater than that of the second Mistress, took up her post. Although the doors to the new wing were still fastened by screws so that there should be no trespassing from the main school, scientific equipment of all kinds, large and small, began to arrive in the Spring term, and was stored in the waiting room, the stationery storeroom, the sixth form room and anywhere else where it would be safe. The teaching of botany was already well established and judged by examination results most successful. Now the teaching of physics and chemistry was beginning with the keenest anticipation and the greatest excitement. As the doors into the science building were unscrewed and the girls were allowed to see the wonders within, Miss Hughes must have been pleased, if not content, with the acquisition of four new classrooms, the physics and chemistry laboratories, the lecture room and the 'three small rooms thrown into one' in the basement, not to mention the quite commodious preparation rooms insisted on by Miss Walter, one of which, the physics preparation room, might be used as a teaching room for a small class. By the end of 1903 there were 352 girls in the School but now, after three years of fitting pupils into the most unlikely spaces, there was adequate accommodation for classes: always provided that the numbers did not continue to increase.

Staff and girls who were in School when Miss Hughes arrived remembered her as beginning a great many new ventures; not just doing things in a different way from her predecessor, as every Head must do, but introducing new ideas and activities. In this their memories were only partly correct. They were remembering Miss Hughes's style, which was very different from Miss Smith's. Even her clothes were different. Miss Smith wore something very similar to what the rest of the staff wore: a pale, high necked, long sleeved blouse and a floor length, simply cut dark skirt: almost a uniform. Miss Hughes's clothes were fashionable. She dressed with care for particular occasions. In her photographs she can never be mistaken for one of the assistant staff. Miss Smith, as we have seen, began by teaching what must have been almost a full timetable and in the face of staff complaints about 'over pressure' probably continued with much more class teaching than would be thought appropriate today. Inspectors of the School in 1905 noted with approval that Miss Hughes taught only two lessons (of Geography) a week and so was free to supervise the teaching in the School in person. Old Girls remembered the effect on a class of her entrance and the vivid interest in the work in hand she brought with her.

Yet it is true that she made innovations. A week after she came she held a meeting to discuss the formation of a Hockey Club, a game which had begun to be taken up by athletic young women in the Eighteen Nineties. Although Miss Smith had had two grass tennis courts laid out in the playground, and these had been much used, there were no organised outdoor games lessons and hockey remained a 'club' – or voluntary – activity for over twenty years. There was evidently a sufficient number of girls interested and willing to pay a subscription each term and provide themselves with the necessary equipment. This was a hockey stick, for the game was played in ordinary clothes. Five days later the first practice was held, and the first match was played three weeks after this. A coach, Miss Dale, was engaged to visit once a fortnight.

In the following autumn the club migrated to stretches of grass more nearly equivalent to a full sized pitch than could be found behind the School in Cheltenham Road and began to play other clubs. Their early scores were dismal but the popularity of the game increased. Team captains were elected and there was competition to get into the 1st XI. The hockey club was followed by a rounders club for younger girls and the opportunities for exercise out of doors in the winter increased.

In the summer, too, Miss Hughes encouraged other sporting activities as well as tennis. A cricket club was started and later swimming was introduced. A Sports Day was held at the end of each summer term. Heats were run off beforehand, a detailed programme was printed on the school copier, prizes were given by the Sports Club, the student teachers, the staff and, in many cases, by Miss Hughes, and Governors were pressed into service to act as judges and timekeepers and finally to present the prizes. As with many of the Head Mistress's special occasions, it had a strong social side. Soon, parents and friends were invited and the programme included a display of gymnastics, which was being taught as an after school activity in addition to the 'Swedish drill' introduced by Miss Smith. Two of the Governors, Mr Jose and Mr Mervyn King, took a particular interest in athletics and gave prizes and trophies. More significantly, they were always there, showing by their presence the importance they attached to the physical wellbeing and enjoyment of the girls.

Within two or three years there were so many clubs organising games and sports that it seemed sensible to merge them into one Games Club, with girls acting as secretaries to arrange the various fixture lists. Practices and matches were held after school at four o'clock in the afternoon and on Saturday mornings. In most games there were matches between forms as well as with other schools and clubs. It must have taken a great deal of staff time. That it was needed is indicated by the sad evidence of the school magazines of these early years of the twentieth century. There is scarcely an issue which does not record the death of a pupil or an Old Girl, and at this point in the School's history there were no old Old Girls. Illnesses, too, lasted a long time, often months or a year. The physical education the girls received, minimal and haphazard as it was by modern standards, actually improved their health and, visitors said, their appearance over the years.

The curriculum received Miss Hughes's early attention. She held separate staff meetings to discuss the syllabus in Arithmetic, Geography, History and French: nine staff meetings in the first term. She re-introduced Latin into the main course of study, and explained why this was necessary for girls who wished to take a university degree before going into teaching. The next term she started a German course. She arranged for sixth form girls studying French to correspond with French schoolgirls and she engaged a native French speaker, a M. Poisson, to give French conversation lessons. This was evidently a temporary arrangement, until she could appoint a specialist French teacher with a good standard in the spoken language. At the time such teachers were hard to find. She appointed Miss Anne Merriman ('Gentle Anne') who was a good teacher but had not been to France. The Governors made her a grant of £10 which enabled her to go to Paris and take a short course at the Sorbonne.

Academic classwork was supplemented among the older girls by the formation of yet more Clubs. The most important of these was the Reading Club which met fortnightly during the two winter terms. Each meeting included some reading aloud, usually by the senior English Specialist, and over a term a book such as *The Vicar of Wakefield* or *Emma* would be studied. The rest of the entertainment was literary: discussions, puzzles and rehearsals for recitations and dialogues. Staff and Old Girls attended as well as sixth formers. The Science staff ran the Field Club, the membership of which was limited to 20 sixth formers, although others might attend by invitation. The Musical Society met every Tuesday evening, from time to time changing its name to the Choral and putting on concerts. The Empire League was most active round about Empire Day on May 25. They usually had outside speakers on the history and more particularly the geography of the Empire. The Art Union was very popular among Old Girls as well as present pupils and they held exhibitions of their work. At least one or more of these 'Club' meetings was held in School after four o'clock every day and on Saturday mornings. It would be easy to explain this enthusiasm for what were essentially complements and extensions to school lessons by recalling that girls and staff had fewer other entertainments and distractions than they have now, but this would be to miss the point. The Clubs offered the girls something they found exciting and which they preferred to doing other things or doing nothing.

Miss Hughes was concerned that all the girls should acquire the habit of reading. They bought their own textbooks but there was as yet no School Library. She encouraged them to set up form libraries, small collections of books brought from home and carefully vetted by form mistresses, or given by friends of the School. She had begun very soon after her arrival to complain about the heating of the School as inadequate. At this time it consisted of gas stoves in the various rooms. The heating engineers recommended heating by hot water pipes and although this system with its bulky radiators will be remembered by generations of Colston girls as less than perfect, it was probably an advance on what was there before. The gas stoves were removed from the classrooms, leaving little alcoves, some of which remain. Miss Hughes had shelves put in these alcoves to house the form libraries. They became a feature of each form room.

The School Museum was in a glass fronted case which from time to time occupied different positions in the School building before coming to rest near the physics laboratory and being looked after by Miss Ison, a member of the science department. All the objects in it were gifts and each gift had to be accompanied by a card bearing the name of the donor and an accurate description of the object itself. It sounds as though it was likely to become a depository for unwanted junk, but it was never that. Every magazine gives a list of recent Gifts to the Museum and, for instance, one of the shorter lists, that for Autumn, 1904, ran as follows: Calc spear, botanical diagrams and a collection of shells, mounted and named from the Curator of the Bristol Museum; fossils from the Eifel region; a Bana Book (part of the Buddhist scriptures); and some pieces of drapery used on the choir stalls of Westminster Abbey at the Coronation of King Edward VII. It is no wonder that soon after this the collection overflowed into the Physics Laboratory.

No effort was spared to stimulate the girls' interest in issues at home and abroad. The first lesson period of every Monday morning was devoted to Address. Miss Hughes talked to the whole School in the Assembly Hall about any event in the past week which she considered important. It might be a matter of school policy or discipline but it was more likely to be national or international affairs, or a mixture of all three. She had a beautiful singing voice and, accompanying herself on the school harmonium, she would teach the girls a new hymn for use at School Prayers. She would give a 'motto' to think about in the coming week. These mottoes were recorded in the magazine and so relayed to Old Girls. Sometimes they had a direct reference to the situation of the School and its pupils: 'Those who trust us educate us' (George Eliot); sometimes they were practical reminders of good behaviour: 'Give us to go blithely about our business all this day' (R.L. Stevenson); sometimes they embodied ideas which would be explained at greater length: 'What is not good for the swarm neither is it good for the bee' (Marcus Aurelius). Very rarely were these mottoes repeated, and one wonders at the ingenuity which found a fresh one almost every week. One, however, was used very frequently, often as the Term's Motto. It was Carlyle's 'Know Thy Work and Do It', and it is clear that she really preferred it to the Colston motto 'Go and Do Thou Likewise', which when combined with a drawing of a dolphin with an arched back can lead to misunderstanding. She herself always seemed to know her work and to do it with ardour.

Today young people learn about current affairs from radio and television bulletins. Then the only way that people could learn what was going on was by reading newspapers and in times of crisis, such as general elections, by attending public meetings. The newspapers, serious and detailed, needed interpretation if younger people were to understand them. A weekly 'newspaper' made of cuttings and explanations was displayed in School in a glass fronted notice board. At first Miss Hughes prepared this herself, but later members of staff took it in turn.

Forms were encouraged to write Form Magazines for publication on the form notice board. Original stories and poems were included in these magazines, but the most important part was a Chronicle of the form's doings, the arrival of new girls, the promotion of old friends and the success or failure of form teams. In July 1902 the first School Magazine appeared. It was to appear termly at a cost of 3d per copy. Old Girls could receive it by post if they paid 11d a year. The first edition contained two short poems by a member of staff, one on the benefits of working together for the good of all and the other a humorous fantasy about the inspection of desks of untidy girls by Edward Colston. There was one page of Editorial, another five of Chronicle, an account of the major events of the term, and the rest of the twenty or so pages is devoted to school and form matters in great detail, reports of the work of the Clubs and news of Old Girls. Examination successes are recorded in full.

Miss Hughes explains the purpose of the Magazine in the Editorial. 'We have for some time wished that C.G.S. should, like so many other large public schools have its own magazine.' She hopes that it will 'prove a real help towards promoting the sound corporate life, and that unselfish care for the honour of the School, which is, I am sure, the idea of each and all of us.' She remained the Editor, although the bulk of the work of producing the magazine was done by the Sub-Editor, Miss A.F. Edwards, who always wrote the School Chronicle at the beginning of each issue. She was one of Miss Hughes's earliest and best appointments. When Miss Potts resigned to take up her appointment as Head of the Leek Church High School, a Miss Greene was appointed as Second Mistress, but she resigned without ever coming to Bristol. The last minute appointment of Amy Edwards was only possible because she had taken a series of temporary posts in G.P.D.S.T. schools for the previous eighteen months and so was free to begin work in January, 1902. She was three years younger than Miss Hughes and had taken the Cambridge degree examination in History, passing with second class honours. As well as being Second Mistress, she was in charge of English and History and the Sixth Form. Many Old Girls testify to the vigour and imagination of her teaching. She was an ideal choice as the compiler of a School Chronicle, for she writes with graceful good humour. The Magazine was published every term until 1914, and then twice a year. Most of it was written by girls and with Staff comments and the news of Old Girls it represents a valuable and moving record of a School growing in self confidence.

Miss Hughes had other methods of promoting the awareness of corporate life. One was the prefectorial system. In her first year in School prefects were appointed from the Sixth form for the first time. As there were then 26 girls in the Sixth it is unlikely that everyone became a prefect but at least all those in their second year must have done. There was a School Captain and a Sub-Captain, nomenclature which was an echo of boys' public schools. Their duties were carried out in the cloakrooms and in the corridors, where conversations were not allowed and 'square corners' were insisted on. The girls moved about the school in single file and when they came to a corner they turned smartly through an angle of 90 degrees, to proceed on their silent way. The next year prefects were appointed from each form. They took the lead in form matters and were supported by a team of monitresses. Early in the next year there was the first 'Honour Day'. The discipline of the School everywhere except in the classroom was taken over by the prefects, school and form. Such days, and then sequences of days, became important events of each term. In the weeks when they occurred the motto was always 'Honour Bright'. Miss Hughes looked forward to a time when not even prefects would be on duty on Honour Days.

She believed that the environment in which girls learnt had an effect on their development and was determined that all members of the School should be actively engaged in trying to achieve the ideal that she called the 'House Beautiful'. Flower Clubs in each form saw to it that flowers were brought to School and carefully arranged and tended. On special occasions the whole building was decorated inside with flowers in the School colours, which were then red and white. Gifts of vases and flower pots were presented to each form, and there was a Flower Shield to be won by the form with the best floral displays throughout the term. Prints were given to the girls to frame for their rooms and gifts and prizes of pictures already framed were eagerly sought after. Disconsolate writers of form notes for the magazine complained when their walls were 'rather bare', and form notice boards were the object of particular attention. Permanent notices were expected to have, at very least, a decorative border. Some which survive have carefully drawn and painted scenes which take up as much room as the text of the notice. All this was never at the expense of neatness and tidiness throughout the building. His Majesty's Inspector commented on the cleanliness, and the care which was given to every room, cloakroom and corridor.

The social education of the girls was a matter to which Miss Hughes devoted a great deal of attention. The table giving fathers' occupations on page 35 shows a remarkable consistency over the years. If the teachers are included in the professionals and the 'merchants' are added to this group, three girls out of ten came from a home where there was likely to be regular entertaining and where the parents enjoyed a respected status in their own neighbourhood. This would not be true of many of the other girls. Miss Hughes's background was upper middle class, as was Miss Edwards's, and both realised that if the girls were to make the most of the opportunities which their education would afford them in later life, they must be enabled to feel confident and at ease when meeting people. In those golden years before the First World War, society had rules in minor matters of etiquette as well as in the major moral ones. The major ones could be the subject of serious, consistent instruction but the minor ones could best be taught by example and by practice. Miss Hughes entertained parties of sixth form girls at her home in Duchess Road, Clifton, and accepted invitations from them to tea in their form room. Other forms attended tea parties in her room at School and reciprocated with parties in their form rooms. She insisted on the niceties of good manners, but she also made these occasions fun, remembered with pleasure by their participants long after they left the School. Form mistresses were naturally involved in these festivities and when in 1903 Miss Hughes added a hot, cooked meal to the refreshments available in the Dining Room in the middle of the day, the Staff ate with the girls. At Christmas time there were parties for Juniors and Seniors. The rule was Fancy Dress, which gave the advantage to ingenuity as against lavish expenditure, and the senior girls had programmes on which to record the names of the partners to whom they had promised dances. The only complaint the girls raised was that the parties were too short, a tribute to the hostess. The Old Girls' Society, a flourishing body founded by Miss Smith, was entertained warmly and regularly. Miss Smith had seen individual parents who wished to consult her every Tuesday afternoon. Miss Hughes continued this practice but soon wished to make contact with parents who had no problems to discuss on Tuesday afternoons, but whose active support and understanding the School needed. They were invited to as many School functions as were possible in the space available, and to evening At Homes, when senior girls with trays of refreshments and knots of red and white ribbons on the shoulders of their white dresses were to be seen practising their skills.

Commemoration Day, celebrated on November 13, Colston's birthday, was an occasion Miss Hughes transformed. Until 1901 it was a full day's holiday, and it is a measure of her inventive flair that she substituted a long working day – over thirteen hours continuous duty for the teaching staff – for a holiday, and was still congratulated on a successful innovation. The day really began the afternoon before, when after school the girls decorated the building with red and white flowers. Morning Service on the day was conducted by Canon Alford. Several parts of it would still seem familiar today. A Bidding Prayer, compiled by the Bishop of Bristol, was used and the lesson was 'Let us now praise Famous Men . . .' Canon Alford read an Extract from the Colston Settlement which must have been even less comprehensible than the one used today, for it omits all reference to the Hundred Poor Boys and concentrates on how the Nominees (incidentally abolished in 1875) should perpetuate their offices. In his necessary explanation of this, Canon Alford abandoned his text and gave a short history of the founding of the Girls' School. The service ended with the singing of Far Down the Ages and then the girls sang the Colston Song which had been very recently composed for them by the husband of the part time singing mistress, Mrs Bunce.

Miss Amy Smith, visiting the School for the first time since her resignation, made a brief speech after this assembly and spoke later to different groups of people throughout the day. It is the first time we actually see her relaxed and generous with her praise of all that had been happening since she left the School. It is as though relief from the burdens of office had enabled her to regain a warmth and spontaneity which she had had to repress for ten years.

The girls and teaching staff trooped off to lessons until the end of morning school, while Miss Hughes took her visitors on tours of inspection. In the afternoon there was an entertainment by members of the staff and of the Reading Club and the Choral Society, more speeches, and the presentation of gifts to the memory of Edward Colston. These were subscribed to by the girls and took such forms as armchairs for the Hall and Honours Boards for the corridors.

On this first occasion the evening was given over to the Old Girls' Society Annual General Meeting and Dance. Subsequently this event was moved to the Spring Term and the evening function on Commemoration Day was an At Home for parents for whom were prepared not only refreshments but also various exhibitions of the girls' work. Old Girls were welcome to come into School all through the day and evening and former members of staff returned too. On that first evening the last to arrive was Miss Potts. It was ten o'clock in the evening before she reached Colston's from Leek High School.

Soon after this Commemoration Day the School was 'recognised' by the Board of Education and given its official number: 13353. This meant that it was now eligible for grants under the regulations for Science and Art day classes, and these began to be paid from September 1903. The financial affairs of the School had already begun to improve although they remained such as would terrify anyone trying to run a small business of a similar size. In 1901 there was a deficit of £140–16s–11d and in 1902 one of £237–0s–11d making a total of £377–17s–10d. In those two years the School should have been paid by the Colston Hospital Trust at least £500 under the terms of the 1875 Scheme, but as Board of Education inspectors reported, payment was 'variable and precarious'. The amount received was in fact £66–12s–7d. Had the Girls' School had what it was entitled to, it would have been solvent. Even as it was, it was a happier state of affairs than Miss Smith had known in the Eighteen Nineties: and now there was the grant from the Board of Education and the £100 a year subvention from the local Technical Instruction Committee to look forward to.

It was recognised by both the parties concerned, the Colston's Hospital Trust and the Board of Education, to whom the powers of the Charity Commissioners had by now been transferred, that the 1875 Scheme needed revision. It had been altered in detail on various occasions; for instance when the Girls' School fee had been increased to £6, and the leaving age was raised in practice to 18. More fundamental changes were necessary, in particular the method of allocation of the endowment income, and it was time for an assessment of how the whole Scheme was working. The process began in 1905 and it is an indication of the size of the task that no fewer than nine drafts were published before the tenth was finally approved in 1910. There had been much discussion about the relationship between the Boys' and the Girls' School. In the original Scheme, the Governors of the Boys' School had appointed eight of their number to be Governors of the Girls' School, with the direction that they co-opt five women. Now the Board wanted one Governing Body to manage both schools

> so as to secure for the Girls' School through the five Women Governors some voice in moulding the policy of the general governors so as to ensure as far as possible the payment to it at a fixed charge of £250 or at all events of some portion of it.

(Letter to the Clerk of the Girls' School Governors, November 1906)

The Girls' School was in favour of the other solution to the problem: that the two Governing Bodies should be separate, with the Society of Merchant Venturers appointing Governors who need not have any connection with the Boys' School. It is certain the original arrangement did present the Governors of the Girls' School with a conflict of interests. While the Boys' School was in such deep financial difficulties there was every inducement to devote all available income to its needs. The Girls' School now seemed to be within measurable distance of becoming viable economically. In 1910, the two governing bodies were made separate from each other.

Miss Hughes' high profile was as much a matter of policy as of personality. At her first Prize Giving in 1901 the Head Mistress's report was read by the Chairman of the Governors, as all Miss Smith's reports had been. It was considered not possible as well as not suitable for a woman to speak in public. The same was supposed to happen in 1902 and that was how the programme was printed. But on that occasion and all subsequent ones Miss Hughes read her own report. She had of course submitted it to the Chairman for approval beforehand. Equally she wanted as much good publicity and widespread recognition for the School as possible. We have noticed how in her Editorial in the first Magazine she refers to Colston's as a 'large public school' and this must have been habitual for before long one of the Governors, the Bishop of Bristol, was using the same description. The matter was taken up by the local papers and produced big headlines – 'A Change of Status?' At the next Prize Giving, Mr Proctor Baker, the Chairman, felt a disclaimer was necessary. As reported by the same paper: 'He might say the Governors had no wish to raise the School out of its place; but they wanted a thoroughly well conducted School for the class of children for whom it was provided – a vigorous School in which the tone should be thorough and sound. And, so far as they could judge, those objects had been maintained, and they would remain just where they were. They had no desire to compete with higher schools, but to do their own work thoroughly and well.' Miss Hughes's report included the news that Dorothy White had a 'free studentship' to Bristol University College, the first University open award to be won by a Colston sixth former. Did she resent the fact that Bristol – and the Merchants – were reluctant to accord Colston's public school status? If so, it seems to have made her even more determined to demand from her pupils the best they could give, and from outside bodies the respect the School merited.

Social status, either for the School or its pupils, was not her primary aim. She passionately believed that every girl should be equipped with the means of securing economic independence for herself. Male speakers at Prize Giving and preachers at Commemoration would commend, often in lyrical terms, the vocation of being wives and mothers, with the unspoken but unquestioned assumption that middle class wives were supported by their husbands and did not have paid employment outside their homes. Miss Hughes and the rest of the staff accepted this. When young teachers married, it was never envisaged that they would continue to teach. The only married woman on the staff was Mrs Bunce, who taught choral singing part time. She also trained choirs and sang in public and was thus an exception to the rule. For almost every woman a career was an alternative to marriage, and a second best. But the staff knew that not every girl would marry and that of those who did some would be widowed early. They were at one with the Head Mistress in trying to persuade every girl who was academically able to go to University or training college. Almost all of these became teachers of various kinds. One of them, Lily Batten, who began winning Garden Prizes in the middle school, became Professor of Botany at Aberystwith University.

Not every girl could continue her education beyond school, sometimes for financial reasons, for there were few grants or scholarships. Miss Hughes was on the lookout for interesting, properly paid work for Colston girls when they left school.

Soon after she arrived she wrote, in longhand but using the old school copier, to all the Bristol employers who might be thinking of adding 'lady clerks' to their staff. ('Lady clerks' is what the newspapers, including the Times, called them. Miss Hughes called them 'girl-clerks'.) At the end of each School Term, i.e. in April, July and December, she wrote 'pupils leave this School whose training fits them especially for Clerkships. Their employers speak in the highest terms of those of our old girls who have gained such posts and I feel sure that in any office where girl-clerks are employed Old Colstonians would prove valuable. Any girl whom I recommend would be a neat and careful writer and would have sound knowledge of English and Arithmetic and would be likely to make a reliable and useful worker in any office. Many girls will have had French correspondence with pupils in school in France and this experience would be an additional point in their favour.'

This assumes that Clerks write letters and keep books in longhand. There was no typewriter, or indeed office, in School. Although the letter just quoted is in Miss Hughes's own handwriting, commercial offices were installing typewriters and employing stenographers who could type. She saw the advantage which a girl with both these skills would have in applying for a job. The next year, in 1903, she arranged classes in shorthand and typewriting.

They were held at four o'clock, after school, and admission was by invitation of the Head Mistress. The teacher was a Mr James Griffiths and they were such a success that the next term they were put on a regular basis, a fee of five shillings a term was charged and three typewriters were bought. Soon the time of the classes altered to the dinner hour in the middle of the day and book keeping added to the curriculum. Keeping a suitable teacher, however, proved difficult. Mr Griffiths soon resigned on the grounds of ill health and eventually a Mr Sykes was found. That these first commercial subjects teachers were both men is an indication of how much this was still seen as a male activity. Nevertheless, when Mr Griffiths was ill and when Mr Sykes too resigned, help came from an unexpected quarter. Miss Openshaw taught the shorthand and presumably the book keeping and Miss G.W. Bunce, the daughter of the singing teacher, the typing. It is interesting to speculate as to how Miss Openshaw came to know anything about shorthand. It may be that at the beginning she acted as chaperone at Mr Griffiths's lessons and was fascinated by a skill which appealed to her quick, orderly mind. Eventually in 1905 an efficient teacher who was prepared to stay was found. She was Mrs E.M. Ord, and the clerical lessons soon ceased to be extras and became alternative lessons within the regular sixth form timetable. In 1909 a separate 'Technical form' was made which concentrated on commercial subjects within a framework of general subjects. They practised their typing on school machines on Saturday mornings – there were still not enough for every girl to have her own – and came back to school at half terms for additional lectures and demonstrations of speed typing. One year they all decided to wear an office 'uniform' of navy-blue skirt, white blouse and navy-blue detachable cuffs to keep their blouse cuffs clean. At the time, the rest of the School only wore uniforms for gymnastics and, on formal occasions, a white dress.

On May 15, 1903, the new science buildings were opened with the maximum publicity. The ceremony was performed in the Hall in the presence of the School, nearly 200 invited guests and the press, a tight squeeze in a Hall smaller than it is today. The Bishop of Bristol took the Chair and the principal speaker was Henry Hobhouse, the East Somerset Member of Parliament. The speeches followed a predictable pattern. The most fitting and useful occupation for the majority of women was that of wives and mothers. Nevertheless, as there were not enough husbands to go round, there was no reason why well educated women should not devote themselves to teaching in country schools and the lower forms of the new schools being established by the local authorities. The event was reported by the three local papers, all of which had run earlier stories on the building itself, and photographs were published in the Western Graphic. A new prospectus describing these improvements in the premises was printed.

The opening of the new wing and the three rooms thrown into one in the basement meant that three forms could, with a little of the shuffling well known to those who allocate classrooms in schools, move into rooms better suited to their size, but it was a tight fit. In September Miss Hughes admitted 22 more girls than the number of leavers. At the end of that term she asked permission to appoint another member of staff and make a new form. It was to be called 'Shell' after the intermediate form at Westminster School which came after the fifth form and before the sixth. The Colston 'Shell' would be of similar character and have its base in the gallery of the Hall. It was probably the first 'travelling' form; when the Hall was in use it must have gone to a temporarily vacated classroom. Its formation signals the Head Mistress's intention to develop the sixth form work. Hitherto the 'VI' had contained anyone who was promoted from VA and sixth formers could remain in the School one or two years, or in a few cases, longer. They took a variety of examinations, and can not all have been taught together. The numbers here, as elsewhere in the School, were rising as it became more usual to stay at school beyond the age of 16.

The Governors agreed to the formation of the new form and, from the financial point of view more importantly, the appointment of another member of staff. They stipulated that the post was to be temporary, for one term only. Their reasons for agreeing to a proposition which would have been unthinkable a year or two before were, apart from the mesmeric effect that Miss Hughes frequently had on people, that the financial situation of the School was distinctly more rosy than it had been only recently. Now that the School was recognised, the three local authorities, Bristol, Gloucestershire and Somerset, were sending it pupils, up to an agreed maximum number, for each of whom a grant to the School was payable. It was necessary to claim these grants on a somewhat tedious form, but once again Miss Openshaw had risen to the occasion. The Governors voted her an honorarium of £5.

They now had 352 girls in the School, 52 more than the Scheme allowed, and neither the skies nor the Board of Education had descended on them. For the past two years the Entrance Examination had been competitive. It was held several weeks before the beginning of each term and there were more candidates than even Miss Hughes would admit. Some were told that they had failed and others that they had reached the required standard but that there were no places available for them yet and their names would be placed on a waiting list. The numbers were small compared with the hundreds who applied annually after 1944 – 73 in July 1904 – but the Governors were reassured that the demand for places comfortably outstripped the supply. The temporary member of staff became permanent within weeks of arrival and without further discussion.

From the opening of the School all school business had been transacted at the Merchants' Hall in King Street. The Treasurer of the Society of Merchant Venturers was also the Clerk to the Governors of the Girls' School and his office dealt with applications for admission by sending them on to the Head Mistress. He received the school fees and paid the bills and the staff salaries.

For this the Society had charged the School £100 a year. Since the Board of Education registration of the School, the administrative work had increased in extent and complexity. As we have seen, some of this was actually being done in School, probably because the information required was more readily available there. The Society could employ more staff in the Treasurer's office and charge the School more, or the Governors could appoint another Clerk and pay him the £100 they had been paying the Society. The Society did not want the work and the Governors might have found it difficult to find a suitable candidate for the post had someone, and we shall never know who, not had the revolutionary idea that the Clerk need not be a man. Once it was conceded that an intelligent woman could, with guidance, do all that the Treasurer's office had been doing there was no further difficulty. The obvious choice was Miss Openshaw, now being paid £95 a year to teach, and doing various pieces of secretarial work in her spare time.

There is no reason to think that she did not make the change very willingly. Besides being obsessively neat in all she did, she had a very clear mind. She might argue – successfully – with a Board of Education accountant about a mistake of five shillings he had made, but she did not let detail obscure her understanding of a whole system. She made herself conversant with all the 94 clauses of the 1875 Scheme, so that she would be ready to offer advice on the amendments which were soon to be proposed. She was to be consulted by Mr Pope, erstwhile Treasurer to the Society of Merchant Venturers and now Secretary to the Merchant Venturers' Technical College, about possible salary scales and the minutiae of a pension scheme. She may have been a stickler, as young teaching staff thought, but she was a very intelligent stickler. Did she miss her classes? Perhaps; but she certainly relished the challenge of problems which could be solved by patient thought. She still took a full part in all school functions, celebrations, parties and picnics.

She had to work very closely with the Head Mistress. Miss Hughes was interested in finance in a practical way, because she knew that if ends did not meet she could not carry out her own educational ideas. She could spend money to good effect, as witness the pictures, plant pots and jardinières of the House Beautiful. Miss Openshaw came to understand money. Most of the Governors were successful business men who not only knew how to make money but also knew how to look after it when it came into their possession. She was an apt pupil.

The School Auditor since 1891 was Charles J. Ryland, a successful accountant with his offices in Marsh Street. When the books were kept at Merchants' Hall he had audited the School accounts there. When the books were transferred to the School, Mr Ryland came to Cheltenham Road and made the acquaintance of Miss Openshaw and, of course, Miss Hughes. He was a childless widower, over seventy years of age, and very wealthy. He probably dealt personally with the accounts that interested him and left the rest to his staff. He came from a remarkable family of clergymen and academics, one of whom founded the Ryland Library at Manchester University. He was a great collector of all kinds of beautiful objects but his great passion was for books. He was not only extremely well read, but he was also knowledgeable about books of reference. When he heard that Miss Hughes wished to institute a school library, his interest was caught at once. He began to be invited to School functions, but he was most at home in the Reading Club. It is good to think of him in the company of young people who shared his delight in the printed word.

Miss Hughes confided her aspirations of further building very widely. To a limited extent she had the support of His Majesty's Inspectors, who conducted the first full inspection of the School in January, 1905. They thought the School needed an Art Room and one more classroom but they urged caution. 'It is impossible to disguise the fact,' they wrote in their report, 'that the present great success of the Girls' School is largely due to the personality of the Head Mistress; and a change of Head Mistress might result in a greatly diminished attendance for which present accommodation would be ample.' They considered that the playground was already too small and would be even smaller if the building were extended, and thought the rooms with windows overlooking Cheltenham Road very noisy. Miss Hughes agreed with this last criticism. At almost regular intervals she had complained about the traffic noise which could be so plainly heard in her room at the front of the building on the ground floor, only feet away from the trams and the horse drawn vehicles of Cheltenham Road. Her solution to this problem had been to ask for double glazing but after the Inspectors' visit she ceased to press for this. She had had another idea.

The Governors could not fail to be gratified by the praise the Inspectors lavished on all aspects of the School's life, including their own performance. This was well deserved: unlike the Boys' School where governors' meetings were frequently inquorate, on one occasion being attended by one governor only, most of the Girls' School governors attended very regularly and visited the School frequently at other times. Some, like Mr Jose and Miss Wait, were there on the first and last days of term, to welcome the girls back or to wish them happy holidays. Now faced with Miss Hughes's dreams of an Art room, five classrooms and some other alterations they put up a token resistance. There would be no problem if the numbers in the School could be kept down. Impossible, she explained. The scholars sent to them by the three counties, Bristol, Gloucestershire and Somerset, were the ones for whom the grants from the local authorities were paid. The School had just become a Pupil Teacher Centre, attracting further grants from the sponsoring local authorities, and the young Trainee teachers must also be accommodated. She was displaying her customary skill in answering a different question from the one asked. They could have rejoined that if the number of scholars could not be reduced, the number of fee payers could; and the School had always had Student Mistresses: what was the difference? But perhaps their own instincts led them to favour expansion rather than contraction. In 1890 they had chosen to build a bigger school than the one prescribed by the Scheme, and they had been right.

They were assisted in their decision by a Memorandum from the Head Mistress and a financial statement from Miss Openshaw. Miss Hughes pointed out that whereas in 1890 classes with an average of 40 pupils were considered quite acceptable, now the Board of Education set a maximum of 34, and required more space for each pupil. Miss Openshaw showed, by a series of meticulously hand written balance sheets, how if the School retained its present number of pupils and received grants from the Board of Education at the present rate, it could pay the interest on a loan from the bank of £4,000, and establish a Sinking Fund which would extinguish the debt in 30 years. She was following a hint from the Inspectors and relying on the fact that over the past two years the School had actually had a surplus of income. The Inspectors had called this 'infinitesimal' but they cannot have been looking at the right line in the accounts. It was actually just over £500. Nowhere does she mention the Girls' School's share of the Endowment Fund, the £250 it was annually entitled to under the Scheme. This would have comfortably covered the 4% interest on the loan, but both she and the Girls' School governors were realists.

By the end of the year Mr Gough's plans for the new extension and the other building work were ready to be sent first to the Colston Trust and then the Board of Education. There was sufficient room to build on at the south side of the building but this would reduce the already small playground again. It is true that when the laboratories were added the opportunity had been taken to build a retaining wall on the northern side of the playground, and level the ground up to it, so that there had been some compensatory gain in playing space, but the School could not afford to lose any more of its playground. The land which the Colston Trust bought from Mr Samuel Robertson in 1888 had two very small cottages on it. One of these was at the foot of a steep embankment and had a garden with fruit trees. The Governors decided at the time that the School had no use for the cottage, and fenced off this southernmost part of the ground by means of palings at the top of the embankment. The cottage became known as Colston Cottage. In 1906 there would be no difficulty in giving the tenant notice. The Clerk was instructed to apply to the Trust to take over the tenancy. The cottage was demolished, and the ground at the foot of the embankment was levelled. The fruit trees were left where they were and the rest was turfed.

This addition to the playground was opened on June 22, 1906, by the Master of the Merchant Venturers. The weather was perfect and the Clifton Zoo Orchestra Band played. The Master led the party of special guests down the embankment by the newly made zigzag paths and named the place the

Pleasaunce. It was at once recognised by the girls as magical and secret, and even today when tarmac has long since replaced the grass and the fruit trees, it still retains its air of welcoming mystery.

The other matter which had to be resolved before work could begin on the extension was the loan. Mr Arthur Baker negotiated this with the manager of the Stokes Croft branch of the National Provincial bank, the bank which subsequently merged with the Westminster bank to become the National Westminster bank. They required not only the title deeds of the School building valued at £95,000 but also an Order from the Board of Education certifying the Governors' right to raise money in this way. Altogether the Bank showed great nervousness for the first two years of this arrangement, making frequent enquiries as to the payment of interest and the repayment of the loan. This suggests that the Bank either thought it unusual for a school to raise money in this way or considered the School a poor risk. In the event the £4,000 loan was repaid in under five years.

Work on the new wing began that summer and it was completed at Whitsuntide in 1907. When the girls returned after the holiday, they found that every form except one had changed its room, a new form had been made by dividing overlarge classes in the middle school and a room had been furnished for a Kindergarten. Conditions for learning and for teaching had in the two previous years grown steadily worse. At one point two forms had used the dining room, much smaller than it is today, as their form room at the same time. The relief for the teaching staff when each girl could be provided with a desk of her own for books and possessions must have been enormous.

The new accommodation consisted of two classrooms and a cloakroom on the ground floor, the same on the first floor and a second floor which contained another cloakroom, a classroom and a large Art room which was at once christened the Studio. It had been designed by the architect, W.V. Gough, who had been responsible for the rest of the building, and the transition from the old to the newer part is particularly well managed. All the rooms except the cloakrooms had big windows overlooking the playground and were as far away as possible from the noise of the Cheltenham Road. One of the ground floor rooms was fitted as combined Library and sixth form room with glass fronted bookshelves along one wall, oak tables, comfortable upright chairs and oak lockers with doors. The Studio with good controllable lighting, running water, store cupboards and easels which could be tilted at any angle from the horizontal to the upright was an indication that the highly valued skill of Drawing had been developed into a wider study in which visual imagination and appreciation were important. It is sad that the member of staff who had brought this about, Miss Edith Anstruther, who was appointed in 1903 as the specialist art teacher, never taught in this properly equipped room, and had to make do with ordinary desks in overcrowded classrooms, and the tables in the dining room which had a very poor light. She left at the beginning of 1907 to take up a lectureship at Goldsmith's College, in the University of London. She was replaced by another specialist and the continuing popularity of the Art Union, the club which she started and which met every week after school, indicates that the enthusiasm she had aroused for the subject continued.

The changes in the rest of the building were almost as remarkable as the new rooms. When the builders arrived, one of their first tasks was to make a new double door at the end of the main ground floor corridor, with temporary steps leading down to the playground. The classroom nearest to this door, beside the staircase, was given a bay window with french doors opening on to a balcony, and two other new windows. It lost some of its area to the corridor connecting the old building with the new and gained two more doors, one under the stairs, the sole purpose of which seems to be to hold a brass trimmed letter box, and the other one communicating with the classroom next door, with the library shelves. An impressive fireplace with an open fire was added and bells to summon the porter and the housemaid. Carpeted with long, pale blue curtains, it was transformed from a classroom into a drawing room and in the autumn of 1906 Miss Hughes took her place there, leaving the Cheltenham Road traffic noises without regret.

With additional teaching rooms it was possible to manage without the one in the basement, and it became part of a larger dining room with a servery. This was an improvement: the Inspectors had remarked that when the girls were seated there was no room for anyone to move between the tables and even so two dining tables had to be set up in the corridor. The number of girls taking the hot school dinner or bringing their packed lunch had risen steadily until it was more than two hundred, half the number of girls in the School. The break in the middle of the day lasted an hour and a half, longer than is usual today, and it had been assumed that most of the pupils would live near enough to be able to go home to lunch in that time. The reason for the increase in the number of girls staying in school all day was not only that many girls came from the surrounding countryside but also that so many extra classes and team practices were held in the dinner hour.

It was at this time that the term 'Kindergarten' was introduced into the School vocabulary. The idea, as distinct from the name, had been in Miss Hughes's mind for some time. Soon after she arrived she asked the Governors' permission to admit girls of seven. She would, she said, be raising rather than lowering the entrance requirement for these younger children. At the time this did not mean very much, for the admission examination was not rigorous for girls of any age. Two years later she was asking for the formation of a Preparatory School, but the decision was postponed to the next academic year, and by then the overcrowding in all parts of the School meant that the formation of a new School, even if it were to consist of a single class, was unthinkable. The extension of 1907 provided the opportunity to make progress with this idea, but she had been putting in some groundwork well before the opening. The girls in Form I, the seven year olds, were asked to invite their mothers and younger sisters and brothers to come to an exhibition of their work. The occasion became a tea-party at which the First Form girls entertained their guests. The next time the invitation was for friends as well as families. Mothers were encouraged to come into School to spend a morning in the classroom with their young daughters. When the new building was in use the room in the front of the building which Miss Hughes had vacated and which had been used temporarily by the sixth form was refurnished with small tables and chairs and the First Form moved in. Some of the chairs, the children remarked, had arms as well as backs. They were delighted with their new quarters and seemed not to be inconvenienced by the noise of traffic. That term one of their number was a boy, Ray, who took on the duty of door monitor very capably. He was joined in the autumn by Wyndham and although there were never as many boys as girls in the lowest forms they were very much part of the Kindergarten. In 1913 they numbered seven and in 1930 fifteen. The First Form, of seven year olds, and the Kindergarten of younger children shared a room at first but sat on the opposite sides of it. Some of their work would be done together and they certainly played together. While the rest of the School was as a treat listening to a lecture on the Succession of Life on the Earth, they played Nuts in May and Rounders in the playground to make up for their deprivation. The wind blew their hats off, which made it even better. The School became a centre for the Froebel Institute Examination and later a training centre for the Institute.

Miss Hughes's interest in the education of younger children was genuine and she could communicate effectively with them. One of the first boys took his two pet rabbits to show her in her grand new room. She had had some prior intimation of this visit, for she fed the rabbits on carrots. But even if she had not had this ease with the very young, she would still have pressed for the addition of a preparatory department. It is common for secondary school teachers to be critical of the training their pupils have had in the preparatory schools and she was no exception. She also saw the new class as a 'feeder form', as the Governors put it, for the rest of the School. By now such strategems aimed at keeping up the numbers in School were works of supererogation, but the habit persisted.

The School now had library bookcases but only a small collection of books. A committee was formed, with Mr Ryland as President, Miss Hughes as Vice-President, Miss Edwards as Secretary and Miss Openshaw as Treasurer. There were three girls and a member of staff from the Upper, Middle and Lower Schools. This committee of sixteen had two functions, to decide which books they needed, and to devise ways of obtaining them. They expected to receive gifts from individual girls, gifts from other people and grants from the governors, and they had designs of three different book plates to be used in these three different categories of acquisitions. It was a long time before there were any grants from School funds but girls and Old Girls raised money in small but useful amounts, and there were a great many gifts from individual girls, leaving sixth forms, staff, and individual governors. Miss Smith and her sister sent a generous donation, enough to provide 42 volumes. Most active of the friends of the School was the Library President, Mr Ryland. A charming note of his survives, written as he says in haste before going off for the weekend to his house in Wales. The list that he encloses shows the kind of books of which he had expert knowledge and also indicates how small the collection was. The next term, Arthur Baker gave 25 volumes which included the works of Jane Austen and George Eliot. Very soon Mr Ryland gave the School bookbinding equipment and provided a teacher for those members of the staff and the girls who were willing to learn. Evidently he thought that many of the books would not be new and would need to have their covers replaced or strengthened for Library use.

'Swedish Drill' had been part of the curriculum from the beginning: ten minutes at the beginning or end of the mid-morning break. In 1905, gymnastic apparatus was fitted in the assembly hall, and classes which had been arranged in the past through the School now took place there twice a week after school, taught by a visiting teacher, Miss Dahl. It was a popular 'extra', and displays were given to girls and parents, the handwritten programme having precise explanations as to the purpose and benefits of each exercise. After Easter 1907, the subject became part of the curriculum, taught by a full-time specialist teacher trained in physical education. Apart from the pleasure that this gave many girls, it had another result. Each girl had to have 'gymnastic dress', and to wear it for gym lessons and on Sports Day. The movement towards school uniform had begun: gymnastic dress was of course the gym slip. It was worn on Commemoration Day, and in School photographs, as well as for gym lessons.

In 1905, the Governors decided to secure the services of a medical 'consultant', a doctor who could be called upon to examine a pupil if the staff thought it necessary. The doctor appointed was Dr Barfield Adams and his fee was half a crown (30 pence) for each visit or consultation. His services were used sporadically. There were no visits in one term and ten in another. In January 1908 an Act came into force requiring all children to be medically examined at some point in their school life. The Governors were doubtful about what they should do and how they should do it, fearing that parents would resent having their children examined by the School doctor. A possible alternative was to require the parents to produce doctor's certificates for their daughters, but this would have involved the parents in paying a doctor's fees, for there was of course no National Health Service then. Miss Hughes, who had a very positive attitude in matters of health and hygiene, negotiated with Dr Adams a new rate of payment: one shilling a child if, when he came to School, he could see several girls, each accompanied by her mother. The staff put forward a list of girls who had recently been admitted but about whom they had no particular health worries, and they were examined. Rather to everyone's surprise this innovation was an instant success with the parents, who were getting a free consultation about their daughters. Such was the parental gratitude that the Governors were encouraged to extend the experiment to all new admissions and to all who had entered the School the year before. The doctor found some conditions which needed further medical attention and the mothers were advised to obtain this. In much greater numbers he found girls whose health could be improved by some alteration in their way of life, their eating or sleeping habits, or by regular exercises of a kind which would today be called remedial gymnastics. There was now on the staff a physical education specialist and she held two 'remedial' classes a week for the girls who were referred to her. The most frequent problems were those of posture. The classes were held out of school hours but from time to time it was difficult to find a suitable room for them and they were held in one of the main corridors.

The advantages of systematic medical examination were apparent both to the School and to the parents. Every girl was seen at least once and those with serious health problems could receive regular attention. The improvement in children's health and physique has been marked in this century. School medical examination did much to start this process.

If middle-class girls whose parents cared sufficiently about their daughters' welfare as to send them to a school like Colston's had such a poor standard of health, the condition of less fortunate children can be imagined. The duty of the better off to relieve the sufferings of the poor and the disadvantaged has been understood in most ages and taught by most religions, but Victorian England had a particular awareness of the inequalities in society. Miss Smith had had a rule that no girl was to bring to school a present for either a member of staff or another girl, fearing that to allow such a practice would draw attention to the comparative wealth of some families compared with the poverty of others. Miss Hughes quietly omitted this prohibition from the Book of Rules when it was reprinted. She herself liked giving. She gave other people attention and encouragement and she also liked giving them things. She saw no harm in encouraging generosity in her pupils, and was appropriately grateful when they clubbed together to give a present to the School, just as she was when individuals brought her flowers. Some of her weekly Addresses were on the theme of charity, and she no doubt reminded her audience that they themselves were the beneficiaries of Colston's charity. The Old Girls' Society regularly gave to good causes in which they were interested, and it was they who suggested that the School should endow a cot in the Children's Hospital. This involved raising £25 a year, the sum for which one child could be nursed in the Hospital for that length of time. A Cot Secretary was elected in each form and she collected an agreed number of pence each week from every member of the class. The Old Girls also made collections and put on concerts and plays to help to raise this not inconsiderable sum each year.

Miss Hughes gave a carved oak and silver shield to be hung above the Cot in the hospital. Except when infectious disease was being nursed in the ward, Cot Secretaries took it in turns to visit on Mondays and Thursdays the child occupying the cot and were then required to write a short account of their visit and the condition of the patient. These were read out at Address, and so the School was kept informed and interested in the enterprise. Usually the children stayed much longer in hospital than similar cases would today, and their names and personalities were known to everyone in School. It was inevitable that some would not recover. One little girl, Minnie Houghton, who had spent months in the Colston Cot, was taken home to die when her mother was too ill to visit her. The Cot Secretaries enquired her address from a nurse, who wrote suggesting presents: a flannel bed jacket, a doll and some eggs. They took these to her and her mother sent a simple, brief note to thank the girls who had visited her, telling them that the doll had been beside her when she died. This was personal giving of a kind we have almost lost today: the donor and the recipient knew each other's identity, and sometimes a good deal more about each other than that. The same was true of the various kinds of foodstuffs brought to School for the Harvest Festival. Each form displayed its gifts on separate tables in the Hall and each form knew where they were going. In one parish there was a Colston Cupboard where the non-perishable food was stored and from which it was handed out to poor hungry people during the winter.

If giving was more personal in the early decades of the Twentieth Century, so was competition. In many subjects there were weekly tests as well as half-termly and termly examinations. Each half term the form mistress prepared an order of merit, called a Schedule. These were read, with comments, to the whole form. The unfortunate expression 'to have the clap' meant that you were applauded as top of the class. On the occasion of Miss Hughes's removal to her new room, each form visited her there and sat on the floor to have its Schedule read.

In the Summer Term there were the Athletic Sports and, on another day, the Annual Flower Show, which had an enormous number of classes, from Table Decoration to Plants Found in a Hedge. Holiday work, which was set every holiday, was laid out for public inspection and individual praise or criticism. The list of prizes at Prize Giving was very long but here Miss Hughes began to award prizes for which the whole forms rather than individual girls competed. It was 1910 before she felt able to abolish what she called the 'somewhat ignoble Attendance Prizes', which could be won by anyone who was never late and never absent and which Miss Smith had introduced to encourage girls to come to School regularly. In that year one of the senior forms had achieved a better than 99% attendance rate in the Summer Term and was awarded the newly presented Attendance Trophy. (The whole School had an annual attendance rate of over 95%; the girls liked coming to School.) Forms also competed for a picture which was given for the best kept form room and for a Challenge Shield for the best work in science.

In 1907 Mr Proctor Baker died, only weeks after he resigned the Chairmanship of the Governors. For several years his health had been poor and his duties had frequently been carried out by Mr W.W. Jose. Two years later his brother Arthur died suddenly. Both brothers had been devoted to the School from its founding.

A surprising number of the 1891 Governors still remained: Mr Jose, Mrs Abbot, Canon Alford, Mr Mervyn King, Miss Wait and Colonel Woodward. Two others, the Revd Charles Cornish and Mrs Pope, resigned only when they left the district. Whatever misgivings there might be about the method of their appointment, they gave their time generously and were loyal in their support of the School.

In November 1909, C.J. Ryland died. His death was unexpected. Shortly before, he had sent a new gardening book to the School and a copy of a life of Colston to the book binding class to be rebound. Miss Hughes could not 'on doctor's orders' attend his funeral at Uphill, Weston-super-Mare, where he was buried beside his wife, and Miss Openshaw and the School Captain went instead. When his will was read it was discovered that he had left all his books and a great many of the other contents of his two houses, one in Bristol and one in South Wales, to the Society of Merchant Venturers for the Girls' School. It was a most important gift to the School, not only because of its monetary value but because it was what an intelligent man of means and taste had collected throughout his lifetime.

The Ryland bequest came at an important point in the development of the School. The new Scheme had reached its final form and was sealed in February 1910; and the Governors and Head Mistress had begun to think about another extension of the School building.

The Scheme had taken nearly five years to produce, from the first discussions in 1905 to the sealing in 1910. Part of the reason for the length of the negotiations was that the Board of Education issued Regulations for Secondary Schools in 1907 and the Scheme had to be brought into line with these. The 1875 Scheme required the Girls' School to award Foundation Scholarships to 10% of the pupils – 20 free places in a school of 200. In the event, money was so short that after the first few years when the School was well able to fill and overfill its places with fee payers, no more Foundation Scholarships were awarded. It came as a shock in 1907 when the Board demanded that 25% of a school's places must be free if it were to qualify for a government grant. It was not necessary for the school itself to fund the free places if a local education authority would do so.

Local education authorities were facing an ever-increasing demand for secondary school places. They built their own fee-paying schools, and awarded free places in them but they needed to supplement this provision by taking up places in other, non-maintained schools. The local education authorities of Gloucestershire and Somerset were very willing to take Colston places and pay for them but there was a difficulty with Bristol. Bristol would only in the first instance award a scholarship to the age of sixteen. If a girl wished to stay on into the sixth, the School might have to take over the cost of school fees. It seems to have arisen from a Bristolian memory that the School had once been designed to have a leaving age of 15. A great deal of correspondence and flourishing of the reports of the General Inspections, which proved that the School had a sixth form, proved in the end to have been unnecessary. The Scheme itself did not specify any particular percentage of free places, but said that the number must be in accordance with the Board of Education regulations at the time. Bristol found the pressure for places too great to resist and in practice the government grant was secured.

The separation of the Governing Bodies of the two Colston's Schools was not achieved without great effort. Not until the tenth, and last, draft of the Scheme did the Girls' School Governors and Miss Hughes get what they wanted. There were to be seventeen Governors in all, eight of them appointed by the Society of Merchant Venturers. (An early draft had proposed that two of these should be women: those drawing up the document had been unaware that there were no women Merchant Venturers.) The local education authorities were to be represented by five members, one from Gloucestershire, one from Somerset and three from Bristol. At least one of the Bristolian representatives was to be a woman. These thirteen members were to co-opt five women.

The Board of Education thought the annual income of the Colston Trust was over £4,000, the figure which Fitch worked on in the Eighteen Seventies. The Boys' School Governors put it at just over £1,300. The cost of administering and managing the real estate in various parts of the country from which most of the endowment income was derived must have been high. In the original Scheme the Girls' School share was to be not more than £250 'if funds permit'; evidently it could be less. In this first draft is a proviso which was retained in all subsequent drafts and which made its way triumphantly into the Scheme in its final form. 'All moneys received as income exclusively in respect of any one of the Schools of the Foundation, whether from the fees of pupils or otherwise, shall be applicable wholly for the purposes of that School.' This can only mean that Board of Education lawyers saw the possibility that fees and other income paid to one School would be used to subsidise the other School. In 1906, when this sentence first appeared, the Girls' School had been able to convince the bank that it was sufficiently sound financially to be lent £4,000. It could not have been borrowing from the Boys' School, which was in financial difficulties at that time.

The division of the net income of the endowment continued to concern the writers of the drafts. By the third one the Girl's School's share was 'not less than £250'. By the eighth draft a new formula was being tried. Five sixths of the available income was to go to the Boys' School, and one sixth to the Girls'. The Boys' School objected and offered one tenth to the Girls'. A letter from the Board considers that 'It would not be fair to fix the proportion of the net income payable to the Girls' School by the Merchant Venturers at any smaller fraction than one eighth.' And this is how it appears in the Scheme. How 'fair' is this? At first sight, most unfair. At the time the Girls' School was educating 490 people, the Boys' School 150. But the Boys' School had to provide free board as well as tuition for 75 boys, and was not as likely as the Girls' School was to have free places taken up by local education authorities.

Where Miss Hughes was not successful was in raising the upper limit of the annual fee beyond £8. She wanted it to be £10, like the Boys' School. Her argument for the higher figure was not, oddly enough, that it was necessary to provide a better education for the pupils. She was not complacent about what the School was offering and was continually introducing improvements and additions to the curriculum, but she did not want the £10 fee for this reason. She wanted it, she said, for the status of the School. Illogical as this seems, it was not unrealistic. Many Bristolians will be aware of an unspoken pecking order in the reputation of their schools. The size of the fee has a great deal to do with this order. When all secondary schools, maintained or otherwise, charged fees, the order was longer, but the principle was the same.

The new Scheme made a distinction between the two Schools in religious matters. The Head Master of the Boys' School had to be 'a member of the Church of England and one that frequents the Holy Communion', a requirement which harks back to Edward Colston's Settlement. There was no such requirement for the Head Mistress of the Girls' School. Religious Instruction in the Boys' School had to be in accordance with the 'doctrines of the Church of England'; in the Girls' School it was 'in accordance with the principles of the Christian Faith'. In both Schools there was a conscience clause, whereby parents could claim exemption for their children from religious instruction, daily worship and, in the case of the boys, attendance at church services. In practice, the religious difference between the two Schools had little effect until after 1944. In 1918 new Regulations for Secondary Schools permitted Governors to give denominational religious instruction if it was requested by parents. The Girls' School then offered instruction in the Doctrines of the Church of England as an alternative to either non-denominational instruction or exemption from all religious instruction or observance. Over the years an average of rather more than 60% of parents chose Anglican instruction for their daughters. After 1944 the Governors applied unsuccessfully to the Church of England to be recognised as a church school. Anglican religious instruction continued for decades after this.

During the period when the Scheme was being drawn up there was a great deal of discussion with His Majesty's Inspectors, correspondence, and even a deputation to the Board. From the pencilled comments in the margins of Miss Hughes's copy of the previous Scheme it is clear that she wanted change in the direction of a wider, more intellectually demanding education for the girls. The successive drafts reflect an increasing sympathy with this. The resulting document is much less prescriptive than the previous one. The competence of both schools to make sound educational decisions for themselves is recognised.

When the new wing was opened in the summer of 1907, there were 438 girls in the School. Less than a year later there were 457 and Miss Hughes reported to the Governors that there was a property for sale in Station Road. This had belonged to a Steam Carpet Beating Company and was not actually contiguous with the school grounds. A small piece of Corporation land and some Railway land lay between. Nothing was done about it at once but two terms later Mr Jose brought the matter up. The 'land with buildings on it' was now used as a Bicycle Factory. A small sub-committee of three – Mr Jose, Mrs Abbot and Col. Woodward – was directed to investigate it and to enquire through a third party what the price would be.

The sub-committee started work at once, went to look at the property from outside and realised that the problem of access had to be solved first. They proposed that the Governors should buy the Corporation waste land and try to lease a strip of the Railway ground. This would give the School a passage way into Station Road as well as the means of reaching the Bicycle Factory premises. Negotiations were opened with the Railway Company and were protracted by the customary dilatoriness of that body: the trees promised in 1890 had still not been planted, so it should not have been surprising when letters went unanswered. If the services of the third party in dealing with the owner of the Bicycle Factory were ever employed, they were soon dispensed with, and the owner, a Mr Pearce, was approached directly. He let them have the plans of the building but by June told them he had another buyer interested. He would give them first refusal if they would match the other buyer's offer. The Governors had still not heard from the Railway Company and could make no decision. They did not get the lease from the Railway Company until December. Mr Pearce had been enquiring their intentions regularly but even when they had the means of access to the Bicycle Factory site, they were still not sure, although they were agreed that some extension was necessary. The number of girls was now 478. Miss Hughes wondered how much longer the Board of Education would allow the use of the dining room as an 'occasional classroom'.

Whilst they tried to make up their minds about the Bicycle Factory, they improved the gas supply to the science laboratories and installed electric light in the Assembly Hall, the lower corridor and, significantly, the dining room. They had a path made through the triangle of Railway land they had leased and installed concrete steps and an iron gate into Station Road. This gave a new way into school for the girls who came by train or lived in St Andrew's and Montpelier. An avenue of poplar trees and flower beds was planted and the area became known in School as Poplar Grove. Perhaps it was the attention which had to be paid to this part of the playground which enabled the Governors to decide against the Bicycle Factory, at least for the time being. They thought it was too far from the rest of the School building and the difference in levels between it and the School grounds would present difficulties. It was just as well that they had delayed. A piece of land 'behind the four Colston shops' became available. It belonged to the two Misses Linthorn of Fishponds who had rented it out and might be persuaded to sell it for about £100, free of ground rent. It would provide another small addition to the playground as well as the site of an extension to the building which could be joined to the new wing by opening the end of the ground floor corridor. The ground was much more nearly level than the Station Road site and it was thought to be solid.

The Misses Linthorn sold for £90 and the legal expenses amounted to about £5. Mr R.C James of Messrs W.S. Paul and James was asked to prepare detailed plans of a three storey building with two classrooms and a cloakroom on each of the first two floors and a library with a small anteroom on the top floor. The need for this anteroom was queried by the Governors. Miss Hughes explained that it could be used as a small classroom and so exclude the use of the Library for teaching. It was her great wish, she said, that the Library from the beginning should be integral, and not an isolated sanctum out of touch with the general life of the School. If this was what she wanted, then the position chosen, on the second floor, at the very end of the School building and entered through a classroom, could not have been less conducive to her aim. Her insistence on this arrangement of the new accommodation becomes more understandable when we hear that she 'strongly urged' that the timbered roof of the Library should be open, so as to give the room a more lofty appearance. At the same time she could not afford to forgo any teaching space. She wanted to turn the lecture theatre in the main building into a cookery room; the time had come when the Kindergarten must have a proper room of its own; the number of pupils was now 490.

Mr James's plans were approved by the Board of Education with few modifications: the most important of these was the addition of a fire escape from the Library. The work went out to tender and meanwhile, test drilling on the site took place. No one with any subsequent acquaintance with the ground to the south of the School will be surprised that 'soft spots' were found. At one place, solid ground was 32 feet below the surface. The necessity for much more expensive foundations than had been expected meant that the cost would be nearer £5,000 than the £4,000 the Governors had budgeted for. Mr Jose's optimistic temperament may have been the reason that the Governors were so little daunted by this: that, and the fact that they were so near to paying off the bank loan they had taken out four years before. The Board of Education pointed out that it would be cheaper to borrow from the Colston Trust and repay the loan to the Trust in the same way that they would pay off an overdraft at the bank. The Governors did not follow this advice. Either they preferred to deal directly with the National Provincial Bank or the Colston Trustees were reluctant to give preference to the Girls' School. The Boys' School was in such financial straits that the Head Master was proposing the use of cheaper butter.

The contractors for the foundations were J. Perkins and Son and work began early in 1911. It was so interesting a project that there were many visitors, including students from the Engineering Department of the University. The main contractor, F. Chown, took over during the summer term; and the alteration of the lecture theatre for its use as a domestic science room was to be carried out in the summer holidays.

Domestic Science was, in 1911, the coming subject in girls' schools. Meetings were held early in the year in Gloucester on the examination syllabus. In May Miss Hughes represented the Head Mistresses' Association at a meeting in Bristol of the Association of Teachers in Domestic Science. In September Miss A.L. McElderry, who had a first class diploma from Battersea Polytechnic in the subject, started teaching at Colston's. In spite of the Governors' plans, the alterations to the lecture theatre were not complete. The tiled floor which had been laid when the raked seating was removed had to be re-laid because the architect would not pass it. There was a stove but more store cupboards were needed. But Miss McElderry began teaching and by January the room was ready. Her classes produced a beautiful cold lunch including salmon with ballymoney sauce for the special guests at the opening of the Ryland Library. At Christmas every Governor received an expertly iced Christmas cake.

While the Library was being built, the Ryland legacy had to be looked after. The Executors of C.J. Ryland's will wanted the books, numbering according to a newspaper report 12,000 volumes, and the prints and pictures removed at once from his office and his two houses. The Merchants would have none of this. They pointed out that the will provided for the houses to be maintained for twelve months after his death so that his gifts could be properly distributed. The wording of the will itself threatened to cause difficulties. He left to the Colston's Girls' Day School 'all my books . . . which may be considered suitable to be kept on the shelves of the Library of the said School and shall be selected by and at the absolute discretion of Miss Evangeline M. Hughes the Head Mistress of the said School and Mr Charles William George of Park Street, Bristol, or by the survivors of them'. Miss Openshaw and possibly Miss Hughes thought that this meant they had to look through all these books and leave behind all the unsuitable ones. This idea would not have been popular with the executors trying to clear two large houses, and fortunately the Treasurer of the Society of Merchant Venturers took a more robust view of the meaning of the will. Miss Hughes must take all the books and sort them out later. Libraries, he said, had open shelves and they had closed shelves. What was all this delicacy about? Admirers of Charles Ryland, and he was an admirable man, can be reassured that there were no pornographic works in his collection. But he was a man of wide interests and catholic tastes. He had a complete set of the works of Oscar Wilde, a 1909 edition, with the pages still uncut. He had 15 volumes of the Yellow Book. He was interested in crime and police work and had accounts of notable trials. He had a three volume Rabelais, illustrated by Gustave Doré. He also had a large collection of medical works, the titles of which suggest that they had once formed a practising physician's reference library. In June 1910 Miss Hughes and her adviser Mr George, the bookseller, signed lists of books the School did not require. There were fifteen books, 42 volumes in all, and none of them can be regretted; although Miss Openshaw, who had to deal with the safe keeping of the rest of the huge number of books, and Miss Edwards, the Librarian, who had to decide which actually should be put on open shelves, both came to wish many more had been relinquished at this early stage. Had this happened, mistakes would have been made. The Decameron was on Miss Openshaw's first list of 'unsuitable books'. When the Library was opened in 1912, it had reached the open shelves, albeit a top one. 'Unsuitability' is a difficult concept, never more so than when the content of a library is being planned. Here they were not able to plan, but were being required to decide about books in their possession. Should a Dickens first edition go on to open shelves; be locked away; or be sold to provide copies of the most up to date edition?

In June 1910 the problem of what to do with all the books and pictures was urgent, and was solved by taking the tenancy of a house opposite the School, 2 Cheltenham Crescent. Miss Edwards in the School Magazine says it was number 3, but there are occasional misprints in the Magazine; and the correspondence with the estate agent and the health authorities always refers to number 2. It does not matter. From then on it was known to the School as the Bodleian Villa. The rent was £25 for a year and it was in a dreadful state of repair. Miss Openshaw's first task was to get the drains attended to and the gas and water supplies reconnected and tested. A gas cooker and meter were hired at a charge of one shilling a quarter each. The books and pictures were moved in and the School housemaid and her mother also moved in as caretakers. The Sheraton and Adam Bookcases went into Miss Hughes's room where, it must be said, they have looked at home ever since.

The list of books prepared by the Executors for probate is sketchy. Sometimes the title is given, sometimes the author. 'Various' with neither author nor title, is a frequent description. Miss Edwards did not doubt that her first task must be to prepare an inventory, both so that the School might know what it actually possessed and also so that she could eventually arrange the books in sections which would make it easy for girls to use the Library to their best advantage. The next term Miss Hughes decided to make Wednesday afternoon the games afternoon for all forms. Outdoor games were still not compulsory, but they were popular and the School had access at Golden Hill and on the Downs to sufficient playing space to permit all teams to practice at the same time. Girls who had misbehaved or not reached an acceptable standard were 'detained', supervised by one member of staff. And the custom of form expeditions to churches and other places of interest, including factories, was made more regular, with at least one form being escorted out every Wednesday afternoon. Miss Edwards recruited a small group of sixth form girls who were prepared to spend their Wednesday afternoons with her sorting out the contents of the Bodleian Villa. Some of the girls recalled these afternoons as hours of bliss reading the kinds of books they had never met before. The School's tenancy of the house in Cheltenham Crescent lasted just two years, from Midsummer Day in 1910 to the same day in 1912. By then the Library was ready and the last book and paper had been carried across the Cheltenham Road.

The formal opening of the Ryland Library by the Countess of Suffolk was on July 6, but the whole wing had been in use since the beginning of the summer term. The School was well used to a general exchange of form rooms at the beginning of a term, as Miss Hughes tried to fit the quart of girls into the pint pot of suitable classrooms, but this time there was general satisfaction that most forms had made a move for the better. The four large rooms in the new building were allocated to: the Technical Sixth, which now numbered about twenty girls but still did not have a typewriter for each girl; another lower sixth; a middle school form; and the Kindergarten. The upper sixth left their room next door to Miss Hughes's for the Library anteroom with some regrets, but these did not last long when they realised that in practice if not in theory the Library too was their territory.

It was the symbol as well as the measure of Miss Hughes's achievement. It looked like the library of a very stately home. The bookcases, the beams in the roof, the imposing fireplace and the panelling under the big windows were all of oak. Deal had been planned for the cupboard doors, but Miss Hughes persuaded the Governors that there should be no penny pinching. The windows were of clear glass, except for the four coats of arms in the upper part of the bay overlooking the garden: Bristol, Colston, The Society of Merchant Venturers and the Diocese of Bristol; and on the opposite side of the room, in one of the three windows was the stained glass memorial to Beatrice Mellor.

The antique Dutch tiles round the fireplace were the gift of a Governor, Mr A.C Powell, and there were Anglo-Persian rugs on the floor. The round, dark oak tables and the rush seated chairs were all old and had taken some finding. There was a fender stool beside the fire. The floor was polished. The wooden floors in the rest of the School were scrubbed until the Nineteen Fifties and long before that had faded to a soft pale grey, but when the Upper Sixth moved in to their new home they got to work with beeswax and turpentine and the floors of the Library and their new form room always shone.

The Library was the meeting place of School clubs and societies and while it is difficult to see how it could be used for individual study during school hours when lessons were going on in the adjoining room, girls did work there at other times, in the dinner hour and after school. Old Girls were allowed to read there on two evenings a week. The top of the fire escape was a favourite place to sit, in summer, with a view over the whole of the School grounds. On the night of March 16, 1941, a bomb fell beside this fire escape and although it was possible to remove the books and bookcases, the building was so badly damaged that it had to be pulled down. Anyone who came to the School for the first time after that date has always been told that the 'old' Library was a special place, and has been tempted to think that memory invested it with qualities it did not possess. He or she would be wrong. The description given by those who worked there and those who visited it confirm its magic: extravagant and not entirely practical as it was, it had a profound effect on the mind and the imagination.

The formal opening in July was as impressive as Miss Hughes could make it. After the Domestic Science lunch served by sixth form girls, the special guests climbed up to the Library. The Bishop prayed, the Countess declared the building open and they all descended to join the parents and friends in the Assembly Hall. The girls sang 'Far Down the Ages Now' and the Chairman introduced the guests. He took the opportunity to mention the additional playground spaces which the School had leased from Bristol Corporation and the Railway Company to enlarge the Pleasaunce, and then described the new building. Miss Hughes told how Mr Ryland had come to know the School and to interest himself in the idea of a Library for the girls. The Countess was presented with a key. His Majesty's Inspector, Mr Cookson, congratulated the School on 'this marvellous inheritance'. The Bishop spoke.

George Forrest Browne was the first bishop of the diocese of Bristol, newly formed in 1896. In the Colston Hospital Scheme amendment of 1899 he was ex officio a Governor of the Boys' School and this was taken to mean that he was also a Governor of the Girls' School. He very rarely came to Governors' meetings – twice in fifteen years – but he almost always came to Girls' School functions and services, and he always spoke. He was a very handsome man, of great charm and geniality. He liked the company of women and they responded to him. His sermons and addresses to the girls over the years, however, make sorry reading. His speech at the opening of the Library is a fair example of what the girls listened to so often. He was a great believer, he said, in novels if they were clean, wholesome and sweet. There were many such books, some of them delightfully comical, some exceedingly pathetic, and some full of instruction about life. But there were those who flooded the world with books which were not fit to read. About five years ago six books came to his house from a lending library. He made a point of glancing through the books before they were circulated in the household. Four of these books were sent straight back, and each one of those four – would they believe it? – was written by a woman. If under the influence of Miss Hughes and Mr Ryland's Library, any of the girls were in the future to write books, he hoped that they would bear in mind the purity of Mr Ryland and of his selection of literature, and instead of being a curse to the world, as those women were who wrote those abominable books, they would be a blessing. In after life when all might seem to go wrong, when everything was like 'sweet bells jangled out of tune', they would have their source of anodyne, a way of getting back their perspective of things, if they turned to their favourite English authors.

This whole passage was subtitled in the Western Daily Press 'The Bishop's Anodyne'. His remarks about the abominable library books were reported in the national press and were given headlines in the Daily Chronicle and the Standard. What did Miss Hughes, the staff and the girls think about it? No doubt they listened with bright attentive faces and laughed in the right places. But some must have found domestic censorship distasteful and the Bishop's view of literature superficial. When Miss Edwards came to write the School Chronicle she twice edited out the abominable books and when Miss Hughes reported an earlier speech on the same library books, she did the same. An interesting feature of the matter is the composition of the Bishop's household. It included two middle-aged daughters, one of whom, Alice, was a Governor of the School. She too was denied the right to choose her own reading matter.

The accounts of successive Prize Givings and Commemoration Days establish the Bishop as the most patronising speaker, but this is only because he spoke so much. He had competition. There was the cleric who warned the girls against gymnastics unsuitable to their sex, and the speaker on citizenship who told them that their part in life was to influence their brothers and husbands. There were honourable exceptions. The Head Master of the Grammar School, Dr Cyril Norwood, told the girls that he did not subscribe to the advice 'Be good, sweet maid, and let who will be clever'. They should try to be both. Inspectors, however quirky their point of view, showed respect for a serious enterprise. Most important of all, the attitude of the male governors made clear to the girls the value they placed on academic achievements.

At Prize Giving of 1912, the Chairman once again defended the policy of the School. A year or two before, Bristol Education Committee had thrown doubt on the School's capacity to provide advanced courses and Miss Hughes pointed out that fifty Colston Girls had entered Universities by that time. Now the School was accused of losing sight of the needs of those for whom it had been built, those who had to leave school at sixteen or seventeen to go into employment, and concentrating instead on those who would stay until they were eighteen or nineteen and go on to University. Mr Jose could have felt some embarrassment over this. He was one of the original governors and knew that it was indeed the case that the School had been planned as one with a leaving age of at most sixteen; and he must then have shared the Victorian fear of the ill effects of educating people out of their social class. By now he had known the School for twenty-one years and had talked to the girls and seen something of their work. 'In a School with such a large number of girls,' he said, 'there was always a certain number of great ability, who were capable of taking the highest instruction.' Today this does not seem an extraordinary observation. At the time, and expressed by such a man, it was a revolutionary statement. The reporter at the Prize Giving could not believe what he was hearing and got it wrong in his account of the proceedings. Mr Jose patiently wrote to the Bristol Mirror and Times to set the record straight.

Since Miss Hughes's arrival the school building had been enlarged to more than twice its original size and there were now 520 pupils instead of 300. The staff was also much more numerous. In the spring of 1913 there were 23 full time teachers with seven part time and student teachers. Most of them were graduates teaching their own specialist subjects. Many of them inspired great devotion in their pupils. Besides the lively Miss Edwards, there was Miss Palin who taught art for twenty-five years in the School and then went to Kashmir to start a new teaching career. Miss Merriman might be known as Gentle Anne, but no one mistook her gentleness for weakness. Only two of the staff were married, both part timers. One was Mrs Bunce, the singer, and the other Mrs Ord, who taught commercial subjects to the Technical Sixth with much success. As for the rest of the staff, it was assumed that when they married they would resign their posts. On the whole, it was a young staff and there were many engagements. One young woman came into School to say farewell after her wedding reception on her way with her husband to the station to go on her honeymoon. Another wrote while actually on her honeymoon saying she missed playing the harmonium for prayers. Some more experienced teachers left for promotion elsewhere and some to look after elderly relatives. They frequently returned as visitors, many of them on Commemoration Day.

These frequent changes of staff do not seem in Miss Hughes's day to have anything to do with dissatisfaction with the level of the salaries paid to them, although this was recognised by the Head Mistress and the Inspectors as being too low to attract highly qualified, experienced teachers. The School had no formal salary scale and the newly appointed member of staff no guarantee that her salary would increase as her responsibilities and her usefulness to the School grew. Every rise in salary had still to be recommended individually to the Governors by the Head Mistress. Applications by the staff themselves were rarely, if ever, successful. In the new maintained schools there were salary scales, with regular increments and recognition of posts of special responsibility. By 1909, Miss Hughes was pressing for the adoption of such a scale. The Governors, much occupied with the repayment of the first loan and uncertainty about grants, put off the decision, although prompted by national legislation they had already introduced a pension scheme and now made proper rules about sick pay.

The salary of the Head Mistress was a different matter. It will be remembered that when the original estimate of the school's expenditure was made, it was considered that the assistant mistresses would have to be paid an average of £100 a year, while the head was to receive £300. In Miss Smith's case this was made up of a stipend of £50 a year and a capitation fee of £1 a head for the first one hundred girls and fifteen shillings for each of the girls beyond that number. In a school of 300 pupils, this does work out at £300. If the numbers fell, she received less but she was guaranteed that she would not be paid less than £200 a year, whatever the size of the school. When in Miss Hughes's time the numbers in School began to rise, her salary rose too. In 1905 the Inspectors had hinted that the Head Mistress should be paid a higher capitation fee, and the Governors promptly raised it to twenty-five shillings for every pupil. In 1913 she was receiving a salary which would have been £700 in a full year. This would have been a high salary for a man in any kind of employment and was surprising for a woman. At the time the Second Mistress was being paid £175. Five full time members of staff were still being paid less than £100 a year.

The principal event in the Summer Term of that year is well told by Miss Edwards in the School Chronicle:

> We have grown so accustomed on our return after the holidays to finding new Wings, new Kitchens, and other little things of that sort, that we were prepared to receive such news with the utmost equanimity. However, the announcement made soon after the beginning of the term was of the nature of a bombshell, and our congratulations to Miss Hughes on her engagement and approaching marriage to Mr Gatcliff were none the less sincere because they were mingled with sorrow for the great loss that the School and all its members would sustain in her resignation.

She was married on Saturday, 19 July, the day before her forty-first birthday, at St John's, Clifton, her parish church. Although the engagement came as a great surprise to Bristol, she had many friends and relatives in other parts of the country and her acquaintance with Geoffrey Gatcliff was not necessarily a short one. The reason that she married when she did, before the end of term, was because her only surviving brother was returning to Canada at the end of July and wanted to attend her wedding. Geoffrey Gatcliff was a year or two younger than she was. The marriage certificate does not give his occupation and he may have had independent means. His father's surname was different from his: a quite usual reason for a man to change his surname is to preserve a family name which would otherwise die out. He visited the School three times, the last time on 15 July when presentations were made to his fiancée. The Governors gave her three silver rose bowls, the staff a tea service and the girls a silver teapot decorated with dolphins. The Old Girls had given her silver fruit and sweet stands. These and a great many other gifts were displayed at a Reception given at the Royal Promenade in Clifton two days before the ceremony. The bridegroom's gifts to the bride were a pearl and emerald necklace, a platinum necklet and an antique Buhl piano. She gave him a camera and an antique dining table.

It was understood that the wedding would be 'very quiet'. Nevertheless, they were married by the Bishop, assisted by the Very Revd the Dean of Bangor, a cousin of the bride, and the Curate in charge of St John's. There were seven other clergy, including another Bishop, another Dean and two Canons. The Governors were well represented and so were the Staff and the University, but many of what must have been a large congregation came from outside Bristol. The wedding dress was 'white satin, trimmed with Carrickmacross lace with an exquisite corsage of old paste and a magnificent diamond pendant'. The honeymoon was spent abroad.

She came into School very briefly on the first day of the Autumn Term, but she spent the whole of Commemoration Day there, accompanying both the service in the morning and the entertainment in the afternoon on the harmonium, and presenting prizes to the winners of the Commemoration Competition. She kept in touch with the School by letter and founded the London branch of the Old Girls' Society, which met in her Kensington home. She again visited briefly on the last day of the next Summer Term.

Within a month of that visit England was at war with Germany and all kinds of small changes which had been taking place in the country over the previous few years were subsumed in this enormous turn of events. Mrs Gatcliff learned to drive a car and took on voluntary war work. Geoffrey Gatcliff enlisted as a lieutenant in the Royal Engineers and they both thought he would be at the Front in a few weeks. Instead he was posted to Beaumaris on Anglesey and she set up house there. Members of staff visited there and she drove them out into the Welsh countryside for picnics. Geoffrey was promoted to captain and moved to Lowestoft on the east coast. An old friend who visited them in the autumn of 1916 thought Mrs Gatcliff looked thin but had no idea that she was seriously ill. She died on Friday, 5 January 1917.

She was buried in the churchyard of St Margaret's, Lowestoft, within sight and sound of the sea. Soldiers carried the coffin in wintry sunshine. Her successor and Miss Openshaw were there.

The Governors appointed a sub-committee of three men and three women to advertise the post of Head Mistress and draw up a short list of applicants, but before doing this they considered the salary which was to be offered. Under the 1910 Scheme, this was a matter for them to decide and they did not have to refer to any scale. They decided to offer a stipend of £100 a year, with a capitation fee of fifteen shillings for each girl in the School. This produced a salary of just under £500 a year, considerably less than the £700 which Miss Hughes was receiving.

They interviewed five candidates, among whom was Miss Edwards, on 24 June and had difficulty in deciding between two of them. By one vote it was decided to offer the post to Miss Beatrice Margaret Sparks, although she had made it plain from the beginning that she would have to give a term's notice before resigning her post as Head Mistress of Wisbech High School.

Miss Edwards had been a strong contender. Her degree, a Second in the Cambridge History Tripos, was better than Miss Hughes's, and she came from the same social class. Sir Vezey Strong, the principal guest at Prize Day in the year that he was Lord Mayor of London, was her cousin. She had served the School with distinction for eleven years, as deputy head, sixth form mistress, head of English and History and latterly as librarian as well. She was also thirty-eight years old at a time when men and women were appointed younger to responsible posts. She had every reason to be disappointed.

The Chairman called another meeting in two days' time to decide what should happen in the Autumn Term. Meanwhile he talked to Miss Edwards. asking her whether she would be willing to act as Head for one term. She told him she would be applying for other headships.

At the second Governors' meeting, he recounted this conversation and also told his fellow governors that he had consulted Miss Sparks about the matter and she agreed with the proposal to appoint Miss Edwards to the temporary post. Miss Edwards was asked in to the room. They told her that she would be paid the same salary as Miss Sparks would have been and that she could return to her post as Second Mistress after Christmas. They were sure that she would be offered a headship elsewhere, and if she were they would not insist on her giving the full length of notice required in her agreement. She asked for time to consider her answer.

There seemed little doubt what her answer would be. Experience, however short, of being a head would be an advantage to her in her applications for headships and it would be much better for the School if she carried on in Miss Hughes's place until Miss Sparks arrived. Within a few days she agreed.

She was a very good caretaker. At times it was almost as though Miss Hughes was still there. There were the weekly mottoes and the many parties. Visitors were welcomed and standards of dress and deportment maintained. Only at Prize Day did there seem a slight awkwardness, when she read the report written by Mrs Gatcliff containing a grateful reference to Miss Edwards, 'a most able and loyal second-in-command'. The prizes were distributed by the Bishop who charmed the prize winners by speaking to each one individually, a feat for a man nearing his eightieth birthday. His address contained the usual reference to their 'beautiful womanhood'. In 1881, he said, he had opposed votes for women because suffrage might spoil their femininity. The girls could see that despite changing Head Mistresses, there was no change in the Bishop.

In January Miss Edwards resumed her post as Second Mistress. She had impressed the Governors by her calm authority and what they called her 'magnanimity and noble spirit', and now it became evident from the Form Notes written for the Magazine that she was held in great affection by the girls. In May she was appointed Head Mistress of Birkenhead Secondary School and true to their promise the Governors allowed her to resign in the summer half-term to take up her duties there.

MISS SPARKS

Miss Sparks visited the School early in December, 1913, and met the staff and girls. On one evening Miss Edwards gave a party for her, so that she could meet the parents.

Like Miss Hughes, she came from a clerical family but she resembled her in little else. She was small in stature, of a fair complexion, her long wavy hair parted in the middle. Even in late middle age her face was rounded. When she came to Colston's she was thirty seven years old and looked much younger. For nine years she had been the first Head of Wisbech High School, and had done well there. She had been educated at Nottingham High School, a Girls' Public Day School Trust school, and St Hugh's College Oxford, where she read mathematics and physics. Oxford did not then award degrees to women successful in University examinations but Trinity College, Dublin, would recognise the Oxford Diploma and her official qualification was M.A.(Dublin). She had a good analytical mind and a formidable memory. Without Miss Hughes's lightness of touch, she conveyed warmth and many Old Girls remember her as 'motherly'. Miss Hughes signed her last letter to the School 'Yours affectionately'. Miss Sparks signed her first one 'Ever your loving Head'; it signalled a difference in style.

She must have listened attentively to what Miss Edwards had to say in December because she does not seem to have needed any warming up period in January. She went into action straight away. The middle school forms were over full. 20 girls had passed the entrance examination for whom there were no places. She proposed a new form and the appointment of an additional member of staff. She admitted the girls, sorted out the other forms in the same year and had a new teacher at work three days after the beginning of term. The argument she used to persuade the Governors is interesting. The new form would generate about £200 in fees and grants a year. The additional teacher's salary would be £105. She always talked very directly about money.

Of course, the new form had no formroom and actually had to share a room with another class: they travelled round the School to temporarily empty classrooms for their lessons. Miss Sparks's solution to this was a new building which would contain a gymnasium and at least one other classroom, preferably two.

This was not a new idea. It will be remembered that a 'Drill Room, with gymnastic appliances, for 100 girls' had been part of the original schedule for the building and had been omitted to save expense. His Majesty's Inspectors had in 1909 indicated the need for a gymnasium. By then ten minutes' drill a day was no longer considered adequate exercise, and Miss Hughes had appointed a specialist teacher of physical education. She taught classes in the Assembly Hall, where gymnastic apparatus had been installed, and the lessons were forty minutes long. Miss Sparks thought most forms had too few gym lessons; and indeed it would be impossible for most girls to have more than one P.E. lesson a week. Besides, she said, it meant that the Hall was not available during school hours for other use. The provision of a separate gymnasium would go some way towards solving another problem, that of overcrowding in the dining room. If the girls bringing a packed lunch could eat it in the gymnasium, conditions in the dining room for those having the cooked meal would be, though not perfect, improved.

Fortune seemed to be favouring this project when a few weeks later the owner of 182, Cheltenham Road, a Mr Collins, was found to be wanting to sell his property. It consisted of the shop with living accommodation above it next to the school and a strip of land running back to Cheltenham Lane. If the Governors acquired this, and also bought the small piece of Corporation land at the end of Cheltenham Lane which they were then leasing, they would have a site for a gymnasium without sacrificing any of the playground. The Chairman was empowered to negotiate with Mr Collins and Mr James was asked to produce a sketch plan of a gymnasium and two classrooms.

As before when they were planning extensions to the School, the Governors discussed how they were to pay for the new building. They had repaid the loan from the Bank for the first new wing in a surprisingly short time but they were still paying off the loan with which the Library wing had been built two years before. Surveyors thought the value of Mr Collins's property was £910, but he was asking £1075 and his legal fees. Mr James's estimate of the cost of the building was £3,500. Another loan would be necessary.

At the same time Miss Sparks was advocating the adoption of a salary scale for the teaching staff as a matter of urgency. The School was due for a full Inspection in the Summer Term and it would be well to have an agreed scale to show the Inspectors. She asked permission to draft a scale which the Governors could consider at their next meeting in three weeks time.

The scale she produced was eventually accepted by the Governors and set the pattern for the salaries of the staff for some years: until in fact the setting up of the Burnham Committee, on which she sat. The salary of the Second Mistress was to rise by annual increments of £10 to £220 a year. The rest of the staff were each given a Grade. There were eight in Grade A, the heads of the larger departments. Their salaries rose by increments of £5 to £170. There were fifteen senior staff in Grade B whose salaries rose by £5 increments to £150 and three junior staff in Grade C whose salaries rose by £5 increments to £120. This was not generous but it was better than the previous state of affairs when staff did not know whether they could expect an annual improvement in their incomes. They were told that it would be possible for them to be promoted from one grade to the next highest and the scale was to come into force in September 1914. The Chairman observed that this would cost the School £140 in the first year and the Governors must realise that this figure would rise annually. He himself had felt compelled to authorise a salary increase of £20 in order to retain the services of Miss Palin.

The School fee had been £7–7s–0d a year for some time although the Scheme allowed for one of £8–0s–0d. It was decided that all new entrants should be charged the higher fee. Canon Alford dissented, fearing that this would prevent poorer children seeking admission. Miss Sparks thought that an application to the Board to amend the Scheme and charge £10 a year was justified.

She was having a very busy first term in the School but that did not prevent her from dealing with another matter. Her investigations into the overcrowding in the dining room had brought to her notice what the girls were actually eating. In the legends of the School she has often been credited with the introduction of hot lunches, but this was not the case. The School had been built with a dining room and adjacent kitchen. Miss Hughes had improved the menu in 1903, so that girls could if they wished have a three course meal; soup, meat and vegetables, pudding and coffee. But it was expensive. The full meal cost a shilling a day at a time when tuition and stationery cost two guineas a term; that is, forty-two shillings. In a thirteen week term parents could be spending sixty-five shillings on school lunches.

It was not necessary to take the full meal and there were other refreshments on offer. You could buy a roll for a penny, potted meat for another penny and jam cost a half penny; but the most popular midday meal, as Commemoration jokes testified year after year, was a roll, a bun and a banana. No one considered that this was adequate nourishment for girls who might have left home as early as seven in the morning and might not get home to their evening meal until after six at night. It was, however, the only part of the whole provision of food in School which made a profit: about £90 a year, the salary of a junior member of staff.

Miss Sparks wanted every girl who could not go home to lunch to have a cooked meal in school consisting of meat and vegetables and pudding. Her enquiries revealed that even if the cost of this were reduced to sixpence it would still be beyond the means of some parents. She put it to the Governors that if parents were charged only the cost of the food, which was four pence, and none of the overheads, and were required to order the school meal on a regular pattern throughout the term, the health of the girls would benefit. She also proposed to abolish the profit-making snacks. The Governors agreed to this, although revenue to the School would be lost in both cases: it would be paying for the gas and labour involved in the production of the school meal and it would lose the £90 a year from lunch time buns.

Well before the end of term a long printed letter was sent to parents. Miss Sparks set out at length and with clarity the reasons for the change and advised very strongly that every girl who could not go home for lunch should have the cooked meal on four days of the week and bring a 'substantial' packed lunch on Wednesdays, the day of the 'free' afternoon. If any girl could not have school lunch on all four days, then she could place a regular order for three, two or even one day a week. No other food would be supplied at lunch time, but girls could buy hot or cold milk, cocoa or lemonade. There was a tear off slip on which parents could place their order. A new boiler and a steamer were installed in the kitchen.

Most parents welcomed the change and there were few bringing packed lunches, although it was beginning in the Summer Term, a time when the idea of picnics is attractive. The girls grumbled but few left much of their generous helpings.

The major event of the Summer Term was the General Inspection in May. Ten Inspectors arrived on a Monday morning and for four days listened to lessons, read records and talked to members of staff. On the Friday afternoon the School was given a holiday and the Inspectors met the Governors.

The Report which was subsequently produced was very different from the two earlier ones, in 1905 and 1909. Then so large a girls' school with such high aspirations was still a rarity and the Inspectors found many innovations to commend. It was different in 1914. The Inspectors had seen many more new secondary schools and were now used to looking in detail at teaching methods and attainment in external examinations. They brought with them new philosophies and policies in education. In all this they had the support of a Head Mistress who was still looking at the School with the critical eyes of a newcomer and who had already shown that she was more than merely willing to make changes.

The next week, when the School was back to normal with the Twelfth Annual Athletic Sports made up of 30 different events and the presentation by the Governors of a silver tea service to Miss Edwards, Miss Sparks began her report on The Report on the Inspection. The Report is a long one, 16 foolscap pages of print. Her report is a fair summary, concentrating on the matters which required action, and she presented it verbally to the Governors at a meeting before the end of term.

She first drew attention to the Inspectors' observation that the majority of pupils entered the School at the age of twelve or older. She wanted to encourage entry at eleven or younger so that when girls reached the upper forms they had had the advantage of several years of systematic teaching. She would use a new prospectus and carefully worded advertisements to secure this. The Inspectors' criticism of the work in subjects such as French illustrated the problem the staff were faced with when trying to teach in a single class pupils who had started the subject at different ages and had reached different stages. We now take it for granted that in day schools almost all the pupils will begin a secondary curriculum at the age of eleven.

This was not the case in 1914, but it was what Miss Sparks hoped for; and what she achieved.

The need for a gymnasium was already very clear to the Governors, but she now stressed the need for another gymnast on the staff. One teacher could not efficiently be responsible for the physical education of over 500 girls. She hoped that the second gymnast would be appointed as an additional teacher and not instead of a present member of staff.

She accepted the two gravest criticisms made by the Inspectors. The first of these was that at the age of thirteen, after one year of science lessons, the girls had to choose between science and Latin. How or when this had been allowed to happen is difficult to discover now and did not matter then. She agreed that every girl should study science to at least the age of sixteen and knew that the more able scientists needed Latin for university admission as well as for their general education. The second criticism was that the girls were generally too passive in lessons. The staff did too much for their pupils, who did too little for themselves. She was concerned to find remedies for this state of affairs and taking the advice offered in the Report proposed that the school day should be lengthened: it would begin at nine in the morning instead of at half past. There would be one Assembly for prayers at the beginning of the day and no Afternoon Prayers at the end of the day.

This reshaping of the school day was an important change. Afternoon prayers had been said in the Assembly Hall every day and Miss Hughes had always welcomed Old Girls to this assembly. Now lessons would continue until a quarter to four. The lunch break would not begin until ten minutes to one, and afternoon lessons would begin at ten past two. The message, that school work was of the greatest importance, was clear.

'Finally,' she said to the Governors, 'there is one other point which occurs to me in connection with the general statement of the Board (of Education) that the work of the School leaves something to be desired, and it is connected partly with the high praise so justly given to my predecessor with regard to the corporate life of the School. It may be that in improving the standard of work it will be necessary to reduce the number of public functions and forms of entertainment. These have their value but quietness is necessary for work. I say this, so that if in the near future you find that apparently we are not doing so much outside work as you have been accustomed to, you may understand that it is because we want to combine a high standard of work with that training in general tone for which the School is noted.'

She already had her eye on one of these 'public functions' – the Flower Show. This consisted of a great many small competitions and attracted hundreds of entries from the girls individually and from forms. It was the occasion of what was a School Garden Party with many guests. She decided that the 1914 Flower Show should be the last one. She also thought that the School took too many external examinations in drawing. The year before she came the girls had been awarded 5 Full Certificates, 280 Honours Certificates and 294 Pass Certificates of the Royal Drawing Society and the School had won the national Challenge Shield for the best results in the Examination and the Society's Exhibition. In 1914 she observed that 'the examination disrupted the work of the School for a week'; and those who have ever had the task of setting up an examination in object drawing, which is what these were, will be surprised that the 'disruption' only lasted a week. The following year the number of candidates was greatly reduced and the names of those who were awarded certificates suggests that entry was being restricted to those who might need a paper qualification in art: Elsie Kohler, Kitty Nix-James and Marjorie Birch (Hicks), the author of *Young Yesterday*, were among those allowed to take the examination.

The Inspectors had advised that the School should do more to foster 'special brains'. By this they meant that it would be an improvement if the ablest girls in every year were taught together and more expected of them. Miss Sparks sympathised with this idea and gradually introduced 'setting' in languages, mathematics and science.

During the Summer Term of 1914 the Governors continued their negotiations with Mr Collins for the purchase of 182, Cheltenham Road. In June he was reported as being still obdurate. By the end of July he had agreed to sell for £1,050 and his costs, and the Governors who were well aware that this opportunity of securing land adjacent to their own might never recur, bought at once using money taken temporarily out of the current account without waiting for the Board of Education's permission to borrow from the Bank. This permission came in October, and the Bank agreed to this, the third loan.

At the same time they explored with Mr James, of Paul and James the architects, the possible form the new building might take. They had been alarmed at the cost of his first plan, a brick building with a gymnasium on the ground floor and two, or even three classrooms above with cloakroom accommodation. They suggested a temporary one storey building of iron and wood which could be much cheaper, but were told that the City Council would not sanction such a building within the city area. Mr James proposed a one storey permanent building with an open timbered roof which could be removed when funds permitted and replaced on top of a storey built above the ground floor gymnasium. A further complication was that the shop and house had a tenant, and he had a right to 'lights'. This meant that no building could be erected so near to the back of the shop as to obstruct light reaching his windows. Miss Sparks and Miss Openshaw thought that a permanent two storey building would be more useful, would be cheaper in the end and was within the means of the School. The fact that they could lay hands on over £1,000 from the School's reserves at the end of a term supports their view.

A week after the end of term war was declared. However often such events are predicted, when they come they come as a surprise and this was peculiarly true of the Great War. In 1939 ordinary people had been talking of the possibility of a second World War to the point of tedium and everyone aged over 25 remembered the last war. In 1914 the last war remembered was the Boer War. No one knew what to expect of a European war of such enormous proportions. There were effects on the Colston gymnasium project.

After the Declaration of War the interest rate on loans rose to 10%. Since the School had started its building programme, it had always been safe to reckon on an interest rate of 5%, with the possibility that it might be lower. A strike of builders' labourers meant that wages might rise and with them the cost of the new building. It was feared that the number of pupils might fall.

By September, however, the picture was more cheerful. There were more applications for admission than ever before and the number of pupils rose to 533. The strike failed and the interest rate came down to 5% again. Indeed, there was an unexpected bonus in the shape of the decision of the tenant in 182 Cheltenham Road to leave on September 29. Any future tenant would be told of the intention to build behind his shop before the agreement was signed and there would be no problem of ancient lights. The Governors had already leased the living accommodation over the shop next door at 184 so that the caretaker and housekeeper, Mr and Mrs Stokes, could live nearer the School; they would not object to the building. In a mood of optimism in October the Chairman recommended trying to get permission from the Board of Education to go ahead with the two-storey building at a cost of £3,500.

In November the plans were studied in detail at a full Governors' meeting. They provided for a handsome brick building of two storeys. The larger of the two classrooms on the first floor could be divided by a partition, so that two classes could be taught in it. Great efforts were made to ensure that the heating system was efficient, and incidentally to improve the heating of the science rooms. A partially covered corridor leading from the main building to the gymnasium was added. Although many Governors still thought it wiser to build only the gymnasium and hope to add the upper floor later, both Miss Sparks and Miss Openshaw advised that in the end it would turn out to be cheaper and more satisfactory to erect the whole building in a single operation, and the plans of the two-storey extension were sent to the Board of Education for approval. Meanwhile the Governors bought the small piece of land at the end of the Lane from the Corporation for £20.

On February 17, permission to proceed was received from the Board of Education and five builders were invited to tender for the work. All five put in tenders and it was planned to open these at the Governors' meeting on May 3. Before that could happen, Circular 903 was received from the Board. This prohibited, because of 'the exigencies of the War', any schemes which involved borrowing money for building extensions. The Chairman had asked Miss Openshaw to enquire whether this applied to schemes already approved. The reply was that it did, and the building of the gymnasium had to be postponed indefinitely. On May 3, he sadly handed the unopened envelopes back to Miss Openshaw to be returned to the builders.

Regrets of the 'if only' variety are useless. One can observe that if Mr Collins had decided to move one year earlier, or the War had started one year later, the School would have had its gymnasium in 1915 and many subsequent limitations to its work would have been avoided. In addition, the quality of the new building as compared with the old would have been maintained.

The girls who returned to School in September 1914 knew that their country was involved in a war which would affect the lives of more people, soldiers and civilians alike, than any previous conflict. They can not have understood that a way of life had come to an end. Throughout the country the response to the declaration of war was positive: many men volunteered for military service before conscription was introduced. In her 1914 Christmas letter in the School Magazine, Miss Sparks wrote:

> The August of 1914 will ever be remembered in your lives as the time when the British people stood shoulder to shoulder in the cause of duty, truth and honour, regardless of the personal pain and suffering which would of necessity be entailed.

Miss Chadwick, who had succeeded Miss Edwards as Second Mistress and was the Editor of the Magazine, saw the need to remind the girls that they must now, more than ever, equip themselves to be of service to their country in the future. The idea that more attention to school work could be part of a schoolgirl's war effort coincided with Miss Sparks's view of the importance of learning. One effect of the war on the life of the School was this greater seriousness of attitude and definition of purpose.

There were many other reminders of war to be seen in School that Autumn Term. There was a great deal of knitting for the forces during spare time: scarves, mittens, belts and, of course, socks. Girls made up three hundred 'toilet bags', each holding a mirror, comb, nail brush, soap and a knitted face cloth. By Christmas there were wounded soldiers in the Bristol hospitals and the domestic science classes made a hundred and twenty pounds of mincemeat for the soldiers' mince pies. Instead of prizes on Prize Day the girls received certificates designed by Miss Palin, and the money saved in this way was sent to the Belgian Relief Fund. Girls stayed after school on Fridays and as well as knitting, darned soldiers' socks, did plain sewing and made bandages. Flowers were sent every week to a YMCA hut on Salisbury Plain and fresh eggs to the Red Cross Hospitals at Eastbourne; a weekly feat of packing in itself noteworthy. When War Saving stamps were introduced as a way of lending money to the Government, they were sold each week in School. Girls stuck them on their War Savings cards, which could be exchanged for War Savings Certificates. These would earn interest and could be cashed after the war for more than their face value. It encouraged the habit of saving but was not otherwise a bargain for the saver: it was soon obvious that inflation was reducing the real value of money.

Although to a much greater extent than in the second World War, young men went to war and their families stayed anxiously behind, some former pupils had first hand experiences. Nora O'Brien was teaching English in a Belgian Convent School when war was declared and she escaped dressed as a nun, arriving home in England with only her borrowed clothes. Alice Wait, returning to her missionary work in Africa just before Easter 1915, was in a boat torpedoed by an enemy submarine. The German captain gave the English crew and passengers ten minutes to abandon ship, sank it and stood watching it go down. Alice was among those picked up by an English drifter but she saw many of her companions drowned or injured. Her long and vivid letter to the School Magazine is infused with an outrage which strikes a modern reader as strange. The English boat was carrying soldiers. Having decided to sink it, the most the German captain could do was warn the passengers. Alice lived in a more innocent age than ours.

In the Summer Term of 1915 each form notice board had its 'Roll of Honour', the names of relatives in the armed forces. In all there were 883 names; one man had won the Victoria Cross, two had Military Crosses, two had Distinguished Conduct Medals and two had been mentioned in despatches. As the war went on the Rolls of Honour were quietly discontinued. Too many girls, and staff too, were mourning their dead.

Miss Sparks had no doubts about the justice of the cause for which the Allies were fighting. They were resisting aggression, in the shape of the invasion of Belgium, and fighting for freedom for all the nations of the world. Perhaps it was this certainty that right would conquer which freed her mind and her energies to confront the problems which still beset the education of girls.

She often communicated with parents by means of professionally printed letters, rather than by letters duplicated at School, or by parents' meetings. These letters are admirably clear in meaning and frequently give very detailed information. They are never informal. In the spring of 1915 the subject was the external examinations which could be taken from School, the Senior and Junior Oxford Local examinations. The examination entry fee was an extra expense for parents, and at twenty seven shillings was not cheap. Girls were not entered automatically and the purpose of the letter was to persuade parents that their daughters should have a qualification which would enable them to go on to further training or better employment prospects.

The next term there was an even longer printed letter on careers. Parents should now expect that girls would, for at least part of their lives, have to earn their own livings. At present it was quite easy for a girl from Colston's to find a job, but unless it was financially impossible she should give thought to training for a profession or worthwhile occupation. Miss Sparks lists a number of careers and describes the entry qualifications. It is an interesting list and of course contains no reference to the Church or the law. The message is clear. It is easy to drift into a deadend job. Decisions ought to be taken before a girl is near the end of her course at School.

In some ways she was reacting to contemporary events. As men were conscripted into the armed forces, women took their places and on Prize Day, the principal speaker, the Chairman of the Gloucestershire Education Committee, could raise a laugh by drawing attention to a new phenomenon, a female bus conductor. But Miss Sparks also saw the danger that women would take on, out of patriotism, work which was less demanding than their education or their ability warranted. Like Miss Hughes in times of peace, she thought the higher the qualification a girl gained while still at school, the less was the danger of her talents not being fully used. The next year she asked the Governors for leave to apply to the Society of Merchant Venturers for a special grant of £300 to buy more apparatus for physics and more equipment for teaching commercial subjects. The improvement of the science facilities was specifically to encourage more girls to think of medicine as a career, and in 1917 Madge Golding, the Head Girl, passed the first examination in medicine while still at School and went up that autumn to Bristol University to start work on her 2nd M.B. The improvement in the clerical subjects equipment, which it is fair to suspect really meant the provision of a typewriter for every girl in the class, was an effort to correct another anomaly which was not eradicated for another fifty years: because girls often turned out to have very good secretarial skills such as organising offices and even writing letters for their less literate employers, office work came to be seen as 'women's work' and was accordingly undervalued. Better training was a good in itself, but it took a social revolution to put right this injustice.

That she had to ask the Merchant Venturers for £300, a sum which could have been provided from income two years earlier, was an indication of the state of the School's finances. At this time the income came from several sources: the School fee, which by the terms of the 1910 Scheme, could not exceed £8 a year; grants from the Board of Education which were dependent on the School's admitting a quarter of the girls to free places; other grants from the Board in respect of girls who would enter the teaching profession, pupil teachers in the main school and student teachers attached to the Kindergarten and taking the examinations of the Froebel Institute; grants from the local education committees – £150 from Bristol, £25 from Gloucestershire and nothing from Somerset; and the eighth of the Colston Hospital endowment income, which averaged £360 a year. Before the war this had enabled the School to expand and in 1914 further developments, the gymnasium and the classrooms, were planned. By 1916 the situation was very different. It was estimated that the cost of living had risen by 50%, and this meant that not only the cost of school meals had increased to sixpence but even the School charwomen were making a good case for a 'war bonus' of a shilling a day.

Although all new building was prohibited, the building had to be maintained and the cost of materials and labour had risen. The new salary scale for teaching staff, modest as it was, meant that there was an annual increase in the bill for salaries. Miss Openshaw reported that the School was running at a loss.

The only remedy seemed to be to try to increase the revenue. Miss Openshaw was instructed to begin negotiations to amend the 1910 Scheme so that the fee could be increased to £10 a year for new girls. She was also to ask all the bodies making grants to increase their contributions. The answers she received were not encouraging. The Board refused to amend the Scheme and could promise no increase in the grants it made. Bristol Education Committee could not improve on its £150 and Gloucestershire would increase its £25 to £100 only if the gymnasium were built. Somerset continued to refuse to assist, although, of course, it duly paid the fees of the Somerset free place pupils. The Governors felt particularly strongly about the attitude of the Local Education Committees. The plain fact of the matter was that if the private and endowed schools of Bristol had not existed, the Committees would have been put to the expense of building more of their own secondary schools. Somerset, for instance, had no secondary school at all in Weston-super-Mare and was only able to provide the secondary places the law required by using the Bristol schools. Miss Openshaw showed that by the end of the academic year the School would be in debt.

Whatever fears for the future Miss Sparks had in this situation she kept to herself. She tried to improve the education being offered to every girl in the School, and from their point of view there was no evidence of retrenchment or even a standstill in expenditure. A second gymnast was employed, and the work in physical education expanded. Although she discouraged entry to the School at and over the age of twelve, she admitted an increased number of girls of eleven and younger and wished she could admit more. She was turning away pupils, she told the governors, who should be in the School. Where they were to be put was the problem. All expedients – lockers in the corridors, shared classrooms, forms housed in specialist rooms, the Library a form room for the Upper sixth – were employed. There could be no new building, but she could improvise. Botany had been taught with outstanding success in ordinary classrooms but there was no Biology room. A lean-to construction of glass and wood was contrived in the small playground on the Cheltenham Road side of the New Wing. It looked like a small greenhouse. It was heated by pipes from the nearby small furnace room, and when it was found to be unbearably hot in summer, it was equipped with blinds. Very good work went on in there. When a biology laboratory was built, this structure in the playground was used for clay modelling. It disappeared only when the Sixth form block was built.

Other essential expenditure was less productive. In 1916 Lighting Regulations came into force requiring windows to be heavily curtained or fitted with dark blinds. £25 had to be spent on meeting these regulations because in the winter months the School had to be cleaned each day during the hours of darkness. Later these Regulations seem to have been necessary not so much to prevent enemy action as to save gas and electricity, and in spite of the School's having an effective blackout, evening functions were prohibited. On special occasions it was possible to get the Chief Constable's approval, but in 1918, for example, Commemoration Day afternoon was occupied by the At Home for parents. The Staff Play, which was the usual afternoon entertainment, was given two days later, on the Friday afternoon, so that the building was not used in the evening. This incidentally, was the occasion when Miss G. Amy Smith, the first Head Mistress, came back to the School for three days. Because the building could not be used in the evening, a great many School Clubs and Old Girls' meetings which had flourished all through the war could no longer operate.

Another necessary piece of expenditure of an unexciting nature was the repair of the School drains. There had been a few cases of diphtheria in the School and Miss Sparks had the drains inspected. There were faults which had to be put right, although they had no connection with the infection. This and the troublesome heating system were an indication that the building, now nearly thirty years old, would henceforth be like all ageing buildings; a cause of regular expense.

A cause for concern, particularly to Miss Sparks and the women Governors, was the School administration. Virtually the whole of it depended on the labours of Miss Openshaw. She had part-time help from Mrs Edith James, who as Edith Sarah had been a pupil at the School. She was a trained musician and was employed as an accompanist and part time singing teacher. She helped in the office part time, as from time to time had other members of the teaching staff. When Miss Openshaw was ill, as she was for two long periods of time, once in Miss Hughes's day and then in Miss Sparks's, there was no one able to take over the duties of Clerk to the Governors, except of course the Head Mistresses. This they both did very capably, although Miss Sparks was notably better at writing Minutes than her predecessor. But there would be something wrong in the organisation if one person could for long discharge the duties of both Head and Clerk, and indeed of School Secretary too, for this is what Miss Openshaw had become. Miss Sparks suggested that what was needed was full time secretarial assistance in the office, preferably for reasons of confidentiality by someone not previously connected with the School. The Governors agreed, reflecting with something like panic on the prospect of a Colston's Girls' School without Miss Openshaw. Miss Eileen Wing, a fully trained shorthand typist from London, was appointed. The next year the Governors still felt that there was too much for the Clerk to do and proposed that part of the work, the accounts dealing with the catering and the ordering of all the supplies used by the School, should be done by another member of staff confusingly to be called the Housekeeper, a title hitherto borne by the Caretaker's wife. They were not able to do this at once.

How well founded was this concern over Miss Openshaw's wellbeing, and the loss of her unique knowledge of School affairs? As far as she herself was concerned, it was amply justified. She was never robust and had been overworking for years, perhaps all her life. She was 47 years old, and in those days many would regard that as elderly, although in public life the eminent were active almost as long as they survived. On the other hand her methods of recording were superb. Her accounts, her memoranda and her minutes never leave the most inexperienced reader in any doubt as to the precise state of affairs. She was perceived to be irreplaceable, and as a woman dedicated to her life's work for the School, she was, but she left the past comprehensible to her successor, whoever that might be.

Elsewhere in School there was no shortage of intimations of mortality. Few families remained in which a son, a father, a brother had not been killed in the fighting. In October, 1916, a Governor, Arthur Bendon Colthurst, was killed in action in France; he was a volunteer well over military age. A few months before, William Wilberforce Jose had died. He was 82 years old, had been one of the first Governors, and was Chairman from 1907. Although occasionally in the last few years prevented by illness from coming to School, he had otherwise been present at every meeting, every School function, courteous, kindly and attentive. He was Chairman of the Colston Trust and a Governor of all the Bristol endowed schools. He had convinced the Colston girls that they were his special interest. Perhaps his best epitaph was written in 1903 by Muriel Salmon, then 12 years old. This is what she remembered him to have said at a morning Assembly:

> My dear girls, the last time I saw you was at the prize giving. When I was going home, I was in a car (tramcar) with several Colston girls; one of them, a little girl, had something very carefully wrapped in paper. I asked her to let me see what it was, and it was a Certificate of Musical Memory, and I thought how lovely it was to have a musical memory, but still better to have musical memories of our early life – memories of kind things done for others, obeying our parents, always willing to help others, bringing flowers to cheer our Mistresses. I hope you will have these kinds of memories, not dull and unpleasant ones. . . .

A choir of seventy-five girls led the singing at his funeral and the School felt it had lost a friend. His place as Chairman was taken by Mervyn Kersteman King, another Governor from the School's beginning and an indefatigable supporter and visitor. He took a great interest in sports and not only gave a challenge cup to be competed for each year but was usually present on Sports Day. He was the prime mover in the acquisition of the Playing Field for the School. In many ways he was a larger than life character. He came from an old Bristol family with a long association with the Society of Merchant Venturers. His great grandfather had done business with Edward Colston and he himself was proud to have been the last Merchant to have used his own ships to trade by barter in West Africa.

Mrs Gatcliff died in January, 1917. Miss Sparks and Miss Openshaw went to the funeral in Lowestoft, and the School Magazine, just about to be sent to the printers with its tributes to Mr Jose and Captain Colthurst, was held up so that an obituary by Miss Edwards could be included. To an extraordinary extent this and the other accounts published in the newspapers of the time catch the charm of her personality. The two representatives, the one of the School and the other of the Governors, returned from Lowestoft to arrange a Memorial Service for her. They had thought first of holding it in the School's parish church, St Andrew's in Montpelier, but it was soon obvious that the church would not hold all who wanted to come and the service was transferred to St Michael and All Angels', Bishopston. The church was full. The Governors were well represented, and so was the University, which had given her an honorary degree, and the Bristol Education Committee, with which she had worked successfully. She had lived so recently in Bristol that most of the people there knew her personally and felt deeply about her. There was a widely expressed desire to commemorate her work in a permanent way.

The Gatcliff Memorial Committee was set up. It consisted of two Governors, Mr Cecil Powell and Miss Mary Wait, two representatives of the present School, Miss Sparks and Miss Openshaw, and two Old Girls, Lily Batten and Joyce Cosh. Mr Powell was the Chairman and Miss Openshaw both the Secretary and the Treasurer. In April, this Committee sent out a printed letter to every Old Girl, former member of staff and friend of the School for whom the School had an address. The letter proposes that the memorial should take the form of an organ for the Assembly Hall, but invites other suggestions if this project should prove impracticable. Some other suggestions were received. Miss Edwards favoured a Scholarship and Miss Farrow, whom Miss Hughes had appointed in 1901, preferred a stained glass window. Almost everyone else was enthusiastic about the organ. It was an obvious choice. On Commemoration Day 1909 every girl had contributed to the nucleus of the 'Colston's Girls' School Organ Fund' and donations to this fund had been made from time to time, so that in 1913 Miss Hughes could announce that they would soon be able to select the particular organ they wanted. By the end of that year the Fund stood at £102–18s–1d. The Gatcliff Memorial Committee members hoped that the response to their appeal would, with what was already in the Fund, enable them to buy and install an organ in the Hall.

Miss Openshaw, with Miss Wait's help, wrote to all known organ builders and learnt that a suitable instrument would cost about £250. By July the Fund stood at £228 and the purchase seemed within its means in the near future. In her investigations, however, Miss Openshaw had discovered the dimensions of an organ to be so much more extensive than the keyboard. The hall was already too small for the School to meet in comfort and no floor space could be sacrificed to the organ. The only solution would be to place the organ in line with the front of the platform and to build an organ 'chamber' behind it. This would cost another £160 which the Committee suggested should be the responsibility of the Governors. They were not averse to this, but the Building Regulations forbade any building at all during the war. The Committee put the money in War Savings Certificates and looked forward to peace.

In 1919 it was discovered that the cost of a new organ had risen to at least £600 – £650 if it incorporated all the features the Committee thought were needed. An organ already in existence in Butcombe could be had for £350, and could be modified and installed when the time came by a Bristol firm, George Johnson and Co. With the help of the War Savings interest and £50 from the Society of Merchant Venturers, they bought the Butcombe organ.

The cost of the chamber was £600. An 'anonymous donor', who must have been Mr Powell, promised £250 with an additional £100 if it was necessary. The present pupils and the Old Girls set themselves a target of £150 and the Committee made a second appeal to friends of the School to contribute the rest. The chamber was built, the organ installed and it was 'Opened' on May 6th, 1922, by a concert given by Mr Hubert Hunt, the Cathedral organist. Miss Sparks and Miss Openshaw laboured on, and by January 1923 had raised the last penny to complete the cost of the purchase and installation. The organ has been played at Morning Assembly for nearly seventy years, lending a special dignity to School prayers. If a non-essential is an extravagance, then that is what it was: but extravagances have also been defined as expenditures on luxuries we could have done without but have never regretted. It is a fitting memorial to Eva Hughes.

The first months of 1917 were some of the darkest of the war. There were severe food shortages which a belated rationing system did not cure. In April the German government warned that from then on it would sink all shipping, not merely military vessels, making for English ports, and the losses in that month were enormous. Yet from the beginning of the year there was a subtle change in people's thinking. In the press and from the pulpits there had been appeals for discipline and self sacrifice. Now the emphasis was on reconstruction, or rather on building a better world when the war was over. Even before the Americans joined the Allies there was a conviction that the fighting would eventually end and the country would return to normal life. Thoughtful people everywhere began to consider the nature of that normality. The education of children and young people began to assume an importance which had a dreadful poignancy. So many young men had been killed and were being killed that it seemed a generation had been lost. Women had done more than nurse the wounded. They had made munitions and some in the absence of men had carried on businesses. It was probable that their services would continue to be needed. The education of girls changed from being socially desirable to being nationally important.

It was possibly with thoughts such as these that the Governors decided to continue with their plans to improve the School administration and to give the teaching staff an increase in salary across the board, without waiting for even the promise of financial assistance. Their confidence was justified. By July new Regulations for Secondary Schools were published. They forecast that the School's grant from the Board of Education would be increased by £900 in 1917–18, and they had hopes that this would be paid retrospectively for the year 1916–17. The whole of this extra money was used to improve the scale of salaries paid to staff.

The two major and ever present concerns for a head mistress in Miss Sparks's situation were the building and the staff salaries. She could do nothing about the size of the building under wartime restrictions on new buildings, although the number of girls in School rose steadily. There were several reasons for this increase. More parents wanted secondary education for their daughters. The City and the Counties wanted many more elementary teachers and wanted places for intending teachers. The population of Bristol had grown as a result of air raids in London. In addition she was being successful in recruiting younger pupils; the problem she said half seriously, was that they were staying longer. The Board of Education recognised the difficulty and allowed the maximum number per class to rise to 35. Staff salaries were another matter. One of her many achievements was the quality of her appointments, but no member of staff was ever attracted to Colston's by the size of the salary. She had already lost two scientists to other work for the government. She considered that the younger teachers did not have enough to live on and that the seniors were not paid enough to encourage them to stay. If she had had to choose between spending money on building or on staff, she would unhesitatingly have chosen staff. That might not have been Miss Hughes's choice, but these were different days.

Colston's was a local school serving an extensive local area with pupils making long journeys each day. Miss Sparks referred to it as a 'great public school' and indeed in point of size it was the third largest girls' school in the country, the other two being Cheltenham Ladies' College and the North London Collegiate School. Unlike Miss Hughes, she did not use capitals when describing Colston's as a 'public school' and meant something different: a school serving the public, accessible to all girls capable of profiting from the education offered, and thus entitled to support from public funds. Although she was clear about the rôle of the School in its own locality, her interests were as much national as local. She was acutely aware of social and educational trends and never hesitated to ask questions of Inspectors and officials of the Board of Education. She could often tell Governors and parents what was going to happen before it actually happened, and in a period of considerable educational change this calmed the nerves of those who would have been worried by changes they did not understand and see the need for. In 1917 she was telling the Governors about 'Mr Fisher's Education Bill' which became law in 1918, and she was anticipating the changes in the system of external examinations for secondary schools which came about as a result of the deliberations of the Examinations Council.

She had always been opposed to the practice of letting girls take as many different examinations as they were likely to pass and insisted that any they did take should be what she called 'useful': by this she meant that the examination should be widely recognised by employers and institutions of further and higher education. The new examinations had her full support. The first, the School Certificate, would be taken at the age of 16 or 17 and would replace the Senior Local examinations. Like the Senior Oxford Local it replaced at Colston's, the new examination could not be passed in one or more subjects at successive sittings. The candidates could only be awarded a School Certificate by passing a minimum of five subjects drawn from at least three different groups (English, Mathematics, Science or Languages) at a single sitting. Exemption from Matriculation – that is, the qualifying examination for admission to a university – could be claimed by the holder of a School Certificate if the right combination of subjects had been passed at a high enough standard. Previously, Matric, as it was called, had been a separate examination. The old Junior Local examinations were eliminated and pupils had to stay at school until they were at least sixteen if they were to have a secondary school leaving qualification. The School Certificate would be sufficient for admission to a training college for elementary school teachers, and to colleges specialising in Art, Domestic Science, Physical Education or Kindergarten.

The greater innovation in the new system, however, was the Higher School Certificate. It had no counterpart in the old school examination system, and was to be taken after two years study beyond the School Certificate. Successful candidates had to pass in at least three subjects but this permitted specialisation. You could, for instance, take a Higher School Certificate in English, French and History, or Mathematics, Physics and Chemistry. The universities would accept a Higher School Certificate from any recognised examining board as evidence of the candidate's suitability to embark on a University Honours degree course, without demanding that the undergraduate spent a year taking the University's Intermediate Examination. This shortened the time the undergraduate spent at university getting his degree, and meant that without more university teachers or buildings, more students could be given a university education. The schools were being given the task of teaching the work of the first year at university.

These Advanced Courses, as they were known in schools, were attractive to teachers who wanted to teach their subject to a higher level. It was also possible to apply to the Board of Education for grants to augment the salaries of teachers undertaking this specialised work and to provide the necessary books and apparatus. On both counts the Advanced Course idea appealed to Miss Sparks and with her customary address she applied for the extra grants and started the courses in September 1917 for a group of eight girls. It looks as though she jumped the gun, for both School Certificate and Higher School Certificate courses were supposed to begin in 1918, but she had evidently assured herself that there would be a Higher School Certificate examination in July 1919. All went according to plan. The eight girls all passed, and three years later six of them were awarded First Class honours degrees by the University of Bristol. The other two had Seconds, one at Bristol and one at Cambridge. The subjects they read were Science, Mathematics, English, History and Modern Languages, an indication that the full range of subjects had been available in School.

Early in 1918 the Board of Education proposed a plan to integrate the Advanced Courses of Colston's and Redland High School. This was to be a pilot scheme lasting two years. Each School would provide half of the subjects needed. There would in this way be a 50% saving of teachers and equipment. The Inspectors assumed that pupils would be exchanged between the two Schools. The two Head Mistresses would have none of this. They were prepared to be co-operative over the best use of scarce resources but a Colston girl must remain a Colston girl to the end of her school life, a Redland girl a Redland girl to the end of hers. The scheme they worked out was ingenious if complicated, and was only possible because the Schools were geographically close. If Colston's started the first year Advanced Course in – say – chemistry, the Redland girls walked down the hill to the chemistry lessons and that group stayed with the same teachers in the same School for the second year of the Course. The next year the first year of chemistry would be started by Redland High School and Colston girls would climb the hill to attend the classes. The same happened in every Advanced subject except biology which was always taught in both years at Colston's, because only Colston's possessed a biology 'laboratory', the glass house in the playground. The other lessons outside the Higher School Certificate courses were taken in the home school, and the girls took a full part in all the activities of their own School.

The Colston's Governors wanted this arrangement because they still remembered Bristol Education Committee's incredulity that advanced work was carried on in the School's sixth form. The Head Mistresses wanted it because they wanted all the subjects in the curriculum to be taught to the level of Higher School Certificate, even if only in alternate years, so that specialist staff would be encouraged to stay and the work of the whole School be enriched by their teaching. The scheme worked well at first, and fairly well for a long time; in fact, until 1940, when air raids made it difficult for both Schools to keep to a rigid timetable. The people who were never really enthusiastic about it were the girls. Officially their line was that they were disadvantaged if they were not taught in their own laboratories and could not spend extra time outside lesson time in the laboratory with which they were becoming familiar. There may have been deeper feelings of loyalty to their own School which made them uncomfortable. At the time of the General Inspection in 1922 members were:

Science and Mathematics	*1st Year*	*2nd Year*
Colston's	11	11
Redland	2	9

Modern Sudies	*1st Year*	*2nd Year*
Colston's	12	8
Redland	6	4

As the Inspectors observed, this meant that over 60 girls from the two Schools were following these courses, a number they found praiseworthy. Had it not been for the joint Advanced Courses, Miss Sparks admitted frankly, she would have needed two extra members of staff.

In 1918 the Governors renewed their efforts to increase the School fee, still limited by the 1910 Scheme to £8 a year. Miss Sparks and an experienced foundation Governor, Mrs Abbot, formed a deputation to the Board of Education and saw a Dr Scott. They proposed that the fee for girls already in the School and for new girls under 12 should be £10, and should be £11 for girls entering the School at 12 years of age or over. They were told that it was not the policy of the Board to allow an increase in fee once a pupil had been admitted to a School, a policy parents of children at feepaying schools today would welcome. The two ladies pointed out that before seeking admission for their daughters, parents had been expressly warned in the prospectus that fees might rise; and an increase limited to new girls would do little to alleviate the School's present financial difficulties. Dr Scott said that parents of present pupils could be asked to contribute on a voluntary basis, and he further advised against asking the counties to increase their grants. This extraordinary advice was ignored by the Governors, who made a formal application to increase the fee for present girls to £10 and for new girls to £12 and the Board evidently accepted that a fee fixed in 1910 was unrealistic after four years of war. The next increase, in 1921, was to 15 guineas (£15–15s–0d) a year. There was no argument then about this not applying to the pupils already in the School. Rising costs and the falling value of money had been recognised as a fact of life, scarcely to be remarked upon.

The Education Act which became law a few weeks after the conversation with Dr Scott took a different line about the relationship between endowed schools and the local education authorities. These new authorities were controlled by a subcommittee of the county council and the old Education Committees, the members of which had been independently elected and were not necessarily county councillors, ceased to exist. The new Act required local authorities to contribute towards the cost of maintaining endowed schools which were part of the local provision of secondary education. This was very much the case of Colston's, which in 1918 was educating 450 Bristol girls and 150 from Somerset and Gloucestershire. The county contribution to the School was ludicrously small. All three counties were of course paying the fees of free place holders but as the fee was not sufficient to meet the expenses of the School and was being kept artificially and uneconomically low by the Board of Education, these payments did not solve the School's difficulties.

The three local education authorities offered more in 1919. Bristol agreed to pay £1,250 a year from April, and this rose to £3,000 the next year and £4,500 in 1921. Separate negotiations with Somerset and Gloucestershire produced results but the grants were calculated according to three different formulae by the three authorities and were not always paid on time. In December, 1921, some of the grants were overdue. The Governors paid the teaching staff and held over the tradesmen's accounts until January when the fees for the Spring Term had been paid. Gloucestershire and the Board of Education paid in January, 1922, and Somerset and Bristol in March. Miss Openshaw could see the costs of salaries, materials and maintaining the building continuing to rise and neither fees nor grants ever keeping up with them.

In 1917 the Governors had given each of the teaching staff a 'war bonus' of £10 a year. In 1918, they approved a new scale which increased the salaries of all members of staff and in particular raised the maximum for heads of departments to £250, an increase considerably less than the rise of the cost of living. Miss Sparks rarely let slip an opportunity to draw attention to the necessity of attracting and retaining the services of good teachers by paying them salaries commensurate with their abilities and responsibilities. Even so, they could not but be astonished at her outburst at a Governors' meeting in July 1919. They had in the latter years of the war fallen into the habit of not meeting between July and December, perhaps because they felt there was little they could do, and they had no plans to meet in the coming autumn. She began by remarking on this, saying that it was her last chance to address them for five months, and continued, 'I have hesitated to speak, but circumstances seem to point to my seizing this opportunity and with much diffidence I wish to lay this matter before you.'

While they must have been struggling with their surprise, for neither hesitation nor diffidence was a noticeable trait in her character, she reminded them how frequently she had told them that the salaries they were paying were inadequate. She gave an example. Six weeks ago a non-graduate member of staff, appointed at a salary of £190 rising to a maximum of £220, had been appointed to a post in another school at a salary beginning at £225 rising to £370. She had not been able to appoint anyone to the post, which would become vacant at the end of term; and she could not offer a higher salary as an inducement without being unfair to other teachers already on the staff. Students from the Kindergarten training department were being appointed to posts in other schools at higher salaries than experienced members of staff at Colston's. All over the country salary scales were being revised upward and while Bristol's scale was still low, those of neighbouring authorities were already higher. She acknowledged that the Governors had done all in their power to give her what she had asked for the staff, but times had changed. Where they had thought in terms of an increase of £10, they must now think of one of £100.

There was nothing the Governors could do, except agree to meet early in the autumn and use all their influence to change public opinion in Bristol about the proper level of pay for teachers.

As misfortune would have it, none of the Governors representing local authorities were present at the meeting, but what she said was very fully reported by Miss Openshaw as an addendum to the minutes. It is interesting to speculate why she spoke so bluntly at this particular juncture. She was doubtless much concerned at her difficulty in filling the vacancy on the staff in spite of the School's reputation, but she began the next term with a full complement of staff. She and a Governor, Mrs Greville Edwards, had attended a meeting of representatives of local Education Authorities in Bridgwater when it must have been borne in upon her that differing scales in adjoining counties would produce unwanted effects. Above all, she could see that times were changing. There was a shortage of teachers and a great public demand for education; but their salaries were worth less than before the war.

The next year she was invited to join the Burnham Committee, recently appointed to devise national salary scales for teachers. These eliminated at least some of the anomalies which came about when each authority drew up its own scale, and the Committee gave the profession a seat at the bargaining table. The Governors paid the Burnham Scales retrospectively from September 1920. They still had to persuade the Local Authorities to increase their grants but in this they were in no worse situation than before.

As soon as the war ended Miss Sparks had drawn the Governors' attention to the need for more accommodation. There were now over 600 pupils, not counting the Kindergarten students who had been given a room in 182 Cheltenham Road. There were by now three travelling forms and several others were occupying specialist rooms. Mr James was asked to attend a special committee meeting in December 1918 and given instructions to draw up plans to provide as much accommodation as possible on the site acquired in 1914. Miss Sparks's guess was that a 'good scale building' would cost £8,000, twice what it would have done at the beginning of the war.

In April Mr James produced preliminary drawings of a building with two floors of classrooms above the gymnasium. Because 'present prices are abnormally high' he said the building was likely to cost £10,000 to £12,000. If it was built piecemeal it would cost even more. They had braced themselves for a cost of £8,000, but they told him to go ahead with detailed plans which could be sent to the Board of Education for approval. This he did in June, and although he now said £12,000 to £14,000 was a more likely figure, they decided to send the plans to the Board. The plans were approved and with some optimism a list of seven builders was drawn up. Mr James said that an independent quantity surveyor would have to be employed, because his firm of architects could no longer provide this service. When the quantity surveyor had completed his work, he estimated the cost of the building as £24,000. This was six times the cost of the two storey building in 1915 and illustrates the price rises and the shortages which were the result of the war. Mr James, whose work must have been limited during those years to military constructions, seems to have been out of touch with the extent of the changes in the building industry.

The Governors decided to ask the three local authorities for help towards the cost of this building, so urgently needed by the School. They did not get immediate answers and received no encouragement to expect that any assistance would be forthcoming. The authorities were willing – indeed, were required by law – to contribute towards the salaries of staff and the maintenance of the buildings of schools to which they sent free place pupils but they were not required to fund new buildings for these schools. They had their own problems in providing new schools of their own.

It became clear to the Governors that at a time when there was constant danger of the School running into debt they could not finance the gymnasium and classroom extension from their own resources, and that they would not get sufficient help from the local education authorities. Just at this time the four small shops on Cheltenham Road to the south of the School came on to the market. The asking price was £750 for one, or £2,880 for the four. Although their proximity to the road meant that any classes in them, or in a building on the site, would be plagued by traffic noises, the idea of completing the purchase of this area adjacent to the School was attractive. It too was out of the question in their present situation and they realised that they must be much less ambitious in their plans. They considered renting a house and even using superannuated army huts. In the end they decided on four temporary wooden classrooms built on a brick foundation on the far side of the grass tennis courts and connected to the rest of the school building by a covered corridor. The bank would make a loan of the £3,000 that this structure would cost and Bristol L.E.A. would make available the money to pay the interest on the loan. The loan itself would be repaid by using the Colston Hospital Trust endowment income. In July 1920 the School was surprised to see workmen removing turf from part of the tennis courts. When the girls returned in September the Annexe was complete. Although there were always grumbles that it was cold in winter and hot in summer, the four classrooms were, compared with several in the old building, spacious and well lit. The number of 'wandering forms' was reduced to one.

From 1916 the School's income rarely caught up with the cost of all goods and services, and then never for long. Only Miss Openshaw, with her succession of seven year forecasts, really understood this. Miss Sparks had a great many other things to think about, above all what she called the 'quiet work' of the School, the devotion to individual, rigorous study which she hoped to instil into each girl. The staff, when they looked at their bank balances, knew that times were hard. The girls, who were experiencing all kinds of shortages at home, still found their School life endlessly interesting and stimulating.

In 1916 Miss Sparks arranged a holiday for Sixth form girls and Kindergarten students who needed one. She took a house in Williton in Somerset for a month and two parties of girls each came for a fortnight. The house called The Poplars must have been large, for there were about 20 girls and three or four members of staff in each party. Miss Sparks was in charge for one of the fortnights and Miss Openshaw for the other. Miss Sparks's housekeeper did the catering. A bell signalled the times for getting up, prayers, mealtimes, going to bed and lights out. The girls, clad in their gym tunics, went on foot and by shooting brake to the seaside and the surrounding country, visiting places of interest. They played tennis, and in the evening made their own entertainment. It was very much enjoyed and was repeated for the next three years.

Miss Sparks was hospitable and gave good parties, although perhaps because of the war they were not on the same scale as Miss Hughes's. In summer some of the junior forms had Strawberry Lunches while others had Strawberry Teas. She invited the staff to a party every summer, too grand to be called a picnic. They went in the evening in brakes to the banks of a river and had wonderful food.

The House system was introduced in 1918 after a great deal of discussion. The girls from each year were divided into seven Houses after west country worthies: Cabot, Canynge, Chatterton, Drake, Grenville, Trelawney and Tyndale. There were House mistresses, captains and committees. Each House met at least once a year. In many school competitions from sport to natural history, successful competitors won points for their House and one House was judged the winner. In the Magazine, where there were once Notes from each form there were now accounts of the year's doings from each House. Soon every original contribution had the author's name and her House. Members of the House Committees were involved in the selection of material for the magazine.

School Houses were welcomed with enthusiasm by the girls although the first House meetings when each girl found herself in the company of girls whose names she did not know were a not wholly pleasant surprise. Once this difficulty had been overcome the system was on balance a success and certainly the competition which had been between individuals or forms was now primarily between Houses. The system gave the School vertical divisions in which older and younger girls could work together and help each other. There were more girls with responsibilities: in addition to the Head Girl and Vice Head Girl there were now seven House Captains and there were seven House representatives in each form. The House was a group to which a girl belonged for the whole of her school life, unlike the form which might be subject to regrouping as each 'year' went up the School. Younger sisters would join older sisters in the same House and daughters of old girls would become members of their mother's House, so that family loyalty could develop.

Many but not all girls' day schools were adopting a House System about this time. The idea and name were taken from the 'houses' in which pupils at large boarding schools lived during term time. While it provides pupils with opportunities it would be difficult to secure in any other way, it has the disadvantage that it is an artificial grouping which does not arise naturally from a similarity of work or interests. Misgivings about organized competition persist to this day.

Although she lengthened the school day soon after her arrival, Miss Sparks did not continue Miss Hughes's practice of giving an Address to the School as the first lesson every Monday morning. She did, however, think it her duty to see that the girls knew what was going on in the world. With no radio or television, the newspapers were the main source of information. Film was beginning to be used to record events and in 1917 the whole School except for the very youngest pupils walked to Jacobs Wells Road to see moving pictures of the fighting in France. The girls were caught in a snow storm on Cotham Brow on the way back, but even so it was the films and not the snow which made the deeper impression on their minds. The length of their walk was not noteworthy: many girls walked as far or further coming to School each day.

Without today's instant dissemination of news, public lectures had an importance and a popularity it is hard to imagine today. Speakers were invited to School to talk to the girls on a variety of topics. Many of these lectures were purely for information, although some, like the one on the Women's Land Army, had a long term recruiting objective. The School branch of the Empire League, later the Victoria League, had a numerous membership, attracted not only by patriotic sentiment but also by speakers on life in remote parts of the world.

Sometimes parents and friends and even the general public were admitted to these lectures. When the Prime Minister of New Zealand, on a tour to advertise his country's exports, visited the School the local press gave a full account of his remarks. He presented the School with a large New Zealand flag.

One controversial issue engaged the interest of both staff and girls: votes for women. It had been debated for many years. In 1870, for instance, the year Fitch came to Bristol, a petition had been presented to Parliament asking that women should have the right to vote under the same conditions as men. In 1906 a joke in the Commemoration Day entertainment poked fun at the idea. A year or two later Bishop Browne was condemning the suffragettes as well as their campaign of violence with his accustomed eloquence. After 1910 women's suffrage was a regular subject for serious debate by the Sixth form and doubtless in the staff room. In 1917, Miss Chadwick wrote in her editorial for the School Magazine:

> It is with feelings of intense satisfaction that we applaud the enormous gains recently achieved by those whose main object for many years has been political emancipation of women, and the according to them of such privileges as shall enable them to develop into capable and self respecting citizens.

In 1918 the Representation of the People Act gave women over thirty the right to vote, if the woman or her husband occupied or owned property worth £5 or more a year. Under the same conditions men were enfranchised from the age of 21. A General Election was held a month after the end of the war. Senior members of staff could vote and girls could see that politics would be their concern, if not immediately, then in the future.

Another sign of the times was noted at Prize Giving in 1920. Miss Sparks wore for the first time an Oxford gown and hood. That University had admitted women as full members. In that year too a token force of 14 Sixth form girls attended the Charter Day service which celebrates the granting in 1552 of a Royal Charter to the Merchant Venturers.

These were years of momentous events, none more so than the signing of the Armistice, and the efforts of successive Head Mistresses to interest the girls in what was going on outside School were on that occasion scarcely necessary. The celebrations in School were worthy of the event. For some days before Monday, November 11, 1918, there had been rumours that there would soon be an armistice and an end to hostilities, but the German envoys had been delayed and there was still uncertainty. On that Monday morning the School was full of expectation. As the mid morning break began guns and sirens were heard. Looking up towards the flat part of the roof the girls saw the Union Jack being raised, and then with more difficulty the larger New Zealand flag. Cheering broke out in the classrooms and in the playground. Ten minutes later Miss Sparks appeared on her balcony, calling to the girls in the garden to come in. Staff and girls hurried together to the Assembly Hall, the rule of silence in the corridors for once broken. What followed was a service of thanksgiving and rejoicing. Miss Sparks said that they must all dedicate themselves again to the service of their country. They were young and had their lives before them. In their joy they must not forget the sorrow of those older people who had lost loved ones. A member of staff whose fiancé had been killed left the Hall in tears.

There were no more lessons that day, and no homework. The next day there was a special assembly at noon, when Miss Sparks read out the news in The Times of what had been happening in London the day before. Wednesday was, of course, Commemoration day with the festivities brought to an early conclusion because of the Lighting Regulations. Thursday was a holiday, and on Friday afternoon there was the Staff Play. It was a week to remember.

The next year on November 11, there was a service in the Hall beginning at a quarter to eleven. There was music, and Miss Sparks read part of Lawrence Binyon's *For the Fallen*

> With proud thanksgiving, a mother for her children.
> England mourns for her dead across the sea . . .

Her selection of stanzas from the poem is interesting. She did not read the lines which everyone knows now:

> They shall not grow old as we that are left grow old:
> Age shall not weary them, nor the years condemn.
> At the going down of the sun and in the morning
> We shall remember them.

Perhaps she thought them unsuitable for younger children. Then at eleven o'clock, the School stood in silence for two minutes.

There was a similar service in 1920, while the Unknown Soldier was being buried with full military honours in Westminster Abbey. The next year, when the sirens went at eleven o'clock on November 11, girls stood beside their desks in their classroom to observe the two minutes' silence. In the streets outside, in shops and factories and offices, everyone else did the same. Only in the second World War, when the sirens could have been mistaken for air raid warnings, did this impressive custom come to an end.

In 1919 the School lost the use of the playing field on Golden Hill, a severe deprivation when one remembers the restricted playing space at the School. Mr King arranged that the Colston Trust should acquire a large piece of land, 32 acres in all, between the Bishop's Palace and Cranbrook Road, known as the Redland Court Estate. The Trust then sold the land on to the Society of Merchant Venturers, evidently at an advantage to the Trust, for the Girls' School's one eighth share of the endowment income increased by about £200 a year. The land included an area, variously estimated as comprising 13 or 9 acres, which was already in use as playing fields. This area the Society proposed to let to the School at an annual rent of £70, with the power to sublet. The rest became part of a housing development, and one of the new roads was given Mr King's middle name, Kersteman.

Outdoor games were still not a compulsory part of the curriculum of the School. They had been a self financing extra and the games fees had doubled since 1914 without any decrease in the number of girls involved. The playing field at Redland was a great addition to the School's amenities, but there was still the question of how it was to be financed. As well as the £70 a year rent, it would be necessary to employ a groundsman and buy grass cutting machines and games equipment. Miss Sparks estimated the total cost at £250 a year although this does not seem to take into account whatever had been spent in the past on hiring other people's grounds. She terminated all the previous tenancies of the field and invited new applications. She was concerned that nothing should curtail the School's use of the field on Wednesday afternoons and Saturday mornings. It is probable that there were hockey and cricket team practices at the field after school when the afternoons were light enough. There were three tennis courts, a welcome addition to the two uneven grass courts at the School. To ensure the fullest advantage to the School, she had to refuse at least two of the applications and this caused bad feeling. She recommended that the Cathedral School should be allowed to rent a cricket pitch at £50 a year and that the West Gloucestershire Archery Club should rent for £10 a year a strip of land on the second, lower field on condition that they used it only in the mornings and on Saturday afternoons. The following year Redland High School also made limited use of the field for a rent of £10. None of these tenants had any storage accommodation on the field and, of course, neither had the School. In March 1920, Miss Sparks thought this matter urgent. She had already tried to negotiate the removal of the Merchant Venturers' School's pavilion from Golden Hill, but had found that the cost would be prohibitive. She now left the matter with the Governors. The Society of Merchant Venturers responded with provision of a wooden pavilion on brick foundations. Sparkling in new paint, it contained storage space for games and maintenance equipment, changing rooms for teams, (although 'changing' was usually confined to shoes after removing one's hat, coat and gloves) and a solid fuel stove and teamaking facilities. The pavilion was opened in the summer of 1921 by the Master of the Society of Merchant Venturers, Mr C. Cyril Clarke, after it had been in use for some months. It was a happy coincidence that he was Master that year. He had become a member of the Society in 1906, a lawyer rather than a merchant. As a young man he had spent time in a Mission in the East End of London. He had seen active service in the war and had been invalided out of the army. He became a governor of the Girls' School in 1916 and although he was not often able to attend Governors' meetings during the war he was soon one of the most devoted and enthusiastic members of the governing body, and remained so for the next 41 years. The evening in early June when the opening ceremony was performed was sunny and the party consisted of the Society, the Governors, the staff and the Sixth form. Tea was served on the pavilion verandah and Mr Clarke opened the door with a silver key to which was attached seven ribbons in the seven House colours. He warned the assembled company against overeating. The week before, when he had been entertaining the Prince of Wales at the Merchants' Hall, the Prince had refused pudding, saying, 'I must keep fit.' Mr Clarke made the girls laugh by quoting Robert Louis Stevenson:

> Happy hearts and happy faces
> Happy play in grassy places
> That was how in ancient ages
> Children grew to kings and sages.
>
> But the unkind and the unruly
> And the sort who eat unduly
> They must never hope for glory –
> Theirs is quite another story!
>
> Cruel children, crying babies,
> All grow up as geese and gabies,
> Hated, as their age increases,
> By their nephews and their nieces.

After tea there was a cricket match between the Society and the School. Although the School team was reinforced by the two Physical Education teachers and by Dr Richard Clarke, brother of Cyril and the School's medical adviser, the Merchants won by 107 runs to the Sixth's 103 all out, an indication not only of the superiority of the batting to the bowling but also of the athleticism of a new generation of Merchants. The captain of the girls' team was Doris Whitaker, sister of the redoubtable Gwen Whitaker who had been appointed to a post in the Treasurer's Office at the Merchants in 1918 and whose portrait, the only one in Merchants' Hall of a woman other than royalty, hangs as a tribute to her thirty nine years of service to the Society. Doris was personal assistant to the Secretary of St Monica's Home, which is managed by the Society, for thirty two years.

In his seventies, Cyril Clarke still recalled this happy evening, the first of many occasions when he presided over a School celebration, with pleasure. At the end of the same term he and his wife Olga gave the School a Georgian silver bowl to be presented each year to the House with the best record in examinations. Filled with roses, it has stood each year beside the books on the table at Prize Day. This was, of course, a personal gift from Mr and Mrs Clarke; the following year the Society again stepped in to rescue the School from a difficult financial situation.

The School had enlarged the Pleasaunce by renting a small piece of land at its end from the Bristol Corporation. This ground had formed part of a larger property known as Rennison's Baths. Now the Corporation wished to dispose of the whole property, including the ground leased to the School. The School architect valued it at £300. Although it was unclear where this money was coming from, he was authorized to offer the corporation this sum. The corporation had threatened to put the whole up for auction. The Chairman and another governor, Mr W.W. Ward, negotiated and secured the piece of ground, small but essential to the School, for £400. The Society actually paid for it and allowed the School a mortgage, repayable in thirty years, on it.

In May 1922 there was a General Inspection of the School, the first since 1914. It was a time to look back at what had been achieved. There were now 620 pupils, 7 of them boys in the Junior School, and there were 14 students doing a threeee year course provided in conjunction with the University of Bristol which would lead to the Higher Certificate of the National Froebel Institute. The results in the first and second School Certificates were very good, particularly as whole forms were now entered rather than only those who were judged likely to pass. On the results of the second School Certificate three State Scholarships had been awarded in the last two years; and one girl, Marjorie Littleton, had won an Open Scholarship in Mathematics to Girton College, Cambridge.

This success was largely due to Miss Sparks's emphasis on 'quiet work', but her admission policy also helped. She succeeded in recruiting the great majority of girls at the age of eleven or younger. In 1921 she only had room for half the number of girls who applied, and she made use of a clause in the Scheme which forbade the School from retaining pupils who were 'unable or unwilling to learn': from time to time, she asked the parents of a small number of unsatisfactory pupils to remove their daughters. But apart from these reluctant leavers there was not much of what she called 'leakage'. The average age of leavers in 1921 was 17 years and 7 months.

As well as requiring the highest possible standards in academic work, she encouraged the active participation of the girls themselves in all school matters. Form committees were followed by the setting up of a School Council made up of the Sixth form and two representatives from each form below the Sixth. They were invited to discuss the running of the School and their views were listened to.

The School had a long tradition of good singing, as the resignation in 1921 of Mrs Wensley Bunce after 26 years of vigorous teaching reminded everyone; and by then there was a small orchestra which could be heard at many functions through the year. This was the creation of Ida Cottrill, an Old Girl who had been chiefly remarkable during her school days for her outstanding work in art. She took her National Froebel Union certificate in School, and was appointed to the art department, where she took charge when Miss Palin had her sabbatical leave. She was also a gifted musician and drew round her a select band of staff and girls. One of the staff was Miss Enid Gibbon, an auburn haired wit who taught French and played the violin until she retired in 1954.

Another advance was the development of drama in School. Miss Hughes, herself an instinctive communicator with a live audience, had produced a full length play almost every year; but the actors were Old Girls, with the occasional Upper Sixth girl playing a small part. In Miss Sparks's time the entertainments given to parents on Open Days began to include the spoken word as well as singing and instrumental music, and involved girls at all stages of their school career. The first play in which all the parts were taken by schoolgirls was *The Water Babies*, based on the tale by Charles Kingsley, in 1919. It was a spectacular production with special lighting effects for the underwater scenes devised by Miss Palin, and a chorus of forty young children trained by Mrs James and Miss Gibbon. It was put on to raise money for play centres for poor children.

This interest in the live theatre may have been an unexpected and welcome result of the war, for travelling companies such as those under the direction of Benson and Ben Greet left London to tour the provinces and gave performances in the Bristol theatres. School parties were organised to see performances of Shakespearean set books; and these were so much enjoyed that theatre visits became a regular if not frequent experience for the senior girls.

There continued to be a number of girls who made long journeys each day to come to School. The rail and 'bus services to country districts were much better than today, but there were fewer parents who had cars and came into Bristol daily to work, and could bring their daughters with them. Some parents arranged that their daughters should stay with relations or friends in Bristol during the week. These arrangements had to be made known to the School authorities, and in an informal way Miss Sparks had assisted in finding suitable families willing to take these weekly lodgers. In 1920 a Mrs Culverwell, a trained nurse with a large house in Cotham called Heathercroft, offered weekly or termly boarding to girls who needed it. Her offer was accepted, on condition that her house could be inspected at any time by the Head Mistress. The fee for full board was about £50 a term, but the parents dealt directly with Mrs Culverwell and the Governors were not involved. The first six girls came into residence at the beginning of the Summer Term of 1920 and two years later there were ten. They were not young children – their pastimes were bagatelle and dancing – and some of them were Froebel students whose homes were even further away than other pupils'. There were never many of these boarders and some years none. Mrs Culverwell gave up in 1934, and her daughter and a colleague with experience of running boarding houses took over. The Culverwells gave their young lodgers a happy temporary home. The house in Cotham had a room known as the 'school room' set aside for the girls. Here they did their homework and amused themselves in the winter. In the summer they had the garden in which to read and talk.

In successive Inspectors' Reports since 1905 there had been adverse comment on the short length of time teachers stayed on the staff, and the 1922 report was no exception. Using the criterion the Inspectors used, the proportion of the staff resigning after three or fewer years' service in the School, the criticism was justified. It was a state of affairs which should not have been found surprising and it can only have been the Inspectors' better acquaintance with all-male staffs which made it so. It was never imagined that a woman teacher would continue with her career after she married. Only if she were widowed or could teach some highly specialised subject part time, would there be any chance of her being employed in a school. During the war a member of staff asked for leave of absence to marry her soldier fiancé before he was sent abroad. Although a majority of the governing body decided to grant the request, the decision was not unanimous and a governor in holy orders was very definitely against it. She returned to the staff a married woman, but resigned as soon as her husband was demobilised. There was naturally no question that he should look for employment in Bristol so that she could continue the work she was doing with conspicuous success. It was obvious to girls in school that a choice had to be made between marriage and a teaching career.

Not all the resignations were the consequences of young staff wishing to marry. Some moved on to take charge of departments in other schools. During Miss Sparks's eight years, six members of staff became head mistresses of other schools. One of these was Miss Edwards: the other five were Miss Sparks's appointments. Three others took posts in teachers' training colleges.

There was, however, a core of members of staff who made their teaching in the School their life's work, and Bristol their home. Miss 'Gentle Anne' Merriman had been appointed in 1902. She functioned, as an Old Girl has put it, as a 'combined community policeman and traffic warden', and taught Scripture and French as well. Miss Palin, appointed in 1910 to teach art, taught the awareness of beauty in and out of the classroom throughout the School. Miss Sparks added to these Miss Stoodley, Miss Gibbon, Miss Beacall, Miss 'Fish' Taylor, Miss Gillard, Miss Street, Miss Page and Miss Clutton.

When Miss Sparks resigned in 1922 to become Principal of Cheltenham Ladies' College, the School, staff and girls alike, was shocked as though a foundation of the structure of life was being removed. One of her many gifts was that of the explicator. She could explain the latest and least familiar educational theory, the most complicated civil service procedure. Such people are often undervalued; the listener tends to take the credit for being able to understand. The girls knew they would miss her kindness and concern for their individual futures. They did not hold her high standard of work, behaviour and tidiness or her custom of preaching on abstract virtues against her. The staff, even more than the girls, respected her intellectual powers and enjoyed the warmth of her personality. She had become a national figure in education. She was Chairman of the Salaries and Pensions sub committee of the Head Mistresses' Association. It was no coincidence that in the year before she resigned the principal speaker at Prize Giving had been the Rt. Hon. H.A.L. Fisher, the President of the Board of Education. But it was as a loving friend that she was missed. She left behind her as Miss Clutton wrote in the Chronicle, an 'indescribable blank'.

She left at half term in the Autumn Term, although she came back to School for a long weekend at Commemoration, and in the following years, as long as there were girls in the School whom she knew she visited from time to time. There seems no good reason why she left so soon after the announcement of her appointment to Cheltenham, but her successor at Colston's had been chosen and Miss Stafford, the Second Mistress, could take over until the end of term.

A pupil of today would have found the Colston's of 1913 unfamiliar, belonging to a much earlier age: she would have found the Colston's of 1922, in spite of its silent corridors and cloakrooms, a school she could recognise by its structures and its ethos. Miss Sparks's work at Cheltenham was in several ways similar to what she had done in Bristol. In her fourteen years there she turned a nineteenth century institution into a modern girls' school. She began with the reorganisation and development of Advanced Courses and the gradual elimination of degree courses. It was a difficult task, performed so sensitively that all involved recognised that she was building and not destroying. She died in 1953. She had had at least two periods of ill health in her life, one in the year before she left Colston's and one lasting two terms just before she left Cheltenham. In spite of this, those who knew her remembered her mental and physical energy.

MISS DREW

That the Governors took a great deal of trouble to find a successor to Miss Sparks can be seen as a tribute to the Head Mistress they were losing. The post was widely advertised, in national newspapers and journals as well as in The Times Educational Supplement. A subcommittee considered all the 28 applications and took up the references of nine. Five of these were invited for interview by the full number of Governors on September 27, 1922. Three were Head Mistresses and two Second Mistresses. After the interviews, three were eliminated in discussion and a vote was taken on the remaining two. It was decided to offer the post to Miss Helen Drew, Head Mistress of Newark High School, and she accepted. Miss Sparks declared herself delighted.

Miss Drew was, like her predecessor, a professional. Her father had been a master at Eton. She went to Oxford High School and then to Newnham College, Cambridge, where she was a Senior Optime in Mathematics and read Natural Science in the second part of her tripos. She had taught at Redland High School, Croydon High School and during the war, at Bradford Grammar School. She was 42, and had been a Head Mistress for six years.

She visited the School during the autumn term, the day after Prize Giving, and met all the staff and many of the forms. When Miss Sparks left, the Second Mistress Miss Stafford took charge for the last few weeks of term and Miss Drew arrived in January. Miss Sparks's departure was felt as a great grief. 'Miss Sparks has now gone to Cheltenham. We miss her at every turn. . . .' wrote the School Captain. Yet Miss Drew was welcomed warmly and settled into her place in the School with great ease. She looked very different from Miss Sparks. She was tall and had dark hair, and she moved with grace and dignity. One Old Girl remembers her as 'regal'. She was, however, in sympathy with what had been going on in School and there was no feeling that there would be a change of direction. In this, she differed from the two head mistresses she succeeded.

Miss Hughes actually changed the character of the School and in at least two instances, the revision of the School fee and the building of laboratories, she reversed previous decisions of the Governors. Miss Sparks, in a very short space of time, reformed the School curriculum and the organisation of the classes, and in so doing affected each girl's experience as she moved up through the School. Miss Drew did not feel the need for such great changes. In any case she was probably by temperament more inclined to gradual planned improvements than to dramatic innovation.

In one matter in particular she was wholly in agreement with her predecessor: the need for a gymnasium both to improve the work in physical education in the School and to relieve pressure on the space provided by the Hall and Dining Room. In her first term in the School there was an ominous indication of the shortage of money available for educational projects. It is sometimes supposed that the depression in the economic affairs of the United Kingdom between the Wars began with the New York Wall Street crash in October 1929. It began long before that. Miss Sparks had told the Governors in 1919 that where in the past they had been thinking in tens of pounds, they must now think in hundreds. The trouble was that they could not convert their thinking into action. Nationally, a committee under the chairmanship of Sir Eric Geddes recommended an economy drive as the way out of the country's financial problems. The cuts which followed bore most heavily on housing and education. Bristol Education Authority requested that the Governors should fall into line with its own practice and from April 1, 1923, should make a 5% cut in the salaries they were paying the Head, the Clerk and the teaching staff. This was the first departure from the Burnham Scale which had been adopted so enthusiastically less than three years before, and it was not to be the last.

Miss Stafford wrote to the Governors saying that the staff accepted the cut, but asked that it should not apply to the youngest members of staff who were paid less than £200 a year. The Governors replied sadly that they would have to comply with the Authority's directive in total and could not give special treatment to the youngest and poorest members of staff. It is significant that the following year there was a petition from the staff that they should be paid at half termly intervals and not, as had been the rule until then, at the end of each term.

In spite of such anxieties, Miss Drew's first year at Colston's went well. There were public lectures and visits to the theatre and to a concert in the Cathedral. At the end of the Spring Term an afternoon was set aside for 'Recitations', when each form had to produce an item to entertain the rest of the School. Some of these were dramatic productions, costumed and stage managed by girls. There had been drama in School in Miss Hughes's time but the performers as well as the backstage workers had usually been members of the teaching staff or Old Girls. Now the girls themselves were being encouraged to perform in public, if only to a school audience. In this we can probably see Miss Clutton's influence. We can certainly see it in the School Magazine, where original writing by girls is becoming the largest single feature. The standard is high and it is noticeable that the girls are not writing to a formula. The test for inclusion is readability, not the close imitation of some published work. The twin highlights of the year, Sports Day and Commemoration Day, were greatly enjoyed. Miss Gibbon was a notable Alice in *Through the Looking Glass*.

In the autumn Miss Drew began to look into possible plans for a gymnasium on the strip of land behind 182, Cheltenham Road. There was no hope of anything but a wooden structure similar to the Annexe, but the aim had to be to get as large a room as possible on the awkwardly shaped site. Mr James, the architect, produced a plan of a building which could be entered at ground level from Cheltenham Lane but had a staircase at the other end to reach the level of the Science rooms. Miss Drew went to see a wooden hall which had been built to his design at Fry's recreation ground on a level site but she also went see the work of a company in Manchester specialising in timber buildings. This firm, Ginger, Lee and Company, had built a wooden gymnasium for Manchester High School and this she also inspected. Mr Ginger, who was evidently the design expert, came to Bristol to see for himself what the problems were. He scrapped his first plan for a conventional hall standing on ground levelled up from Cheltenham Lane and concentrated on achieving level entrances from the covered corridor running alongside the physics laboratory to the Annexe.

By February of the next year the Governors had approval in principle from the Board of Education for both the erection of a wooden building and a loan from the Bank of £1,300. They accepted Mr Ginger's revised plan. The gymnasium, with a small dressing room, and a cloakroom with lavatories and washbasins, would be made in his workshops in Manchester and erected by his workmen at a cost of £960. Before this could happen the ground had to be cleared and foundations built. This part of the work cost almost as much as the gymnasium, but there is no doubt that it was money well spent. The restricted site had buildings on three sides and the lane on the fourth. By raising the structure on brick pillars to the level of the adjoining corridor lighting and ventilation were improved. The opportunity was taken to put in yet another boiler in a brick built heating chamber in the small triangle of land between the end of the gymnasium and the lane. This was the fifth solid fuel boiler in the School building; they all had to be stoked by the caretaker. His consolation had to be that the four anthracite stoves in the Annexe classrooms were replaced by hot water radiators heated by the new boiler.

The gymnasium was erected during the summer holidays, and was ready for use in September although the necessary apparatus was not installed for some months. Before this, at the Governors' Meeting in June, Mervyn King had resigned the chairmanship, although he continued as a governor and came to School regularly until his death in 1934. It is said that on the day he died he was planning to come to the School Sports the next day. He was 79 when he ceased to take the chair and he may have felt the problems not only of paying for the gymnasium but also of ensuring an adequate income for the School in the years to come were better tackled by a younger man. Cyril Clarke, who had been a Governor for eight years and had already shown himself to be a generous friend to the School, was voted in to the chair.

Early in the new year the girls held sales of cakes and sweets to buy materials for Bazaar Working Parties. The goods they made and many other gifts were sold at the great School Bazaar on July 1, and the sum of £300 was raised. A production of *As You Like It* made over £40. The Old Girls gave a performance of *David Garrick* and the younger children held small sales. How much the Governors and their friends gave is not recorded, but the Society of Merchant Venturers gave £250. At the end of the academic year the new Chairman decided that it was unnecessary to borrow more than £1,000, instead of the £1,300 for which the School had permission from the Board of Education.

Colston girls and Old Girls had a long tradition of charitable giving – to missions overseas, to poor families in particular parishes and to the maintenance of a cot in the Children's Hospital – and this continued. Raising money for themselves was a new departure and one had to go back to the Sales of Work in the Eighteen Nineties to find anything comparable. Then what was sold were articles made in needlework lessons. Now schoolwork and the effects of the School Certificate and Higher School Certificate examinations prevented lesson times being used in such a way. The money for the gymnasium was raised by activities out of school time. Miss Hughes had been given a grant by the Colston Hospital Trust and had been able to borrow from the bank. Her strategy for repaying the loans had been to increase the number of pupils, which she found easy, and the School fee, which had been more difficult. She had left problems for her successor. Miss Sparks had added to these a further, although not so dramatic, rise in the number of pupils, a firm intention of developing and systematising the curriculum and a determination that the staff should be paid more adequate salaries. In her time smaller amounts had been borrowed and the buildings erected were on a more modest scale. She contended that if the country wanted free and subsidised places in endowed schools such as Colston's it must be prepared to pay for them nationally and locally in the form of grants. When Miss Drew arrived in January 1923 this equilibrium between the running costs of the School and the help it received in grants was at best uncertain, and there were signs that it would disappear. Nor, with the number of the unemployed rising through the decade, was it likely that permission to raise the School fee would be granted. The decision that the School should help itself when it needed a new amenity was inevitable in the circumstances. There is no evidence that the Governors, staff, girls or parents resented it, and Miss Drew was decidedly in favour.

Besides the acquisition of a gymnasium the other unusual happening in 1924 was the visit on June 19 to the British Empire Exhibition at Wembley. Miss Drew and Miss Openshaw had collaborated on the arrangements. They saw 245 girls accompanied by 22 staff off to London on a special train at half past six in the morning. At Wembley the girls divided into groups of a dozen or so, each accompanied by a member of staff and senior girls, and they spent the day exploring the huge exhibition. It rivalled the Prince Consort's Great Exhibition of 1851 and the Festival of Britain after the Second World War and made a great impression on the minds and memories of the young. Its purpose was to renew confidence in the stability of the Empire and Britain's power to recover from the effects of the war. In fact, the girls

1. Miss Amy Smith, Head Mistress 1891–1900.

2. Mr W Proctor Baker, Chairman of Governors 1891–1907.

3. Miss Amy Smith and academic staff 1893. Miss Edith Openshaw is seated to the right of Miss Smith with tennis racket.

4. Colston's Girls' School from Cheltenham Road at the turn of the century.

5. Miss Evangeline Hughes, Head Mistress 1901–1913.

6. Opening of the Science Laboratories, 1903.

7. Cast of the first School Play, 'Palace of Truth', 1904.

8. Opening of the Pleasaunce, June 22 1906. The New Wing was to be built in 1907.

9. *Entrance Hall, 1906*

10. *Assembly in the Hall, 1906.*

11. Head Mistress's sitting room, 1909. Miss Hughes moved from the front of the school to this former classroom to which she added the bay window and balcony.

12. Mr Charles Julius Ryland shortly before his death in 1909.

13. The Ryland Library, 1912.

14. *Miss Hughes and the Domestic Staff, 1913.*

15. *Miss Sparks and staff, 1923. Miss Openshaw is sitting to the right of the Head Mistress.*

16. Miss Beatrice Sparks, Head Mistress 1914–1923.

17. The School Cricket Team who played the Merchant Venturers' XI at the opening of the new Pavilion in 1921. Dr Clarke to the left.

18. Chemistry Room, 1922 (from a collection of photographs donated to the school by the family of Cicely Monkton).

19. Miss Helen Drew, Head Mistress 1923–27.

20. Miss Gladys Morgan, Head Mistress 1927–1945.

21. School holiday in Geneva, 1930.

22. The Kindergarten, 1940.

23. *Swedish drill on Sports Day in the Pleasaunce, 1940.*

24. *Farm holiday, 1940.*

25. Queen Mary's visit, 1943.

26. Domestic Science, 1948.

27. Miss Mary Green (latterly Dame Mary), Head Mistress 1945–1953.

28. With the Sixth Form in 1952.

seem to have had a glimpse of the complexity and interdependence of the world.

They all met for lunch during the day and boarded the train home at six o'clock in the evening. They were met at Lawrence Hill station by Miss Drew.

The next year's magazine as well as recording all the money-raising efforts for the gymnasium records Miss Drew's absence for a fortnight in March because of illness. That this should have been thought noteworthy is interesting. Miss Sparks was away for several weeks at the end of a Summer Term so that she could receive treatment for rheumatism at Harrogate and it was never mentioned in the Magazine. No doubt she made very firm plans as to what should happen in her absence.

That year Sports Day was held at the Playing Field instead of in the Pleasaunce. For 25 years it had been remarked that the sun always shone on Sports Day, but this year it had to be postponed to the next day because of heavy rain. Nevertheless it was an important occasion, with a refreshment tent and banners for each of the Houses. The winning House had a silver cup. The runners-up had chocolates sent by Miss Sparks. Later generations will believe that the secret of guaranteed good weather was lost that day.

In the autumn the old institution of an Honour Day was revived, when the staff merely taught and all the school discipline was in the hands of the girls. The suggestion came from the School Council, inaugurated by Miss Sparks and taken very seriously by Miss Drew, who passed Council resolutions on to the Governors if she thought them of sufficient interest. The Governors tended to agree to suggestions which would not cost them or the parents too much money. School Captain after Captain deplored the triviality of the suggestions, usually about the school meal or uniform, sent in to them: they were serious-minded young women.

Miss Drew's standards in professional matters were high. She gave encouragement to young members of staff who wished to improve their teaching methods and she kept her eyes open for signs of lack of discipline or interest in classes. The School Certificate results in Latin had been poor for three years, with nearly half the candidates failing, and she enlisted the help of local and Board of Education inspectors to discover what was wrong. They told her that the subject was taught too slowly in the early stages and without conviction to the upper forms. She recommended to the Governors that the senior classical specialist should leave the staff at the end of the Summer Term and a new appointment be made for the following September. This had never happened before at Colston's. Teachers had not had their appointment confirmed at the end of their probationary year, but no head of department had been dismissed after five years on the staff. The teacher concerned seems to have been one of Miss Sparks's very few unsuccessful appointments. She had a second class honours degree in classics from London University, but neither her own education nor her professional career had been continuous. Her successor, Miss A.L. Burton, with a first class honours degree and an impeccable teaching record, put matters right. She gave the School ten years of distinguished service until her sudden death in 1936.

Apart from Latin, academic results at the top of the School were good. Most girls seeking degrees went to Bristol University but there were some at the London colleges and at Cambridge, and now three at Oxford. They wrote letters, for the most part light hearted, for the School Magazine: an encouragement to younger girls to join them. Sporting results against other schools, on the other hand, were at the very best mediocre.

1926 began with wintry weather. Miss Openshaw slipped on the ice and broke her wrist. International affairs had been much in the minds of staff and girls for months and there were great hopes for a lasting peace as the result of the talks at Locarno. At a meeting of the School branch of the Association of the International League, Miss Black described her schooldays in Germany. She was Miss Drew's cousin and kept house for her. In emergencies she would come into School to give German lessons. Miss Elspeth Clark, the Second Mistress and senior historian, resigned on her appointment as Head Mistress of a school at Westcliffe-on-Sea. She was lively and amusing and everyone was sad to think of her leaving.

Towards the end of March Miss Drew became seriously ill and was operated on. The finance subcommittee had already arranged to meet on March 30 and granted her a term's leave of absence on full pay. The Governors also had to deal with the problem of who should run the School in the absence of the Head Mistress and with the present, experienced Second Mistress leaving at Easter. They decided to ask Miss Openshaw, Miss Merriman, by now the most senior member of the teaching staff, and the Second Mistress designate, Miss Florence A. Stoodley, to take charge together. Miss Stoodley, who taught English and history and had been on the staff for eleven years, was a newcomer compared with the other two. Although it was an unusual arrangement, it was probably the best that could be managed at the time. One of the important administrative tasks of the Summer Term is the appointment of new staff and this the three of them did by enlisting the help of heads of departments. They were concerned that the work of the School should continue as normally as possible and in this they succeeded. There were if anything rather more expeditions, visits to theatres, concerts and factories than usual. Mr Mervyn King arranged for a party of girls to visit a flotilla of minesweepers at anchor off St Augustines's Quay and the Master of the Merchants, Mr Victor Eberle, gave prizes for the best essays on the subject. The General Strike in May made life difficult for the girls who came to school by train. The miners did not return to work for six months after the Strike ended and in the autumn Miss Openshaw had to find logs to use in the furnaces instead of coke. It was said she chopped them herself.

MISS DREW

Miss Drew was back in School during July, working quietly in her room and seeing people one at a time. When the Autumn Term opened she seemed to be fully recovered and the term began on a high note of excitement. The Chairman and his wife had a baby son, Charles Nigel, and the whole School was invited to be his Godmother. When he came with his parents to Sports Day his reception was rapturous.

Three days after Commemoration Day Miss Drew was away from School again. The Chairman said she must take six months' leave with no responsibility for School affairs at all. Miss Stoodley was appointed Acting Head Mistress. The earlier triumvirate had done well, but all three had full time jobs to do apart from the work of the head. Now a temporary member of staff was appointed to take most of Miss Stoodley's time table.

The Magazine records with joy Miss Drew's return in September but says nothing of her later absence. Very great anxiety had been felt about her illness earlier in the year. It was a time when sickness necessitating prolonged nursing and rest was much more common than it is now and a teacher's absence for a term because of her, or her parent's ill health was not unusual. The silence about Miss Drew's third absence is an indication that the staff had little hope of her return.

She wrote short letters to the staff and the School for the beginning of the Spring Term and sent a telegram to the meeting of the Old Girls' Society in January. At the end of March the Chairman received her resignation. She died on Easter morning, April 17, and was buried at Wolvercote, Oxford, where her family lived. Although the School was on holiday it was well represented at the funeral. At the beginning of the new term there was a week of quiet mourning. A memorial service was held in St Michael and All Angels' church, and Sports Day was cancelled. By sad coincidence, Miss Elspeth Clark, so recently Second Mistress, died on June 3, and news came of the death at her home in the South of France of Mlle Renée Anroux who had taught French since 1913. The staff and all but the very newest new girls knew all three and there was a general feeling of bereavement throughout the Summer Term.

The School suffered in every way through the loss of Miss Drew. When she was in School and in good health she displayed qualities of both vision and energy. She had, Miss Stoodley wrote, 'a large simplicity and a certain directness of outlook' before which artificiality and insincerity could not stand. 'The world seemed a better and a simpler place when she was near.' She inspired confidence and helped people, girls and staff alike, to perform at their best. The fact that for most of two years the staff did not have the support of her presence or her guidance and still managed to keep the corporate life of the School going is a measure of their skill and dedication.

MISS MORGAN

The Governors advertised the headship, received 36 applications and interviewed four candidates at the end of their meeting on June 24. They selected Miss Gladys Mary Morgan, Second Mistress and senior historian at Berkhamsted High School, and it was made possible for her to start in September. She was appointed a few days after her thirty third birthday and so was considerably younger than either Miss Sparks or Miss Drew. It is interesting that all three heads appointed during Cyril Clarke's long chairmanship were of this age.

She had been educated at Blackheath High School and St Hilda's College, Oxford, where she read History. She was a tall, impressive figure. She drove a yellow, open topped car and was credited with a sporting life outside School. Several Old Girls remember her as looking like George Eliot. She once attended a Sixth Form fancy dress party as King Charles II: they thought the likeness striking.

She had to wind up her work at Berkhamsted in a very few weeks. She did not dispose of the country cottage where she had been living, but went abroad for a holiday, driving alone. She gave a lift on a deserted road to two women walkers, one of whom had a well simulated limp. The actress was Miss Gibbon and her companion Miss Rashley, Miss Openshaw's assistant. She discovered who they were, but did not enlighten them as to her own identity. She still had time to spend several days in School before the beginning of term, listening to Miss Openshaw and going many times to every part of the building and the garden.

Later she described her first impressions. She liked the graciousness of such rooms as the Library and the feeling that the building, inconvenient and inadequate as it might be in some places, had been cherished. She was surprised by the smallness of the kitchens and when she saw them being used she was amazed that such quantities of good food could be produced in such conditions. She thought the Hall, built it must be remembered for a school of 300 girls, was small for nearly 600. She had still to see it on state occasions when there were visitors. She was also doubtful about the provision of laboratories but thought that the enlarging of the Hall was the most pressing need. She saw how it could be done. There was an empty space between the end wall of the Hall and 182, Cheltenham Road, the shop where the Froebel students had their base. If the Hall were extended to join the shop, the kitchen could be rebuilt below the new part and the dining room could be enlarged. Meanwhile she had to get to know the School, the staff and girls, the Governors and the parents.

MISS MORGAN

She is so far the only Head Mistress to begin her work in the School in the Autumn Term. At Colston's it is the heaviest term of the year. Not only does it contain Prize Giving and the Christmas festivities but Colston's birthday and the day on which the Merchant Venturers celebrate the granting of their Royal Charter in 1552 both fall within it. Since Miss Hughes's time the School had kept November 13, the birthday, as Commemoration Day and new staff were told then, as they are today, that once they had experienced the marathon which is 'Commem' they would no longer feel new, in any sense of the word. She threw herself into all these activities with spontaneity and vigour. Girls remember her as having a slight stutter in her speech. It was no handicap. She was a communicator, both with large groups of people of every age and on paper.

The staff welcomed her with relief. The editorial of the School Magazine takes as its subject the legend of the phoenix, rising resplendent from the ashes of its former self. Few if any of the teaching staff can have had any idea of the problems she faced. There were some comparatively minor matters of which they were aware. Some of the mathematics classes were too large, a state of affairs which should have been foreseen in July and dealt with then. Miss Morgan re-divided the classes and Miss Openshaw obligingly taught the extra ones. She probably relished teaching again and by this time she had good help in the office. Miss Evelyn Rashley, in her early thirties, was a Classics graduate with a clear mind and steady nerves. The Governors were dismayed to think of the Clerk taking on yet another responsibility and authorised the part-time appointment of a mathematician.

Other problems could not be dealt with so quickly. In 1922, when Miss Sparks left, there were 620 pupils. This number fell each year and reached its lowest point, 551 girls, in the year after Miss Drew died. The average age of school leavers also fell from 17 years 7 months to 16 years 10 months. A number of girls were leaving each term below the age of sixteen. They were the subject of discussions in Governors' meetings. When their parents accepted the place in School, they had undertaken to let their daughters stay until they were sixteen. Now they pleaded poverty, and in some cases the girls were not doing well academically. Other schools in similar circumstances imposed a financial penalty: the amount was usually the equivalent of a term's fees. The Governors saw difficulties in this. One term's fees would not compensate for an empty place in the senior school. If the parents were financially embarrassed it did not seem right to add to their burdens, and in cases of real distress the School would remit part or all of the fee. If the girls were unhappy at School, they were unlikely to do better if they were made to stay against their will. The debate went on for years, Miss Morgan at first being in favour of the penalty. Eventually the Governors decided to word the agreement form which parents signed much more strongly and to insist on the payment of a penalty. By then this particular problem had disappeared. In the late twenties, however, it was one of the reasons given for the decline in the number of pupils, along with a fall in the birthrate during the war and the current rise in unemployment. The counties of Somerset and Gloucestershire had built secondary schools and no longer wished to send so many Free Place scholars to a Bristol school. This would not prevent fee paying parents in the two counties from choosing Colston's for their daughters if they wished. None of these 'reasons' touched the underlying state of affairs: a loss of confidence, a lack of excitement in the School itself.

The external examination results tell the same story. In the summer of 1927, when Miss Morgan arrived, only five girls had been awarded Higher School Certificates. When she saw the School Certificate results she decided to make a new Sixth form group for girls who would retake the examination in the hope of improving their performance sufficiently to be able to claim exemption from Matriculation.

At the same time the financial situation of the School was becoming perilous. A change was being made in the way grants were calculated. The Board of Education made a fixed per capita grant, the total sum depending on the number of pupils over 11 years of age. The Local Authority asked for the accounts of the past year and an estimate of expenditure in the coming year before deciding on the size of its grant, which would be larger if the School were able to show that it needed more. This deficit funding was about to cease. In March 1927 there had not been enough money available from the endowment income to make the annual repayments on the three outstanding loans and an overdraft was taken out on the current account. This led to complaints from Bristol Local Authority that money from grants was being used for building projects. Bristol rates were to be reviewed and it was feared that the rateable value of the building would be assessed more highly. New Board of Education regulations would soon require the Governors to make a contribution to the value of 2% of the salaries bill to a superannuation fund.

Whether, in her first months in the School, Miss Morgan fully appreciated the extent of the financial problem is doubtful. Miss Openshaw was there to explain, but the new Head Mistress's temperament was impetuous as well as generous and in those early days she found it difficult to accept that there was so little money available for what seemed to her essentials if the work of the School were to develop as it should.

In February 1928, Miss Openshaw fell ill and within six days she died. The reaction in the staffroom was incredulity as well as grief. Fears had been expressed for her health, but only by the Governors who saw her at intervals. The staff, who saw her every day, noticed her cheerfulness and her infectious pleasure in solving practical problems to everyone else's greater comfort. They had felt a great personal affection for her, smiling at her unceasing striving for perfection but recognising its selflessness. They were less vividly aware of her success in handling the School's affairs. She was fifty eight years old and had been entitled to a pension at the age of fifty but had continued with the work she so much loved.

Her funeral in St Alban's church, Westbury Park, was attended by girls in the middle school and senior forms. Her sister Grace, with whom she lived, asked that they should sing her favourite hymns, those associated with Commemoration and the ends of term. Merchants, former members of staff and representatives of other Bristol schools were there to pay tribute to someone who had been involved in a great educational venture from its beginning.

Partly because she had known every Old Girl but also because of her genuine interest, she had collected news of former pupils for the School Magazine. Now the Old Girls wanted to subscribe to a Memorial to her. A committee, similar to that which had organised the Gatliff Memorial, was set up with the same Governor, Mr A.C. Powell, as Chairman. Miss Morgan said that before Miss Openshaw's death the staff had wanted to commemorate Miss Drew's work in some way. At first the committee thought there would be some awkwardness in asking for contributions to two separate memorials at the same time. In fact it worked very well. The staff had thought a loan fund, from which girls in School and recent leavers could borrow to continue their education when they were in temporary straits, would be a fitting tribute to Miss Drew, and the Old Girls wanted an Edith Openshaw Scholarship Fund which would enable a girl to go to university. Miss Morgan drafted an appropriate letter which went out to all Old Girls and friends of the School inviting contributions to either or both of these funds. The secretarial work was done by Miss Rashley, but the cost of paper, printing and postage was borne by an anonymous donor; this was likely to have been Mr Powell himself. The response was excellent. By early autumn over £1,200 had been given to the Scholarship Fund and over £250 to the Loan Fund. These are very large amounts collected quickly. It took nearly six years to get together a much smaller sum to buy and install the organ in memory of Mrs Gatliff.

The Helen Drew Loan Fund benefited girls and Old Girls frequently in the years to come. The principal was invested but the interest was kept in an account accessible to the Head Mistress so that it could be used at short notice. The existence of the fund was referred to but it was not thought suitable that the names of those who borrowed from it should be made public. This was not the case with the Edith Openshaw Scholarship, which was to be awarded for exceptional achievement, and Miss Morgan thought there should be a special honours board for the names of the holders and also a bronze plaque recording Miss Openshaw's service to the School. She asked Sir George Oakley, the architect responsible for among other notable buildings the Great Hall of Bristol University, to design the plaque, which would have cost £55, but the rest of the memorial committee objected that the money had not been given for this purpose. The School could not afford such a sum and the project of a plaque was abandoned. Mr Powell himself gave the wooden board on which the list of Scholarship winners was to be inscribed.

The 1910 Scheme enabled the Governors to give up to £100 a year to girls going on to Universities. This had never been done and was out of the question now that the School was in debt. Nevertheless, the School was becoming better able to help those leaving for higher education. Mr Proctor Baker, the first Chairman, had left a sum which brought in £50 a year for an undergraduate scholarship, and a legacy from Mrs Gatcliff produced £25 a year, earmarked for girls going on to train in Art, Music, Domestic Science or Physical Education. Both the Proctor Baker and the Gatcliff scholarships had the same limited usefulness: each could only be held by one girl at a time, and if the winner of either embarked on a course lasting longer than a year, no one else could benefit until the previous holder had finished her course. The new Openshaw Scholarship improved matters. Miss Morgan applied for further help to the Trustees of the Gamble Fund. The Revd John Gamble, Canon of Bristol Cathedral, had left a substantial legacy to endow university scholarships to be held by students at women's colleges; in practice, this meant the universities of Oxford, Cambridge and London. The Trustees of the Fund made a grant to the School of stock to the value of £3,600 which would produce an annual income of £150, enough to assist three undergraduates in any one year. The Governors wrote a letter of thanks to the Trustees. Miss Morgan wrote to them asking them whether if there was any money left when the funds for scholarships had been distributed they would consider making a grant towards school building, for she was still hoping to build in spite of the financial anxieties, of which she must by this time have been fully aware.

In March 1928 there was a surplus on the year's account of about £25. Miss Rashley, well instructed by Miss Openshaw, explained that this was because a change in the accounting procedure required by the Board had resulted in the School balancing eleven months of expenditure against twelve months' income. In the coming year they would save £250 on the Head Mistress's salary. Miss Morgan was starting at the bottom of the scale while Miss Drew had been at the top. Incidentally, it was a sign of the times that the salary of the head of a school did not now differ so greatly from that of an assistant. At her peak, Miss Hughes was paid more than four times as much as the highest paid assistant. Miss Morgan's salary was a good deal less than twice that of the Second Mistress. Miss Rashley went on to remind the Governors that they would be paying £100 a year less towards her pension than they had towards Miss Openshaw's. Nevertheless, at the end of the next financial year there was a deficit of £996, and the outlook for the year after that was bleak.

The expenditure in these years was not abnormal, given the age of the building and the nature of the site. The house used by the students at 182, Cheltenham Road, needed a good deal of attention, as did the roof of the annexe and the studio ceiling. There were signs of subsidence in the playground near the Library wing and in the corridor beside the Head Mistress's room. The outside of the building needed painting but this at least could be postponed. The remaking of the drains of the new gymnasium could not. There was an urgent need to increase the School's income. Miss Morgan asked whether the Board would permit an increase in fees, and proposed a modest ten shillings a term. She was told that there was no possibility that this would be agreed to. Some Governors thought the Society of Merchant Venturers should be asked for help for the next two or more years. Experienced Merchants were not surprised to be told that they must make a 'formal, detailed appeal' to the Bristol Local Education Authority. The Society thought Bristol's declining support for the School could not be justified and did not intend to encourage it by providing alternative funds.

The School's outgoings were scrutinised not once but several times by a subcommittee of the Governors. Such economies as could be made were small and unwelcome. There happened to be no suitable candidate for the Gatcliff Exhibition; in such circumstances the annual income of £25 could be used for the Library and the annual Governors' grant of the same amount for new books could be withheld. It had been customary to pay a member of staff an allowance of £25 a year for work as the Librarian. Instead, a recent school leaver was given free lessons in shorthand and typewriting in return for part time work in the Library. It was proposed to use part of this to clean and overhaul the organ, but the School put on two entertainments which not only paid for the organ repairs but also helped towards repaying the gymnasium loan. The £50 saved on the Library went on the ordinary expenses of running the School. A right of way which existed between the Pleasaunce and Bath Buildings was sold for £40 but the Board insisted that this should go to reduce the loan which had been taken out to buy the extension of the Pleasaunce. It is doubtful that this comparatively small sum was sufficient compensation for the loss of access from the south to School property.

It fell to Miss Morgan to propose and carry through the only major reduction in the School's spending. Every school offering a complex timetable geared to individuals needs at least one member of staff who can understand and manipulate the timetable. In the confusion of Miss Drew's absences there had been no such expert but in Miss Morgan's first year she demonstrated that she had timetable skills. She considered that outdoor games should be available to every girl who could not show good reason for being excused. Many girls had gone home or elsewhere on Wednesday afternoons. By revising the timetable so that games were taught every afternoon, better use was made of the field and every girl had a games lesson. The new arrangement was generally liked by the girls and the few seniors who wanted to sketch in the Cathedral or go for a long walk one afternoon a week could be accommodated. The staff were surprised by the novelty of this arrangement, which reveals how inflexible the timetable had seemed before. It would be pleasant to record that the School's success in matches against other schools improved at once. It did not. The only sport in which Colston's excelled was swimming.

Miss Morgan's examination of the timetable had by the end of her first year convinced her that it was possible to provide a satisfactory education with a smaller teaching force, and in her second year she brought to an end the contract of three full time members of staff. It will be remembered that this was the year in which the decline in the number of pupils in School reached its lowest level. One of those leaving had taught in the Kindergarten: Miss Skeet, who was in charge of music, had Kindergarten qualifications and now divided her time between main school music and the youngest pupils. Another taught French, and Miss Morgan secured the services for the coming year of a French assistante. The third was a mathematician. The reduction in the number of staff seems to have been accepted as inevitable both by those who remained and those who left, but neither a shrinking staff nor declining numbers of pupils is ever a cheerful prospect.

At this gloomiest point both Miss Morgan and the Chairman displayed a steady optimism. There were some encouraging signs. The Board of Education produced new scales for the direct grant to schools such as Colston's, an increase of £2 a year for every fee paying pupil. The Chairman's personal plea to the city council to reconsider the rating assessment was successful. The 'formal and detailed' appeal to the Education Authority was presented with great care, and listened to with courtesy. It was turned down, but it improved relations with the City. Most importantly, the number of pupils began to rise. In Autumn 1929 there were 610 pupils and 12 Froebel students. There were fluctuations after this, but in the Thirties the trend was always upward. At the Finance Committee in July 1929 the Chairman produced plans he had asked Mr James to draw up for an extension of the Assembly Hall.

There was general agreement that a larger Assembly Hall and Dining Room were the most pressing among the several needs of the School, and this view was supported by the Inspectors who visited the School in 1930. Their list of priorities was: the Hall extension; asphalting the Pleasaunce; and the provision of at least one more laboratory. Miss Morgan, in talking to the Governors, put these desirable improvements in a different order. After the enlargement of the Hall and kitchens, she listed science teaching accommodation. It is probable that she was concentrating on the two most expensive projects. Mr Powell, the Governor who had so generously contributed to the organ fund, provided a hard tennis court in the Pleasaunce and this went some way towards solving the problem posed by a grass playground in winter. If more teaching space were provided anywhere in School, it would be possible to free the Library from use as a formroom. The immediate task was to find the money needed for building.

Cyril Clarke did not favour more loans for building; or, more precisely, he did not like inflicting a burden of interest and repayment on the future. He set about inviting his acquaintances to make gifts to the School. Mr W. Melville

Wills, who had been given the freedom of the Society of Merchant Venturers in 1929, promised £1,000; a Mrs Yda Richardson promised an equal sum; and he collected £250 from other sources. Mr James thought the Hall extension would cost about £4,300. Six builders were invited to tender for the work, and the lowest bid, £3,996, from Frank Wilkins would with professional fees be close to this figure. The Chairman decided not to go ahead until he had the promise of £4,000 without counting what the School might be able to raise. He wrote to the Pilgrim Trust, but received no help. Miss Morgan's letter to the Gamble Fund did produce another £1,000 and, eventually, permission to use this money for building. The rest of the £4,000 must have come as individual donations. In June 1931 Wilkins was instructed to start work.

For almost the whole of the year 1930/31 the School had been intent on money raising. Two days in June were announced as the date of School Bazaars. Preparations began in the autumn and by Christmas over £107 had already been collected in various ways: sales of cakes, fruit, lavender and handkerchiefs and a mile of pennies. Mrs Richardson opened the Bazaar on June 5 and Mrs Hiatt Baker the one next day. Besides the stalls there were refreshments and entertainments, and many Governors came on both days. The sum raised was £550, enough to ensure that there would be money remaining in the Building Fund when the Hall extension had been completed. The enterprise in which so many people, parents and Old Girls as well as present pupils, had been involved gave the School confidence in its capacity to help itself.

Building, or rather the preparatory demolition, began before the end of the Autumn Term. The organ was dismantled and the pieces laid out in the gallery. The Hall was partitioned and the roof removed from the platform end of it. The dining room became the builders' workshop and the work of reconstruction began. The new kitchen was made, joining the old building to 182, Cheltenham Road. Above this the Hall was extended by the removal of the old very narrow dais and the construction above the new kitchen of a rectangular platform which, like the kitchen, joined 182. A door at the back of the platform opened on to steps leading down into 182, and for the first time it was possible to reach the house where the students had their classroom and common room without going out into Cheltenham Road. Another new door, with steps leading down into the kitchen yard, was made at the same time. The original plan had been that the exterior of the building should be 'of plain brick with freestone windows but no decorations'. Shortly before the plans went out to tender, this austere directive was amended to include 'with buff stonework stripes so as to be in keeping with the existing building'.

The new kitchen was not ready until a fortnight after the beginning of the Autumn Term and it was not until half term that the partition in the Hall came down and the glory of the new platform was revealed. It was so much better than the old one that it was greeted with pleasure and excitement, but producers of plays soon found that not even the possibility of using the house behind the platform as a green room made up for the very small spaces on either side of the stage. The organ was replaced at the side of the platform, but the pipes were behind a wall, presumably erected in the interests of tidiness and symmetry, and the sound was much impaired. This was a strange mistake for the architect to make, for he had been responsible for the original organ chamber. As on several other occasions, Mr Powell came to the rescue and had the wall removed: it turned out not to be necessary to the structure of the Hall. Another noteworthy feature of the new part of the Hall were two great plaster columns supporting the roof where the arch over the old dais had been removed. These seem to have been overlooked by everyone who examined the plans and came as a great surprise. At first the Governors were all for getting rid of them. Although the pillars do not bear any load, they conceal the quite slender supports which do, and it was a matter for debate whether these supports would be any less unsightly than the pillars. Finally the Governors decided to leave the pillars where they were for the time being and discover in practice whether they obscured the stage or unduly obstructed the use of the floor. Over the years they have become accepted as part of the Hall, although visitors sometimes question their function.

As yet there were no curtains for the new stage, but these were expected in the new year and at the Commemoration Day entertainment, movable screens were used to good effect. A substantial wooden screen which could be folded back when the whole Hall was in use was erected between the ceiling and the edge of the platform, so that the platform could be used as a classroom while some other activity was going on on the floor of the Hall or in the gallery. This was never a very satisfactory arrangement for the screen was not soundproof, particularly when music was involved, but it is one more indication of the shortage of teaching spaces from which the School has suffered throughout most of its existence. Because of this, the door at the back of the platform which led into the house next door was of real benefit, and enabled better use to be made of the rooms there, cramped though they are.

Miss Morgan's achievements during her first four years in the School had been remarkable. She had arrested the decline in the number of pupils in the School. The Inspectors thought that this had been the result of the lower birthrate during the war and would be corrected by the increased number of eleven year olds in 1930 who had been born when the war was over. She did not dissent from this theory, although it was scarcely applicable to a school with a Kindergarten and Junior department. The plain fact was that girls were not staying at school as long as they had ten years before, and were either leaving before they were sixteen or not staying on in large numbers into the Sixth form to take the Higher School Certificate examination. The reason given publicly was the continuing industrial depression and the consequent widespread unemployment, which not only reduced family incomes but also tempted young people to take the first paid employment they were offered. Miss Sparks had encountered this last problem during the war and had met it with letters to parents, lectures on careers, talks at public functions and a great deal of individual counselling. Miss Morgan quickly came to see that rules and financial penalties would not cure early leaving. She arranged for outside speakers to come into School to talk about various careers. Old Girls were encouraged to describe their work both on visits to the School and in letters to the School Magazine. She devised occasions when she could talk to parents. She held a separate Prizegiving for the Junior School so that more people could hear her account of the School's work during the year. It had been the custom on the evening of Commemoration Day for the Head Mistress to greet parents in the flower decorated Library, standing beside the glowing fire. This meant she saw parents for at most a few minutes. As soon as the Hall was enlarged she used it to talk to groups of parents at greater length on Commemoration Day, and was able to report to the Governors that a thousand visitors 'many of them fathers' had been reached in this way. Above all, she was always ready to talk to girls about their own doubts and aspirations. Many former pupils describe their surprise that the Head Mistress they had regarded with so much awe should listen to them attentively and advise them in so friendly a fashion.

She was able to maintain a warmly encouraging relationship with sixth form groups. She had from the beginning made it her practice to give a weekly talk on Civics and Current Affairs to the Clerical Sixth and to the group which was repeating the School Certificate year, and the Inspectors in 1930 encouraged her to allow the Academic Sixth to attend this course. She made a Sixth Form Play part of the afternoon entertainment on Commemoration Day and so introduced a new dimension to the satirical messages delivered on that occasion. She attended meetings of the School Council and convinced the members that she was there to facilitate and not to dominate the discussion.

One among the many School Clubs, the International League, had developed into the League of Nations Union. It was strongly supported by both staff and girls; in 1932 nearly 150 senior girls were members. They sought to inform themselves about world affairs by going to lectures and by studying the literature put out by the Union. From the early years of the century Colston girls had left the United Kingdom, some as missionaries. Others had made their homes in the Colonies: this was not felt to be going 'abroad'. Now interest increased in what was happening in Europe and, to a lesser extent, in the United States. With memories of the Great War, if not in their minds certainly in their parents', they noted the changes which were taking place. In the later thirties their reaction was one of growing apprehension, but in the early years of the decade the mood was of sympathetic optimism. The aeroplane as the usual means of foreign travel was still a quarter of a century away but journeys by train and boat became cheaper, easier and much more common. The School took advantage of this. In 1930 a party of girls accompanied by three members of staff went to a fortnight's conference in Geneva organised by the League of Nations. The programme included some sightseeing but was formidably instructive. The next year two separate parties went on camping holidays in Germany. Their itinerary included Trier, Cologne and Aachen and their pre-Hitlerian impressions seem to us today to belong to a distant past. It became the custom to make at least one expedition abroad a year and parties of girls accompanied by several members of staff visited such places as Normandy and Denmark.

The notable academic successes of these years came about almost by chance. The new Gamble Scholarships could be held only at women's colleges in universities and by now these colleges had been provided by benefactors with a number of open scholarships and exhibitions awarded on the results of an entrance exhibition. Girls who a year or two earlier would have gone to Bristol University and lived at home now took these entrance examinations hoping to benefit from the Gamble money. In 1929, Hilda Short won an exhibition in mathematics at Royal Holloway College and the next year the seventeen year old Barbara Bowell won a scholarship, also in mathematics, at the same college. The year after that Hilda Davies had a scholarship to Westfield College, Barbara Gadd an exhibition at Royal Holloway College and Eileen Tanner one at St Hugh's College, Oxford. There were three more open awards the next year and a precedent had been established. The number of girls staying for either two or three years in the Sixth to take entrance examinations as well as Higher School Certificates increased.

Although the Society of Merchant Venturers decided in 1928 not then to make a grant of money directly to the School, it bought 180d, Cheltenham Road when it came on the market later that year. This was the house and shop nearest to the School on the south side and the intention was to let it until the School had both a use for it, and the means to rent it. When the Governors were asked by the Treasurer of the Society how long a lease should be offered to the existing tenant, their despair can be gauged by their answer: seven years. The Society did not act on this estimate of the likely duration of the School's financial troubles, and gave the tenant a four year lease. After the 1930 Inspection and the recommendation that the Library should no longer be used as a formroom, Miss Morgan asked that the lease which she believed would not end until March 1936 be shortened. She found to her pleasure that it could end in March 1932. By this time the School could afford the 'very favourable terms' of £90 a year, with a new fire escape and nine washbasins, on which the Society would rent it to the School. The tenant moved out on Lady Day and the Governors made a gateway through the School fence so that there should be easier access to the back of the now empty house. Miss Morgan's first idea was that she would move the Kindergarten and the Clerical Sixth form into the new premises, but before the actual move took place in the summer she had decided that it would be better to have the Froebel students, now nineteen in number, in the same building as the Kindergarten, and so gain another classroom in the main building and the use of the whole of 182 Cheltenham Road for sixth form groups. From September 1932 there was a distinct improvement in the amount of space available in School.

There was also evidence that the School's finances would soon be in a much healthier state. This was not the case elsewhere in the country. The year before the Board of Education had cut the direct grant to such schools as Colston's and had directed that the Governors should reduce the salaries of all full time members of the teaching staff by 10%, and this had, as before, fallen with worst effect on the youngest members of the staffroom. Of the cut 5% was restored from September 1934, and the rest from July 1935. There was never any question of a back payment. Bristol Local Authority also cut the grant to the School.

Nevertheless, the Governors felt able to think about improving the accommodation for science teaching. The matter had first been raised by Miss Drew and strongly recommended by the Inspectors in 1930. Then Mr James had produced sketch plans and estimated the cost at £2,000. This had always seemed a small sum. In November 1933 the Governors considered the various possibilities: improving the glasshouse in the playground; adding another classroom to the annexe and converting a classroom in the main building for science teaching; or extending the present physics laboratory and building a biology laboratory over it. This would be relatively expensive, but no ordinary classrooms would be lost and there would be the least possible loss of playground space.

Mr James was instructed to draw up detailed plans and care was taken to consult the science staff about the provision of cupboards and the position of the various services within the new rooms. The plans were sent to the Board of Education for approval, with a request for permission to borrow the necessary money from the bank. The plans were approved and permission was given for a loan to cover the cost of the building but not the furniture. The Governors responded with a renewed appeal to be allowed to borrow a sum which would cover the whole cost and even include improvements to the lavatories beside the basement cloakrooms. The Board of Education agreed to this without further demur, and the bank made available the sum of £5,500 for 30 years at 4% or the bank rate, whichever was the higher.

That the Chairman proposed to borrow from the bank when three years before he had been totally opposed to such a course of action demonstrates the great change which rising numbers of pupils had made in the School's financial situation. No longer was it a question of the Governors taking two years to decide whether to repaint the outside woodwork and then doing the Cheltenham Road side one year, and the back of the building the next. In 1935 they were not only able to retile the Pavilion roof, buy a new motor mower, effect the perennial repairs to the flat roofs, improve the lower cloakroom lavatories and deal with unexpected weaknesses in the retaining wall on the Cheltenham Road side of the Pleasaunce, all out of income: they also paid off one of the existing loans. He seems to have been quite confident that this improved state of affairs would continue; as indeed it did. Miss Morgan worried from time to time about the size of classes.

Work began, 'noisily' according to Miss Morgan, on the new science rooms during the Summer Term of 1935. It had been necessary to employ one team of builders for the foundations and another for the superstructure. In 1900 the Governors had allowed the city authorities to build a culvert, the Cutler's Mills Brook culvert, under the playground. It had been a hazard when the Library wing was built, and now the extended science laboratories would be built over it, and care had to be taken not to damage it. Building proceeded during most of two terms. Relations between School and builders never seem to have been cordial, unlike the state of affairs when the Hall was extended. The physics laboratory could not of course be used and a classroom elsewhere in the building was temporarily fitted up for the teaching of science. The gymnasium was used as a classroom and swimming substituted for gymnastics in the curriculum: it would appear that Bristol North Baths were not then so well used by other schools as they are now. A certain amount of inconvenience was to be expected when building was going on in such close proximity to a school at work, but in November Miss Morgan made a formal complaint to the Governors. Her most important criticism was that neither the architect nor the clerk of the works had succeeded in coordinating the work of the builders and the subcontractors or in getting them to follow the plans in detail. It was precisely this detail, the position of an electric socket and the capacity of a cupboard, which had been so painstakingly considered by the people who were going to work in the new rooms and the science staff were understandably disappointed. Some though not all the matters complained of could be put right. The Governors resolved that in any future building, the specifications should include the detailed requirements of the Head Mistress and that supervision of the work as it progressed should ensure that these requirements were met. Such a resolution is very frequently passed as new buildings come into use. The sadness is that in the case of the Colston building there was, because of world politics, no opportunity to put it into effect for the next twenty years.

The new laboratories, two large and two small, were light, airy and well furnished, in spite of the disappointing details. It had been planned to hold the formal opening and Prize Giving in January, but because of the death of King George V the double function was postponed until March. The principal guest was the Vice-Chancellor of Bristol University, Dr Thomas Loveday, who was presented with a golden key at the door of the biology laboratory. He told the girls they were very fortunate to be studying science (he was himself a classicist) at a time when it was the greatest of intellectual ventures; but scientific discoveries could be used to destroy as well as to benefit life, and it was for them to ensure that liberty was maintained and the gifts of science used for man's happiness and not his destruction.

The Thirties saw developments at the playing field. When the Society of Merchant Venturers bought the land in 1920 from the Redland Court estate it was open country with at least two working farms in close proximity. Although the part of this purchase which the Society rented to the School had been in use as playing fields for some time, its condition would not today have been thought acceptable for any athletic activities and one after another improvements were made. An asphalt path was laid round the pavilion. A Governor, Mr Charles S. Clarke, provided the labour to drain first the upper field and then, next year, the lower. Bit by bit a perimeter fence was erected and hedges planted. This marking of the boundary was necessary as the rest of the land bought by the Society was being developed. By the early Thirties the houses both on Redland Court Road to the west and Kersteman Road to the south had been built and this had necessitated some infilling of uneven ground. The builder had not used the whole of the area and plots of ground behind the back gardens of the houses were added to the space rented by the School. There were problems on the other boundaries. Cows from one of the farms were permitted to graze on part of the field, but they strayed on to ground, known as the Tips, which was in the process of being made up by one of the builders, and injured themselves. Neither the School nor the Society would accept responsibility for this. A small pond was drained and filled in. Electric light and a telephone were installed in the pavilion. In honour of the coronation in 1937 lime trees were planted. Members of staff cared for flower beds and Miss Page gave one of the technical sixth forms gardening lessons there. Miss Morgan introduced lessons other than games at the field for younger girls. In good weather they spent most of one day a week there. She also proposed that two hard courts should be laid down in memory of Mervyn King and undertook that the girls themselves would raise as much as possible of the money needed. It was 1936 and the remarkable exhibition of Chinese Art had opened in London. The School play, *Lady Precious Stream*, was much enjoyed and raised £100 of the £400 the girls contributed to the £600 the courts cost. The rest came out of income. Mr Charles Clarke, who had done most to transform the playing field, agreed to be President of the Athletic Sports Club which Mervyn King founded.

A new Scheme for the Colston's Hospital Trust schools was sealed in 1936. The principal changes seem to have been made at the request of the Governors of the Boys' School. The Bishop of Bristol ceased to be an ex-officio Governor of the Girls' School. His place was taken on the Governing Body by a representative of the University of Bristol. The first University Governor was Professor G.C. Field, who was an active friend of the School for twenty years. Nothing was lost by the ending of the Bishop's formal connection with the School: he continued to come every so often to take School Assembly and to attend School functions. The Palace adjoined the playing field and he was a kindly neighbour. Another change in the new Scheme was that the old seven eighths to one eighth formula for the division of the endowment income between the two Schools was abandoned and the Society of Merchant Venturers was given the duty of deciding how the money was to be allocated. It can only be presumed that the criterion was to be the greater need. In one important section the old Scheme was retained unchanged in the new: religious instruction for the girls was to be 'in accordance with the principles of the Christian Faith' and there was no requirement that the Head Mistress should be a communicant member of the Church of England. These seem to have been regarded as unimportant matters at the time.

In School the first steps were being taken towards the acquisition of the battery of audio-visual teaching aids which were used later in the century. A wireless set was bought out of profits from the dinner fund and used experimentally for two years. Schools programmes put out by the BBC could only be used at the time of transmission, for there was no means of recording them, and the timetable had to be built round the times of the broadcasts. The programmes in modern languages and current affairs were found helpful, a radiogram of a type approved by the BBC was provided and several rooms were wired so that loud speakers could be used. There was only one receiver, and only one programme could be heard at a time.

Earlier, Inspectors had commented on the rapid turnover of staff and deplored the lack of a good number of elder statesmen in the staff room. No such criticism could be levelled at the School in the Thirties. It was still true that younger teachers left to marry but in 1937, for instance, 14 of the 34 staff were aged 40 or older, and had taught at Colston's for at least 13 years, many of them considerably longer. The women Governors drew attention to the frequent and quite lengthy absences of these teachers. Some of these were not significant of anything in particular: three were injured in the same motor accident and one tore her Achilles tendon playing netball. There was an epidemic of influenza and 16 members of staff were away, 14 of them at the same time. What alarmed the women Governors was that in these years eleven members of staff were away from their work for periods of from half a term to longer than two terms. Even by the health standards of the time this suggested a high degree of stress which could be related to their work. Miss Morgan herself had been away for the first half of a Spring Term with bronchitis and a year or two later would be away for most of another Spring Term. She obviously used up a great deal of nervous energy in her work, but the record of the rest of the staff suggests she was not alone in this. There can be no doubt that many of the women who devoted themselves almost exclusively to their profession did overwork and impaired their health. Miss C.I. Taylor, Miss Phillips, Miss L.E. Wilson, Miss Rogers and Miss Skeet all retired early, though it must be remembered that the usual age of retirement, which had been 50, was now 60. Miss Burton, Miss Smith, Miss Spraggett and Miss Clutterbuck died before they reached retiring age. The Governors asked Miss Morgan to keep a close watch on the older staff and to suggest that they took time off before they became seriously ill. It is not always easy to detect signs of strain and little came of the Governors' suggestion.

There were, however, the survivors: Miss Horne, Miss Clutton, Miss Gibbon, Miss Rashley and Miss Page. One of the most remarkable of these was Miss Palin. Gwynedd Marion Palin was born in 1877 and trained for four years from 1896 to 1900 at the Birmingham School of Art. She taught in various schools and took further examinations. She began work at Colston's in 1911, a good draughtswoman and watercolourist with firm views on the central place of art in a liberal education. In her holidays she travelled as widely as she could and one of the interests of many an autumn term was her lively account of some distant part of the world and the display of her paintings, delicate, atmospheric and superbly drawn. When she had been at School for twenty years, Miss Morgan arranged that she should have a year's leave without pay to go round the world. She retired from Colston's in 1936 and among her leaving presents was a supply of drawing and painting materials for her next venture. She went to teach in a school in Srinagar, Kashmir, where the language of instruction was Urdu and the pupils, mostly Moslems, had never had any lessons in art. She returned to England in 1938 for a brief holiday and then made Kashmir her home. At the end of the war when missionaries were expelled from China, she gave help and comfort to an Old Girl, Marion Parsons, who had been working there. Miss Palin went on teaching until nearly ninety and each Christmas the School would receive one of her beautiful cards, a painting of the Kashmiri countryside, usually of trees and water.

The School had a long tradition of active interest in foreign affairs but even without this the girls would in the second half of the decade of the Thirties have been aware of fears for the future. Italy had invaded Abyssinnia, as Ethiopia was then called, and the League of Nations had been powerless to stop the invasion or effect the withdrawal of the troops. Civil War had broken out in Spain, but the opposing sides had been backed on the one hand by Fascist and the other by Communist regimes, so that the struggle was seen to have dimensions which crossed the frontiers of a single country. The devastation of Spanish towns, particularly by aerial bombardment, was a revelation of what war in future would mean. Early in 1938 local committees were set up to plan air raid precautions and a circular from the Board of Education spelled out the implications of responsibility for large numbers of children together in a single building. The Governors considered the possibility of vacating the two upper floors, and concentrating everyone on the ground floor and in the basement. The staff must have been horrified by this.

By the summer even such expedients were thought to be too risky and Bristol Education Committee decided to close all its schools if there was a war. War seemed to be very much a possibility in the early autumn, only just averted by the Munich Agreement. The relief was enormous and the staff felt they could concentrate on their school work once more, but the Governors commissioned a report on whether the School building could be turned into what they called an 'air raid refuge'. The report was long and detailed but the short answer was that it could not. There could be no protection against a direct hit; but, they were told, most of the casualties in Spain had not been of this nature. Much more general dangers were blast and fire.

The last year of peace, 1938–39, was so full of schemes and further schemes to be put into practice in the event of war that it seems remarkable that Miss Morgan was able to do anything except attend meetings and study reports. At one stage only the complete evacuation of the School seemed feasible, with camps being set up in some undiscovered safe place. It was understandable, but nevertheless an unattainable dream. Then there was the plan to build a shelter under the upper playground entered at the level of the Pleasaunce; or a steel strongroom for a skeleton administrative staff; or a contraption of steel tubes and sandbags in the basement. Any one of these constructions would have been extremely expensive and the School had no large sums available. The Board of Education would not give financial assistance to direct grant schools for such works but if local authorities gave help they could claim back half the cost from the Board.

Meanwhile Miss Morgan pursued another line of thought. Bristol Education Committee had now decided that if war came, schools without any air raid protection would be closed and only those with some sort of protection would be used. This was setting a much lower standard of safety than the Colston Governors and architect had been working to. She set about finding places where the girls could work with a degree of protection. The academic sixth form would be welcomed in the Bishop's House near the field, and the technical sixth could go to the YWCA Wayfarers' Club in the crypt of St George's church. She wrote to other schools – Clifton High School, Redland High School and Fairfield School – asking for part time accommodation and received encouraging replies. She began to plan the deployment of staff as visiting teachers.

War came at the beginning of September, 1939. Almost at once a number of assumptions on which prewar planning had been based were found to be wrong. Aerial bombardment did not begin at once, even in places like London which were seen as being in the front line. The kind of defences which the country could muster made raids by bombers carrying big bombs of high explosive much more likely at night than during the day. Day schools were not at quite so great a risk as had been supposed.

Term had been due to start on Tuesday, September 19. The Governors met on the Wednesday before, still of the opinion that no teaching could be carried on in the Cheltenham Road building. There was a directive from the Board of Education that Schools without air raid shelters should remain closed, and the architect had not been able to produce workable plans for strengthening the basement, or building shelters in the playground. Miss Morgan's ingenious plans for dividing up the School between various sites and the exertions of the staff in producing assignments of work which could be sent out to the girls at home would not provide an education comparable with the one they were missing. The Bristol Education Committee representatives among the Governors announced flatly that the following week they were going to open all their schools, protected and unprotected, and parents could choose to send their children at their own risk. (The teachers were not to be given the choice.) A majority of the Colston Governors would not agree to take this responsibility but they did change their minds on another matter, to which they had previously been opposed: they agreed that the parents should be consulted.

Miss Morgan had a very fair notion of the response she would get. A few months before she had analysed the addresses of the girls aged ten and over. Nearly half came from the 6, 7 and 2 postal districts and although there were some girls making very long journeys, most parents would judge that their daughters would be as safe in School as at home. A notice was put in the local papers and on September 26 the term began, a week late. It was planned to make up the five lost days later in the year. Fifty-five girls did not return immediately, but their parents said their daughters would return as soon as shelters were built. Twenty-six girls left, to train, to take up employment or to go to schools nearer to their homes. There were 111 new girls.

Meanwhile, the construction of the shelters began. The idea of underground bunkers giving protection from direct hits from high explosive bombs was finally abandoned, as it was all over the country. Shelters which were in essence a trench covered by a concrete superstructure were accepted as the best that could be done, and in practice saved a great many lives from blast, falling masonry and incendiary bombs. Two concrete structures in the Pleasaunce would each hold 50 girls and these were put in hand at once. Two years before, the Society of Merchant Venturers, pursuing a policy of buying property near the School, had bought the piece of land between Cheltenham Lane and Station Road which adjoined Poplar Grove. This at the time was known as Pugsley's Yard and had been the site of a Steam Carpet Beating Company and then a Bicycle Factory. Thirty years before, Miss Hughes had had her eye on it when the School had been looking for somewhere to build a library; thirty years later it was the site of the Dolphin Building. Now there was evidently no problem about possession, for the work of clearing the site began at once. Four shelters of the nationally approved type would be built here, one in Poplar Grove and four on the upper playground. They were completed by January and there was room for the whole School in them. The girls had air raid drills, like fire drill, and practised getting themselves safely and quickly into their proper shelters.

The early months of the war were just as confusing as the last months of peace had been. People called it the 'phoney war'. Nothing seemed to be happening, except of course for the black out. This was much more carefully observed than in the earlier war. There was no street lighting and Air Raid Wardens patrolled to see that no chink of light was visible from any building. It would have been quite impossible to black the School out to the standard required and as the autumn days shortened, after school activities had to be abandoned. Afternoon school ended at 3.15 p.m. so that girls could begin their journey home in the light. There were no lessons on Wednesday afternoons so that the school could be cleaned then and on Saturdays. There was already a feeling, which grew stronger as the war went on, that every minute in School was precious and must be used in the best possible way.

1940 began with a prolonged cold spell and snow lay on the ground for several weeks. It was impossible to use the field. Miss Morgan fretted about the lack of playing space for the girls and the general unsightliness of the grounds with the raw shapes of the shelters and the damaged gardens. In the end the most obtrusive of the shelters, the ones on the upper playground, were covered in earth, and grass and flowers planted on them, but this did not happen for some time.

With the coming of spring the 'phoney war' ended. There began to be air raid alerts during the day. At first the girls sang songs and played guessing games in the shelters but soon taking shelter became so ordinary a part of life that they took their work with them and did what they could. France collapsed and the British forces were evacuated from Dunkirk. In the School Certificate examination the candidates had to repair to the shelters during no fewer than eight papers.

Few families were able to plan summer holidays. Apart from the difficulty of fathers who were in the forces or could not leave war work there were few places to go. Enemy invasion was a constant threat and coastal resorts were out of bounds. Miss Morgan arranged a 'summer school'. For four weeks there was a programme of activities in School and at the field, organised and supervised by relays of staff. Staff also took a sixth form party walking and cycling in the Quantocks at Easter and other parties hop picking near Ledbury in September. In other years there was potato planting and harvesting, pea picking and still more hop picking. For teachers and pupils it was part of the pattern of the years of war.

The term which began in September was the first in the Jubilee Year. On January 19, 1941, the School would have been in existence for fifty years. A Jubilee Book was planned, with Miss Clutton as its editor. It was impossible to hold any suitable celebration during the winter in wartime, but a Service of Thanksgiving in the Cathedral was arranged for July. There were several occasions during the year when it seemed doubtful whether anything other than a Memorial Service would be appropriate then.

In the autumn, air raids on Bristol began in earnest. From November the school day began at half past nine in the morning because the girls had had such disturbed nights and because the crowded 'buses had difficulty in negotiating the damaged streets. After a bad raid everyone was shocked and short of sleep. At the end of the school day there was a scramble to get home for an hour or two of peace before the sirens sounded again. Two sisters in the Junior School, one aged ten and the other seven, were killed with their parents when their home received a direct hit. There was an A.R.P. (Air Raid Precautions) warden's post in the School building but fire watchers were needed to concentrate specifically on putting out fires. Members of staff, four at a time, slept in School each night ready to do what they could. From time to time they must have raised their eyes to the Hall roof and wondered what they actually could do when the incendiaries came. In January they had some relief from this particular fear. Forty ratings from H.M.S. Cabot were billeted on the School and had their bunk beds in the gymnasium. At the sound of the sirens ten of them looked after the School building and the other thirty assisted the Wardens in the surrounding streets. The bunks took up a good deal of precious space but the School was grateful for the nightly presence of the sailors and presented them with a wireless set.

On the night of Sunday, March 16, there was a particularly heavy raid on Bristol. Merchants Hall, in King Street, the headquarters of the Society of Merchant Venturers, was hit for the second time and irreparably damaged. The scene in Cheltenham Road the next morning was not of such complete devastation but it grieved staff and girls to an extraordinary degree. There was a big crater in the road, the débris from which had holed roofs and broken windows. A second bomb had fallen in the playground at the foot of the external fire escape staircase of the Library wing, and a third in the Pleasaunce at one corner of the hard tennis court. The next two days were spent in clearing up. The roofs were mended and the staff repaired the windows and cleared the floors. Mr Meredith, the architect, who had now taken over from Mr James, inspected the Library wing and declared it unsafe for use; and he thought the adjoining studio and the classroom below it were also dangerous.

On the Wednesday the girls in the fifths and sixths preparing for public examination returned to school and were taught. By the following Monday the timetable had been rearranged so that every class had lessons on five half days a week and worked at home for the rest of the time. A parent living in Elmgrove Road nearby offered the hospitality of her home to the Kindergarten. Miss Morgan, looking for a place for the Junior School, had found Upton Lodge in Cotham. It was a house with seven rooms and a good basement, suitable as a shelter, and it belonged to Alderman Byrt. He was the grandfather of Mary and Kathleen Byrt who had been Colston girls. Kathleen was now on active service, a doctor in the Royal Air Force, and as Dr Kathleen Faulkner she later succeeded Dr Richard Clarke as School Medical Adviser. Alderman Byrt proved to be a kind and sympathetic landlord. As well as the installation of school equipment, the house needed more lavatories and washbasins, the basement strengthened and some additional paving in the garden. This had all been done by the beginning of May and the Junior School with the exception of its top class, the ten year olds, moved in to, for the first time, a separate home of its own. The departure of the younger girls was regretted on both sides but it made possible the return to a normal timetable for the senior school.

In the meantime decisions had to be made about the shattered Library wing. The Local Authority offered to blow it up, a quick and inexpensive way of disposing of a dangerous structure. The Governors decided that it should be dismantled by demolition experts from London. All the contents and any re-usable materials were to be salvaged, and most of this was housed with Mr Charles Clarke's permission at Tracy Park. The bookcases were re-erected in the Assembly Hall and the books were once more in use, though not without further incident. In the Good Friday firebomb raid of April 11, the Hall roof was set alight. The whole building was saved from destruction by the sailors. Although some of the books were soaked by the water used to put out the fires, the roof was repaired with sheets of corrugated iron and the Hall was in use again at the beginning of the Summer Term.

The loss of the Library, which for generations of girls and many staff had symbolised the grace of learning, was a blow to the whole School, past and present. It had a particular effect on Miss Morgan, whose strong and generous emotions were never far from the surface. Miss Rashley who as Clerk worked closely with her said later that after the Monday morning when she saw the effect of the bombing it was 'never glad confident morning' with her again. It is probably true that the joy which gave her words and actions such vitality did desert her then. If so, she did not allow her private feelings to prevent her from dealing efficiently with problems as they arose. We have seen how quickly she had the girls working normally, albeit in cramped quarters, after the bombing. There were other problems.

At the beginning of the war, Bristol was a neutral zone as far as evacuation went: it did not propose to evacuate children but it was not designated as a reception area either. Parents who wished to send their children into the country or abroad to the Dominions or the United States made their own arrangements. This changed when Bristol was bombed and the Local Education Authority offered parents the opportunity to send their children away from the city, and widened the scheme to include children at independent schools. The Governors considered a plan to evacuate the School as a unit and realised that they did not have the resources to run a large boarding school in the country even if they could find a suitable building. Miss Morgan still thought that most parents who chose to send their daughters to Colston's would want to keep them at home. The threat of invasion, which had led to the removal of all road signs, was by no means over, although Germany's declaration of war on her erstwhile ally Russia had added a further dimension to speculation on the enemy's intentions. In the Summer Term after the bombing there were 83 fewer girls in School than there had been a year before. 60 of these were girls who had been sent away from Bristol by their parents and the rest were accounted for by a drop in admissions. This represented a considerable fall in revenue. There was another financial difficulty. The Government had promised help to institutions which had to modify their premises to make them safer in wartime and which had to spend money on 'first aid' repairs after enemy action, but this help had to be claimed and the claim investigated before it was paid. In the early years of the war the School had a large overdraft at the bank. No sooner had the claim for the erection of the air raid shelters been paid than it had to borrow again to meet the cost of extensive repairs necessary because of war damage. In the course of the next three years these difficulties disappeared. The evacuated girls returned home and the applications for admission increased. In 1945 the number of pupils was the highest it had ever been: the senior and junior schools together totalled 747. The School's current account was healthy.

Miss Morgan shared her anxieties with the Governors, but with no one else. For girls and even staff the abiding feature of School life was its normality. In the July after the bombing, Jubilee year was celebrated by a very good production of *Tobias and the Angel* by James Bridie, performed on two summer evenings in the book lined, corrugated iron roofed Hall. Later in the same month the School processed into the Cathedral for a thanksgiving service, conducted by the Dean and addressed by the Bishop. It was the first time the School had worshipped together in the Cathedral. In the following autumn the Commemoration service was held in St Andrew's church near School. The Cheltenham Road shoppers were astonished to see the girls marching along with their chrysanthemums, but St Andrew's proved too small to hold everyone who wished to attend, and from 1944 a service in the Cathedral became the first part of every Commemoration celebration.

In the summer of 1941 parties of girls had a fortnight's holiday at Wycombe Abbey School and at a hotel in Lynmouth to which Badminton School had been evacuated. This was by special invitation of the other two schools, and was in addition to the harvest camps.

The younger girls settled into Upton Lodge, the house in Cotham Grove, very quickly. They could keep tadpoles and chrysalises and count the different insects in the garden. They had to remember to close the garden gate so that their two tortoises did not get out, but with petrol rationing there were few cars or lorries passing. The danger to the tortoises was escape, not extinction.

The children were near to the playing field, and had a vegetable garden there, specialising in marrows. Class Upper II wrote, produced and acted in a Greek play, *Perseus*, in the garden in front of the summer house. They charged two oboli (pennies) for admission.

Less than a year later the house next door, Osborne House, became available and the Governors rented that too. Now the ten year olds could join the others, vacating much needed space in the Cheltenham Road building. There was now room to prepare and serve a midday meal for those who wanted it, and there were rooms for the students. The Junior School became a separate entity and flourished. The Government was encouraging married women to return to work and there was a great demand for school places for young children.

In fact the juniors were much more appropriately housed in Cotham Grove than they had ever been in the various rooms they had occupied in the main school building. There had been a succession of very gifted teachers, many of whom had, after their experience of training students doing the three year Froebel course at Colston's, gone on to posts in teacher training colleges. One of the most outstanding of these was Miss H.M. Berry, who came in January 1940, after her predecessor who had put in an appearance on only twelve days in the Autumn Term had been dismissed. Miss Berry had methods which even today would be recognised as progressive. The children were encouraged to do everything possible for themselves, to observe and record, and to learn from their own experience. Her particular strength was in teacher training. The National Froebel Foundation asked the School to arrange a two year course at Upton Lodge for trained teachers and the Education Department of the University of Bristol sent students to observe the most up to date educational practice.

Miss Berry had to engage the interest of parents whose children were receiving an education in many ways different from their own. She welcomed them to the School and never tired of explaining its aims and demonstrating its methods. From this unusually close contact between teachers and parents came the idea of a Parents' Association, an idea taken up enthusiastically by the parents. The Junior School Association was followed by others in different parts of the senior school. They met regularly to hear talks on subjects of interest to them in promoting the welfare of their children, and to enjoy social occasions. By 1945 the various associations had merged to form a body of parents actively loyal to the School.

The retraining programme for teachers which Miss Berry had pioneered was one of the signs of an increasing shortage. Teaching had not been a reserved occupation when war began and, indeed, two members of Colston's Staff had joined the forces. Now when every child was to have a longer school life the problem became acute and plans for the recruitment and rapid training of suitable people mature in age were put into effect. In 1944 the Board of

Education asked that Miss Berry should be seconded to be principal of an emergency training college for primary school teachers. At first she divided her time between her work as head of Junior School and her preparations for the opening of the new college. She took up full time duties there in September 1945.

The Parents' Association was not the only innovation which Miss Morgan encouraged in these years. She experimented with a six-lesson day in place of the usual seven. As a temporary measure while the school day was necessarily shortened it was considered by the staff to be a success. She also introduced sex education, not then considered an integral part of general education. Dr Griffiths from the Middlesex Hospital spent three days in School, talking to the various age groups. His visit was welcomed by members of the Parents' Association and was repeated in following years.

Some of the casualties of the war were the after school clubs of which there had been many, meeting regularly. The impossibility of an effective blackout and the need to get home before the alert sounded meant their decline. The war brought compensations. The cinema was already established as a means of entertainment, but air raids and air raid damage in London brought theatre, ballet and above all music to the provinces. There were lunch time concerts in the Colston Hall, to be enjoyed for 6d by those who could both walk and eat quickly. Bristol had three full sized theatres and Bath one. When the bombing had abated it was possible to see a succession of London productions and the greatest actors and dancers of the time. To many young people the war gave an introduction to the live performing arts which they enjoyed for the rest of their lives.

It was a war in which women and children were involved at the same time as men as the victims of violence and so shared a common experience. Communication was more sophisticated than it had ever been before. There was still no television set in everybody's home, but there was a wireless set in a bakelite case and families everywhere sat down together at nine o'clock in the evening to listen to the BBC radio news. Young people followed the progress of the war with concentrated interest, convinced that their own hopes and fears would have a decisive effect on the future. They felt an exceptional closeness to other people of their own age and a need to cross barriers. As early as the summer of 1941, the sixth forms of the Bristol secondary schools formed the Bristol Youth Group and with the encouragement of heads of schools worked out a programme of shared activities, discussions, musical events, plays and service to the community. Fifth form pupils were later included but membership did not of course extend to that great majority of pupils who did not attend secondary schools and left formal education at the age of fourteen. The group gave many able boys and girls an early experience both of working together and of independence from their elders. Because individual membership of such a group is of short duration – two or three years at most – it did not survive in its original form, but it was a symptom of a new attitude. However loyal one might be to one's own school there was a vast area of opportunity and responsibility outside it. School was never again a sufficiently satisfying world for the capable and idealistic young person.

Just as in that earlier war, plans were being made by the government for a better educational system; it would be part of a more equitable, more caring society, already known as the Welfare State. The new Education Act, the Butler Act, came in 1944. Its provisions were based on the thinking of several reports produced in the Twenties and Thirties. The minimum school leaving age would be raised to fifteen. Instead of the secondary school being an alternative to the last years in the elementary school, there would now be secondary schooling for everyone. The elementary school, to be called more precisely the primary school, would take children from five to eleven years. Then all pupils would proceed to a secondary school which would be one of three kinds. The present secondary schools would continue to take pupils from eleven to sixteen years of age, with the possibility that they could stay on in the sixth form until they were eighteen. These schools would now be called grammar schools. New schools would be provided for pupils who would benefit from a technical, more vocational education. There were in practice very few of these. All other pupils would be accommodated in modern schools where they would pursue a curriculum, judged appropriate to their needs and abilities, until they were fifteen. A selection procedure at the age of eleven would determine what kind of secondary school a child would attend. All these local authority schools, grammar, technical and modern, would charge no tuition fees and there would be no extra charges for textbooks and stationery.

In all this it was not clear what rôle would be played by Direct Grant schools. One of the conditions of the grant direct from the Board of Education was that at least 25% of the places in a school must be free. Would parents be prepared to pay fees for the other places when their children could attend local education authority schools free? Early in 1943 the Chairmen and Heads of the Bristol Direct Grant Schools met to consult each other and to put into words what they thought they could offer: academic excellence and the moral, cultural and personal benefits of tradition. At about the same time it became known that a subcommittee of the Bristol Education Committee had declared itself opposed to any further use of the Direct Grant Schools. The Schools felt themselves to be under threat and remained watchful. The Act became law in 1944, and the Direct Grant Schools found that they had a significant part in the pattern of education. They had to admit 25% of their pupils to free places and to reserve another 25% of their places for pupils who had had at least two years' education in local education authority schools. Although Colston's had admitted elementary school candidates in the past, the Junior School eleven year olds could hold their own in competition for the remaining 50% of places. In the first half of 1945 negotiation began with the Chief

Education Officer of Bristol, Mr George H. Sylvester, as to the number of Colston's Girls' places Bristol would want and how many could be offered to Somerset and Gloucestershire.

In April 1945 Miss Morgan tendered her resignation. She had been appointed Warden of Manor Hall, a Hall of Residence for women students at the University of Bristol. She had been Head Mistress for eighteen years. She had seen the School through almost to the end of the war: victory in Europe came in May. The numbers in the School were the highest they had ever been and admissions in September were well on the way to being settled. The School's finances were sound and the problems in the Junior School were those of success. In 1942 and 1943 there had been five University Open Awards in each year, three of the ten Oxbridge. Rebuilding was thought to be imminent and the new architect, Mr Ralph Edwards, had surveyed the building preparatory to producing plans for a new library wing. She had been ill again and was tired, and she knew she needed a change of occupation.

The Governors accepted her resignation with regret, for she had made many friends and was greatly respected, and they set about finding a new Head Mistress. In July they interviewed six candidates from a field of 22 applicants and chose Miss Mary Georgina Green, who was teaching French at the William Hulme School for Boys in Manchester. She could start in January 1946.

Miss Morgan was concerned to make her successor's task as trouble free as possible. Reconstruction after the war would bring its problems and its opportunities but she did not foresee any changes of particular moment. In June a routine application had been submitted to the newly styled Ministry of Education for the School's continued recognition as a Direct Grant School. The changes which the new Education Act required in the relationship between such schools and the local education authorities had been put into practice in the current year. In July there was a General Election and the wartime all-party government was replaced by Labour. Ellen Wilkinson became Minister of Education in place of R.A. Butler.

On October 22 a letter from the Minister announced that Colston's Girls' School was to be removed from the Direct Grant List from January 1, 1946. The School could receive grants from the Local Education Authority 'until the future status of the School was determined'. No reason for the change was given.

The effect on Miss Morgan of this wholly unexpected blow was crushing. She had more than once by her energy and professional skill rescued the School from disaster and had thought she was handing on to her successor an assured basis on which to build the future. The Chairman reacted with angry incredulity that the School which had received its first grant from the Board of Education more than forty years before and which had served Bristol and the surrounding counties by providing inexpensive education of the highest quality for over fifty years could be treated in this way. He called an emergency meeting of the Governors for November 6 and in the meantime set about finding out all he could about the reasons for the Ministerial decision. No doubt many of the other Governors were making their own enquiries.

At the emergency meeting the Chairman strongly advised an appeal. The Foundation Governors shared his anger and bewilderment. He directed their attention to the many Bristol schools retained on the Direct Grant list. How did they differ from the two, Redland High School and Colston's Girls', which had lost the grant? His answer was that the two rejected schools had no overt denominational bias. The Roman Catholic schools had, conspicuously, been retained on the list. Discussion on the subject went on in all kinds of places for the next ten years, but he never wavered in his opinion. The two rejected schools had, in fact, other features in common. They were girls' schools and they were day schools.

Alderman F.C. Williams, who over the years had emerged as the spokesman for the Local Education Authority governors, denied that the Authority had influenced the Minister's decision in any way. They had seen the list but had 'offered no observation'. He hoped that there would not be too much emphasis on the religious question. He went on to enumerate the possibilities for the future of the School. It could become an independent school, fully fee paying; it could become a voluntary aided school, with the Local Authority responsible for the cost of running the School in return for the right to fill all the places, while the Governors retained the ownership of the building and responsibility for maintaining certain parts of it; or it could become voluntary controlled, which left less responsibility or initiative to the governors. He advised that they apply for Aided Status.

The meeting decided to send a deputation to the Minister to plead for the retention of the Direct Grant and to ask that in any case the withdrawal of the Grant should be postponed. In the meantime every effort should be made to arouse public opinion in support of the School.

At the Governors' meeting in November the Chairman had to report that the Minister refused to receive the deputation. He had however been more than once to the Ministry and had talked to the civil servants who were dealing with the matter. They told him that the decision had been made because Bristol Local Authority was short of places for girls in secondary grammar schools, and this answer was also given in letters from Members of Parliament which were published in the local papers. There should have been little surprise at these revelations. Alderman Williams's denials had been too prompt. The 1944 Act's requirement that an appropriate secondary school place must be provided for every child, girl as well as boy, had merely made public a state of affairs which had always existed. There were too few grammar school places for girls in Bristol.

There was enormous support for the School from the Parents' Association and the Old Girls' Society, who wrote letters and sent deputations. Miss Morgan could see little to be hopeful about in the future. When the Governors were not receiving either fees or grants, how were they to fulfil their financial obligations to an Aided School? Their right to a proportion of the Colston's Hospital Trust income had not been strengthened by the 1936 Scheme and had been precarious in the past. Nor was she in sympathy with the tripartite system of secondary education. Colston's had not been a highly selective school academically. It did outstandingly well by clever girls as they reached the sixth form and it gave self confidence to many a girl who could not pass School Certificate. Its strength lay in being able to educate successfully girls with a wide range of abilities. In her farewell speech to the Old Girls she said,

> I do not believe that any good thing that has been achieved here in the past can be lost – but I do fear lest the School – and other Schools – ceases to be a community, a living growing thing, a corporate life; and comes to be regarded as a mere public service, something provided to be used, as a 'bus, a streetlight, a swimming bath, a public library . . .

She had never sounded more like Miss Hughes. To her the School as a community was now in jeopardy and she left with a heavy heart. She remained a firm friend and supporter. She became a Governor in 1955 and took up her duties with enthusiasm. She found to her dismay that the rift between the Merchant Venturers and the Local Authority Governors which had been occasioned by the loss of the Direct Grant had never healed. She died in 1957.

MISS GREEN

Mary Georgina Green was born in Wellingborough, Northamptonshire, in 1913. Her father died in the influenza epidemic of 1919, and her mother returned to teaching. Mary – or Molly as she has always been known to her friends – attended Wellingborough High School and was awarded a State Scholarship. She read French at Westfield College in the University of London, and took a first class honours degree. After her appointment to the Colston's headship in the summer of 1945 she visited the School in the autumn, three days after the letter breaking the news of the loss of the Direct Grant had been received from the Ministry. She had to return to Manchester to finish the Autumn Term there but Miss Morgan kept her informed of developments and when she arrived in January Miss Rashley could bring her up to date: the Direct Grant had been extended for two terms, until the end of August, 1946. After that, a new rôle had to be found for the School.

Miss Green made an immediate impression of friendliness and energy. She was tall and slender, and had short curly red hair. In School she was a forceful disciplinarian who set high standards of efficiency. In her dealings with the world outside School she soon showed that she could put her point of view with tact as well as clarity.

She found herself and the School in a totally unexpected situation. When she had accepted the post nearly six months earlier no one could have foreseen the present problem. Few heads can have been faced with so many unknown possibilities in their first few weeks in a new post. When Miss Sparks took up her duties in 1914 she had two terms of peace before the first world war came; and the war was a great potential for disaster which was being faced by the whole country. Miss Green arrived in the middle of a crisis which affected a very few other schools and none in the particular circumstances of Colston's. Anyone taking over the running of an institution which has a long history likes time to get to know the people already involved and the ethos which they have combined to create in the past. She had no such running-in period. When she was asked for advice or decisions she had no greater background of relevant experience than any other party – Governors, Local Education Authority, the Inspectorate or even officials of the Ministry – involved.

With hindsight it is questionable whether at this stage in the School's history she could have made any difference to what happened. It seems likely that all the decisions had, consciously or subconsciously, been made. On receipt of the Ministry letter the immediate reaction of the Local Education Authority Governors was that the School should become 'Aided'. The effect of this would be that the Colston Trust, through the Society of Merchant Venturers, would continue to own the School buildings in Cheltenham Road; would be responsible for a proportion of the cost of improvements to them and of external repairs; and would retain two thirds of the seats on the Governing Body. The Local Education Authority would meet the cost of all the running expenses of the School, including staff salaries, and have a third of the places on the Governing Body. School fees would be abolished. Admission at eleven would be by the selection procedures of the Local Authority.

The other options were that it should be closed, that it should be taken over and fully controlled by the Local Authority or that it should become an independent, or private, fee paying school. Closure of so large a school when there was a great shortage of secondary grammar school places could not be contemplated by the Local Authority: nor did the Authority want to take the School over completely, which would have involved buying the site and building in Cheltenham Road from the Trust. The option of independence needs further examination.

As soon as the parents, or more particularly the members of the Parents' Association Committee, heard of the loss of the Direct Grant they petitioned the Governors to 'Save the School' and there is no doubt that they meant that it should become independent. The Governors replied that they could not do this without being certain that a sufficient number of parents would be forthcoming to pay the necessarily increased fee, and they asked the Parents' Association to reassure them on this matter. The Committee of the Association wrote to all the parents asking whether they would be willing, or able, to pay the increased fee, quoted as a notional £45 a year. There were 735 children in the School. The parents of 250 of them did not reply. Just over a hundred were unequivocally in favour of independence.

It is instructive to look at what happened elsewhere. At Redland High School, which as well as being the nearest neighbour was also in the same position of having been removed from the Direct Grant list, a meeting of all parents was called. They were addressed by both the Deputy Chief Education Officer for Bristol and a Professor of Education of Bristol University. They were able to ask questions and have the principle of 'tapering' the Direct Grant explained to them: all the girls with Direct Grant places then in School would retain them, and if the School became independent the new fees would apply only to those who entered in and after 1946. The Professor also told them that once the School had become 'maintained' by the Local Education Authority there was no guarantee that it would preserve its identity. It might at some later date be merged with some other school or schools. 97% of Redland parents voted for independence.

The Colston's parents had no such opportunity to ask questions and to have them answered. The 'tapering' principle was not explained to them. Most important of all, the questionnaire should properly have been addressed not to parents of girls already in the School but to parents who might want to send their daughters there in the future. Here we return once more to the idea which had been behind the many discussions about the school fee in the past.

Whenever the Governors had seen that an increase in revenue was needed to enable the School to keep up the standard of the education it was offering, they were met with the argument, first from the Charity Commissioners, then from the Board, then the Ministry of Education and always from their own members, that an increased fee would exclude those pupils for whom the School had been established. The idea of the School as a Charity had shaped the thinking of the Governors, of the Colston's Hospital Trustees and of the Merchant Venturers from the beginning: indeed, it went right back to Colston's original foundation and the Hundred Poor Boys for whom everything was provided free of charge. But the Schools as well as society had changed. Until 1944 every parent except the very poor expected to pay for secondary education. The Colston's fee had been kept low by injections of public money in the form of grants and sometimes by a fraction of Colston's Hospital endowment income. How many parents would have been willing and able to pay more? This question had never been addressed, and January 1946 was late in the day to begin such an investigation. On February 4 the Finance committee recommended an application for Aided Status, the Society of Merchant Venturers agreed and the full Governors' meeting on February 28 concurred. The local papers which had asked repeatedly for information were given the news. After that, the matter might be thought to have been settled, and it remained to Miss Green to see to the day to day running of the School.

It was not a case of merely taking over the reins of a vehicle in motion. In the first weeks of her arrival she had received six resignations from the senior school staff, two of them to take effect at Easter. A seventh was likely, for the Second Mistress, Miss Burnett, was being interviewed for the headship of Walthamstow High School. In the event, Miss Burnett was appointed and took up her duties in Walthamstow in May. Resignations and new arrivals are unsettling at any time and particularly so in times of crisis. It is a measure of Miss Green's speed in controlling the situation that there was no panic in the staff room and that no sense of fear or uncertainty was communicated to the girls or their parents. She made three temporary appointments for the summer term, all of them satisfactory and one of them, Mrs Pedley, the Classics specialist, able to continue as a permanent member of staff.

Miss Morgan and the staff had succeeded to an astonishing degree in maintaining during the years of war a spirit within the School of lively activity as well as of corporate identity. Now that the fighting had ended in Europe and in the Far East it might be expected that a return both for the School and the country to prewar freedoms was possible. This did not happen. Wartime restrictions remained and were even extended. For instance, food rationing, accepted as necessary during the war, continued after the ceasefire. In 1946 bread rationing was introduced and in the next year the meat ration was reduced. Clothes were rationed until 1949. In spite of this austerity the staff and the girls felt that new ideas could now be entertained, the hopes and experiences of the war years could be built on, and both expeditions and experiments could be made.

While there was still any possibility of bombing it would have been unthinkable to take a school party to London, but during the Easter holiday of 1946 a party of staff and sixth form girls spent a week's holiday in London visiting theatres and art galleries, concerts and churches, and generally getting to know the capital. A Member of Parliament, Mrs Middleton, who was an Old Girl, arranged for them to visit the Houses of Parliament, hear the Court of Appeal in session, listen to a debate and finally a privileged few had tea on the terrace. Nearer home, it was again after six years possible to hold Sports Day for the whole School at the field with parents and visitors watching. During the war the numbers had to be limited to the numbers of places available in nearby air raid shelters.

The School Play was Gilbert Murray's translation of *The Trojan Women*, Euripides's heartbreaking account of the plight of the women after the fall of Troy, waiting to be taken as slaves to Greece by their conquerors. It reminded the audiences of the 'displaced persons' in refugee camps for whom the war was not over, and most of the money raised was appropriately sent to the Lord Mayor's Fund for the Relief of Distress in Europe. In the summer there was again a Harvest Camp and for a month girls lifted potatoes, thinned cabbage, planted and hoed.

In these last two terms of the Direct Grant Miss Green had a further task to perform, perhaps the most difficult and most important of all. The country was witnessing the inauguration of the Welfare State, a series of social reforms designed to guarantee a minimum acceptable standard of living for all citizens however underprivileged, and including the sick and the unemployed, the young and the old. The 1944 Education Act which provided secondary education for every pupil, abolished school fees in maintained schools and raised the minimum school leaving age to 15 was part of this great movement, which had almost universal support. It had less than universal understanding and it was Miss Green's aim to persuade the girls to take the opportunities which the new state of affairs afforded them. With no school fees to pay, and with grants available for those who qualified for admission to Universities and Training Colleges there was no need for any girl to cease full time education before she had achieved everything of which she was capable. Now that financial obstacles had been removed the only limits to success were the limits of ability and application and, she said, they owed it to the School as well as to themselves to make full use of the opportunities which had come their way. This seems an obvious message, but it was one that had to be repeated many times. Apart from the small number of outstanding students in School who regularly distinguished themselves in open academic competition year by year, there was a great majority content with very modest ambitions. Miss Green may well have sensed the unrealised potential of this majority even in the short time she had been in the School. She knew that, from the coming September onwards, when admission was by competitive examination and had nothing to do with parental ability to pay the fee, it would be proper to expect much more from many more girls. It was a theme to which she returned in the future.

The problem presented by the Junior School remained. Although it no longer shared the Cheltenham Road site it was still an integral part of the School. Parents had entered their young daughters on the understanding that if they reached the admission standard of the main school at the age of eleven they would be guaranteed a place. Now the main School would no longer conduct its own entrance examination and eleven year old entrants would be selected on the results of a procedure administered by Bristol Local Education Authority: the Eleven Plus, as it came to be known. Parents could list secondary grammar schools in the order of their preference, and the children who did best in the examination would be offered a place in the school which their parents had indicated was their first choice. The girls in the Junior School had to compete on equal terms with the rest of Bristol for places in the main School. By the spring half term it was known that 15 of the 30 girls in the top class of the Junior School had not passed the first stage of the Eleven Plus. Even if the successful fifteen were all given preferential treatment – and Miss Green would press for this concession – and allowed to take up places in the senior School, there remained fifteen sets of parents who naturally felt that the understanding upon which they had chosen to send their children at an early age to Colston's Girls' School had not been honoured. Their disappointment had an immediate effect on parents of still younger girls who were removing their daughters from the School and sending them to preparatory departments where a promise of admission to the senior school could be kept.

From the financial point of view this sudden drop in numbers in the Junior School was serious. While it had its full complement of 150 pupils the School had been running at a small loss, in contrast to the senior School which ended the 1945/46 financial year with a healthy credit balance. The loss could be made up from this balance: the advantage to the School as a whole of having a successful preparatory department would have outweighed the cost of this, if the senior School had been continuing as a Direct Grant School. But from September the School would have only its miniscule endowment income to dispose of, and this was already earmarked for the maintenance of the building.

Two members of the small Junior School staff were leaving in the summer, one because she had married and the other because she had accepted a post in a Training College. Two more were likely to go, one to get more experience and the other because she was ill. Miss Green was faced with the probability of having to replace more than half the staff and the impossibility of making appointments while the future of the School was uncertain. As she pointed out, no one would accept a post in a School which might not exist in a few months' time. Another complication was the responsibility the School had for the Froebel training department. There were three second year and eight first year students who had embarked on the three year course. If these young women were to find training places elsewhere they must be warned as soon as possible.

The Junior School Management Committee, composed of women Governors and the two past and present Head Mistresses, held the one and only meeting of its existence in March. By then, the Education Authority had yielded to Miss Green's plea that the successful candidates in the Eleven Plus from the Junior School should be given priority of entry to the senior School, but there was no guarantee that this would happen again. The Authority would accept no financial responsibility for the Junior School and, indeed, the Management Committee had no brief to discuss this aspect of the problem. The various other difficulties were rehearsed and the Committee came to the unanimous decision that the parents should be given a term's notice and the School closed in July. Through Miss Rashley's temperate and businesslike minutes there comes the feeling of a sad despair; and perhaps also, in what she records of Miss Morgan's contributions, of grief for the destruction of a flourishing school.

The small Finance Committee met two days later, and a few days after that an Extraordinary Meeting of Governors was held. At that meeting a letter was read from a member of the Junior School staff, Miss Fowler. She asked the Governors to keep the School open, at least for a few more years, so that its valuable experimental work in primary education might continue. By the end of the meeting the Governors had to some extent departed from the resolution before them from the Management Committee. They decided to ask the Bristol Local Education Authority to take over the School and run it as a primary school with a training department; and, if the Authority refused, to close it.

It would be interesting to think that the Governors had in mind the preservation of a progressive school, but it would be a misunderstanding of their attitude. They were not wholly in sympathy with educational experiment, unless it was being pioneered by someone like Miss Hughes, and they had had a sufficient number of complaints from parents that their daughters were being made to work too hard to confirm them in their prejudices. They did on the other hand feel an obligation to parents who had sent their daughters to the School believing that it would continue to exist for the length of their children's junior school life. Among the Governors were representatives of the Local Education Authority. They knew that places did not exist in the Authority's primary schools for even a minority of the Junior School pupils. It would be much less expensive for the Authority to take over and run the School than to build either a new school or extensions to existing ones. The Foundation Governors found they had an effective argument in the threat of closure.

At the end of this truly extraordinary meeting Alderman Williams made an evidently considered speech. It was a matter, he said, of great personal regret to him that the Minister of Education had decided to remove the senior School from the Direct Grant list without consulting the Local Authority. This action had led not only to the present difficulty with regard to the junior department, but had also made a fundamental change in the status of a school which had played an outstanding part in the life and traditions of Bristol. He was listened to in silence and thanked at the end. Nothing would alter the conviction of the Foundation Governors that the Bristol Authority had somehow influenced the Minister's decision. They wondered whether the Authority was now belatedly realising that had the Direct Grant list been left as it was there could have been more places available to it at Redland and Colston's than there were now at Colston's.

The future of the Junior School and of the students in the Froebel training department was now assured, although the staff regretted that they would no longer be part of Colston's Girls' School. The school has continued to this day as a local education authority primary school on its Cotham site. It has earned the respect and affection of its pupils. Soon after its status was changed there was controversy, which spread to the columns of the local papers, as to the propriety of its retaining the name of Colston. Happily, no official notice was taken of this smallmindedness.

After the February Governors' meeting the Clerk wrote to the Ministry applying for Aided status, and enclosing a copy of a letter she had written to the Chief Education Officer about the future of the Junior School, both matters which seemed to her then of extreme urgency. She was surprised not to receive any reply until the middle of April. Later, a delay of a mere six weeks would strike her as a swift response. The letter from the Ministry asked for the Governors' comments on the Instrument and Articles of Government proposed for the School and enclosed a copy of Form 18 Schools.

If there were a draft Instrument and Articles they have not survived. The Governors thought they were being asked to produce a draft themselves, and this the Finance Committee did, using all the available Ministry statements and publications, and sent it to the Bristol Chief Education Officer so that he could forward it to the Ministry with the Local Authority's comments. In the same way, they sent him the Form 18 Schools of which a section was to be completed by the Local Authority before it too was returned to the Ministry.

Form 18 Schools became an important part of the Governors' work. Its purpose was to discover whether the Governors had sufficient resources to enable them to fulfil their responsibilities to an Aided School. It required a statement of the income the School was entitled to from the endowment. This was difficult to answer. Under the 1936 Scheme the School was entitled only to such a share of the Colston Trust income 'as the Society of Merchant Venturers might decide.' It asked whether the School had any outstanding loans and, if so, at what rate they had to be repaid. It asked whether the School had received any promises of grants 'from Diocesan or other sources.'

There were even more alarming questions. Under the 1944 Act a Local Authority was required to ensure that all the secondary schools for which it assumed responsibility met the standards set out in the new Building Regulations. If the School did not already meet these standards, how much would the improvements cost and how did the Governors propose to pay for them? It was unnecessary to enquire into the Regulations. Quite apart from the corrugated iron of the Hall roof and the missing Library wing, both of which might be the subject of successful war damage claims, the building had other deficiencies with which the Governors had become only too familiar over the years: the small playground, the temporary classrooms, the lack of showers in the gymnasium. Nor was this all. The Local Authority was also required to produce a Development Plan which would improve the educational provision in the whole of Bristol. Could the Governors make an appropriate contribution to this vision of the future, as yet vague but likely to be expensive? Miss Morgan's misgivings seemed to have been well justified.

The first draft of the Bristol Development Plan reached the Governors in June. The Preamble is full of good intentions and is careful to commit the Authority to doing little more than the 1944 Act prescribes. Its greatest novelty – 'An experimental Multilateral School is proposed in the early stages of the programme' – is well buried in the blandness which does not try to conceal the backlog of repairs and the new buildings which the City requires. As far as an official document can go, it is honest in revealing the local state of affairs: one of ignorance as to what could, as well as to what should, be done to improve the education of Bristol children. This state of ignorance was national as well as local. The end of the war, the change of government, educational theory and material shortages combined to produce a situation where it was very difficult to get clear answers to any queries. After the Preamble there was a list of Bristol schools, with a note on the future of each one. The entry for the School was short, five lines of typescript. The Governors' feelings are indicated by their reaction. They objected that the name of the School had been changed to 'Colston's School for Girls' and they wished to retain the old one; that the date when the Direct Grant ceased was incorrect; that the number of pupils was also incorrect; and that they did not understand the last sentence: 'Consideration of the future of the School has not yet reached a stage at which any definite statement can be made.' The Chief Education Officer's reply, placatory in response to the first three objections, was specific as to the last. The future of the School depended on a survey which the City Architect would make of the school buildings.

So the school year came to an end, with nothing in the future settled. The School was to be 'transitionally Assisted' from September. In practice this meant that Miss Green and Miss Rashley made detailed estimates under various headings of what was needed to carry on the work of the School, and the Authority made 'block grants' based on these estimates. The first instalment of £5,000 should have been paid in October. Neither this nor the residue of £6,000 still owing from the Direct Grant had been paid by December and there was a large overdraft at the bank. The Local Authority money, which had been withheld because of a misunderstanding on the part of the City Treasurer, was paid in the New Year and the financial arrangements with Bristol City Corporation thereafter worked well. They gave the School a great deal of independence, and were evidently convenient to the Bristol education officials.

In the early months of the transition from Direct Grant to Aided status a feeling of isolation was disquieting. There was no other Aided secondary school in Bristol. In other parts of the country there had been such schools since 1922 and in London there were fifty of them, many of them very well known. Some but not all of them had endowments and some were the protegés of liveried companies. Some were denominational. Miss Green wrote to several Heads of these schools, including Miss Bishop of the Godolphin and Latymer School in Hammersmith and Dame Dorothy Brock of the Mary Datchelor School in Camberwell. She found to her surprise that they were almost as ill informed about the future as she was, and perhaps even more apprehensive about the effect of changes under the 1944 Act than she yet had reason to be. From them she discovered that there were three matters which might require special attention in any settlement with a Local Education Authority.

They were all agreed that it was of primary importance that the Governors should appoint the head, and through the head the assistant staff. In order to make this relationship clear, the teachers' contracts should be with the governing body and their salaries paid by the governors, even though the money to do so was provided by the local education authority and the salaries calculated by local government officers. The reason that the Aided schools set such store by this was that they were afraid that if the Local Authority were the employer teachers could be moved from one school to another within the Authority's area and the idea of loyalty to a particular school would be lost.

They wanted the money in block grants to be paid into the School's account so that it could spend the agreed total as it chose. They wanted to select their own books, furniture and equipment and not to have to accept whatever the Authority had chosen to buy in bulk.

Finally they wanted to be able to fix their own dates for terms and holidays. The Act prescribed a maximum and a minimum number of days to be worked in the school year. Some Authorities insisted on the maximum. The Aided Schools wanted the maximum length of holidays.

A further possible bone of contention, the selection of the pupils, never seems to have aroused so much feeling either in London or Bristol. It was soon clear that there would be great competition for places in these notable but now non-feepaying schools and the schools seem quietly to have accepted that by leaving this task to the Local Authority not only the exertions but also the opprobrium connected with selection could be avoided. In the case of Colston's Girls' School there was an added complication. The counties of Gloucestershire and Somerset still took up a few eleven year old places each year and held their own selection procedures. Mr Sylvester, the Bristol Chief Education Officer, and Miss Green facilitated an agreement between the three Authorities.

In London the three contentious matters were the subject of lengthy consultations between the Aided Schools and the London County Council, each side aware that the Ministry would make the final decisions and incorporate them in the Articles of Government of each School. In Bristol there were consultations too, but at lengthy intervals with Mr Sylvester speaking for the Authority and Miss Green keeping the Governors informed about what was happening in London. These meetings do not seem to have been in any way acrimonious and practical working arrangements were established before the last consultation in 1950. The reason that the question whether the School could be given Aided status took so long to decide was nothing to do with whether the School was viable under a partnership of Local Authority and Governors. As Mr Sylvester had said, the future of the School depended on the building in Cheltenham Road.

As soon as the first aid repairs which followed the bombing in 1941 had been completed the Governors began to plan the reinstatement of the Library wing and the improvements they wanted to make when the war was over. They had appointed a new architect, Mr Ralph Edwards, to claim the compensation for war damage and to draw up preliminary plans for a new library and additional classrooms. His first proposal was rejected because it occupied too much of the playground. He objected that he had received no plans of the building from his predecessor and was working under difficulties. The Governors negotiated with the Society of Merchant Venturers a long lease of the Cheltenham Lane site which they had rented for air raid shelters. While they were doing all this they recorded, almost casually, their decision to stay on in the original building in Cheltenham Road. Evidently the idea of a move had been raised but immediately dismissed. In this there was some sentiment. Everyone remembered the old Library with affection, and there may too have been some lingering memory of the prestige enjoyed by the purpose built school of the Eighteen Nineties and the extended building of the early years of this century. Whatever the reasons, there was a strong feeling before the loss of the Direct Grant against moving the School anywhere else.

In 1947, in Miss Green's second year, there was a General Inspection followed, as was the custom, by a meeting between the Inspectors and the Governors for a preliminary report. Mr Sylvester attended this meeting. He had already begun to think about the School's accommodation problems and he raised the subject of a possible move to the site of the old Bishop's Palace, adjoining the School playing field in Redland Green. The Palace had been bombed and burnt out in the heavy raids of 1941, the Bishop had moved to the present Bishop's House in Clifton, and there now remained only the ruins of Bishop Browne's mansion. Cyril Clarke had seen the possibility of extending the playing field by adding this ground to it and had tried to buy it but at that time the Church Commissioners would not sell. Now that it was for sale, but with its acquisition linked to the idea of a new school building, he was much less sure that he wanted it.

The Inspectors' formal report was not expected immediately and did not arrive until June, 1948. In the meantime the City Architect made his survey of the school building and produced a report which Mr Sylvester sent on to the Ministry. It is quite short and unequivocal in its verdict. The building could not be adapted to meet the Building Regulations of the Education Act. The site would have to be more than doubled in size to provide the pitches required for outdoor games, and this could only be done by buying adjacent properties, most of which were commercial in character. The building itself could not be properly ventilated and many parts of it had insufficient natural light. The additional classrooms and specialist rooms which were needed were listed.

The Ministry sent a copy of this report to the Governors, asking that another Form 18 Schools should be completed to explain how they proposed to finance the new building. Before this could be done the Inspectors' report arrived. There could be no question, it said, that the School would have to be moved ultimately to a new building elsewhere – 'There would seem to be possibilities in the neighbourhood of the excellent playing field' – but this was not likely to be practicable for many years. It therefore recommended that, as soon as circumstances permitted, a limited number of building works should be undertaken, some of which should, and probably could, be put in hand without delay. In particular it listed the rebuilding of the Library wing, the provision of changing and showering rooms for the gymnasium and the removal of air raid shelters from the playground.

The Governors felt they were being given conflicting instructions. There is no doubt that there was a great deal of confused thinking. Both Mr Sylvester and the City Architect were good friends of the School. The adverse report of the survey was intended to facilitate the School's removal to a site they considered altogether more salubrious than the Cheltenham Road. The Ministry was saying that this could not happen immediately, and the present building should be improved. There was much talk in Bristol and in London about the Governors' responsibility for the building, both for extensions and improvements to the old and for the provision of a new one, but no one at this stage paid any attention to the question of who had to provide the site. Cyril Clarke paid visits to the Ministry and made the often very friendly acquaintance of a series of civil servants who told him what they could, which was initially not a great deal. In the fullness of time Alexander and Barraclough produced their authoritative handbook *County and Voluntary Schools* and what had not been understood before became clear. The Governors owned the site and the buildings in Cheltenham Road and could sell both to provide the funding for a new building. It was the Local Authority and not the Governors who had to provide the site for the new building and also, incidentally, the playing fields for an Aided School.

This made a difference to the Chairman's thinking. For over two years he had avoided committing the School to the purchase of the Bishop's Palace site while it appeared that the cost of both it and a new school building would fall on the Governors. His tactics were quite simple: when a meeting with the Chief Education Officer at the field was suggested, his rheumatism prevented his standing about in the cold. At other times he had an appointment at the Ministry in London or was going abroad. Now he agreed to ask the Education Committee to buy the land for use immediately for sports activities and eventually for a new school building, but stipulated that the Authority must clear and level the ground. The Committee passed the necessary resolution, but the year was 1949, the year in which the pound was devalued and public spending curtailed. The Ministry refused to permit the purchase. The 1944 Building Regulations were already seen as demanding too lavish and expensive a standard. There was much essential building to be done and old buildings were to be improved rather than replaced. The greatest obstacle to Aided status, the fear that the Governors would not be able to find the funds for a new building, was thus removed.

The Chairman may have been dilatory in coming to a decision about the additional ground at the field but he was being very active in other ways. He decided, early in 1947, that Colston's Girls' School should be a Church of England school. The idea may have been growing in his mind for some while but several matters combined at that time to produce a conviction which he never abandoned. He had noticed that the Roman Catholic schools had retained their place on the Direct Grant list. He had made the acquaintance of the Revd Mervyn Stockwood, then the vicar of St Matthew Moorfields and later the Bishop of Southwark, who understood local as well as national politics and who gave him advice. He caused searches to be made into Colston's original settlement and the Colston's Hospital Schools Scheme of

1875. There was no doubt where Colston stood on the subject of religious instruction and observance; and the first Scheme which included the Girls' School required that the Head Mistress should be a communicant member of the Church of England and that religious instruction should be given 'in accordance with the doctrines of the Church of England'. This had been altered – 'watered down' in his phrase – in the 1910 Scheme to 'in accordance with the principles of the Christian Faith' and the requirement that the Head Mistress should be an Anglican was specifically omitted. It has to be said that the new Scheme of 1936, when he was already Chairman, and the draft Articles of Government which he supervised in 1946, did not revert to the original terms. Now, however, he was adamant that the School should return to what he considered was legitimacy.

No one who knew Cyril Clarke, or even met him briefly, could doubt his profound and abiding reverence for the Church. He was devout in practice as well as theory. He loved the School and spoke as though he was proposing to return a treasure to the safe keeping of the Church, where it belonged. There were other advantages of a return to the original regulations. He wished to establish a Building Fund, so that the Governors would always be able to meet their obligations and avoid any diminution of their powers. It was hopeless to look for financial help to the Society of Merchant Venturers, now concentrating on the problem of the Boys' School for which not even Aided status was an option. But there were educational charities and monies from the sale of redundant churches which he hoped would be more accessible to a church school and he worked very hard to interest the representatives of these funds in the School. More important even than financial security was the separate identity of the School. He and, it must be said, the Merchants thought that there was a real danger that the School would be taken over completely by the Local Education Authority, its assets dispersed and the special work it had always done for the education of girls discontinued and merged into some other project.

One of the several versions of the Form 18 Schools which Miss Rashley completed required the form to be sent to the Diocesan Education Committee or the Bishop before it was sent on to the Local Education Authority for transmission to the Ministry. This was because a number of Aided schools were denominational schools and received support from church funds. The Chairman took this as a sign pointing in a new direction for his campaign. He was the kind of layman who besides giving money to the Church did a great deal of unpaid work for it and he had many contacts. He was on first name terms with the Bishop, the Rt Revd Arthur Cockin, and was a member of the Diocesan Conference. He appealed to the Bishop, the Conference and the Diocesan Education Committee to recognise the School as a church school and was appalled to be met with a lack of enthusiasm. The Diocesan Education Committee was engaged in delicate negotiations with the Local Authority about the agreed religious syllabus to be adopted by the Authority's schools; and it had no spare cash to give to individual schools if, as its members feared, it was being asked for money. The Chairman let it be known that he would address the Diocesan Conference on the subject. The Bishop asked him to refrain, saying that the Diocesan Education Committee had too much on its mind to think about Colston's Girls' School. The Chairman said nothing could be more important than Colston's Girls' School, and spoke at the Conference, to no avail. The general tone of the exchanges can be savoured from the last four paragraphs of a letter from the Chairman to the Bishop in March 1949:

> I consider Edward Colston's Settlement is our Charter, not any Order of the Education Committee.
>
> This is enough to give me a heart attack.
>
> Would you care to telephone me tomorrow morning.
>
> I am just off to a funeral,
>
> Yours very sincerely,
>
> Cyril.

The Chairman, as was by now his custom, sought a series of interviews with civil servants at the Ministry, and the subsequent letters from these hardworking officials reveal some sympathy and even more admiration for his efforts. He was a man of feeling, very articulate and full of ideas. His friends at the Ministry were at pains to discover from him the nature of the religious life of the School. He was able to tell them that in fact all the Head Mistresses had been Anglicans to whom their personal religious life had been important; that Miss Sparks had introduced denominational religious instruction and since then parents had been able to choose Church of England instruction for their daughters; that Miss Morgan, the timetabler, had ensured that parents had a completely free choice by arranging that all Scripture lessons in any year happened at the same time, and this had meant that she employed a clergyman as a part time member of staff; that all school services were Anglican in form and conducted by Anglican clergy; and that recently Miss Green had arranged confirmation preparation classes and corporate communions. No member of another denomination had complained about any of this, and it was true that many parents welcomed the fact that religion played so vigorous a part in School life.

This factual account could not fail to prompt the question, at the Ministry and elsewhere, as to what more recognition as a church school would give the School than it already had in the way of allegiance to Anglican doctrine. In particular, whatever the status of the School, the Diocesan Education Committee was not going to give financial support. The Chairman believed that the long term advantages of a separate identity and the hope of future funding were sufficient, but the Ministry could not see that recognition by the Church conveyed any practical benefit at present. The last application for

Aided status as a Church School was the result of a split vote on the Governing Body. The Foundation Governors voted for it, the Local Education Authority Governors either voted against it or abstained.

In August, 1950, the School was granted Aided status, but not as a Church School. The transitional period, expected to be a few months, had lasted four years. The School had come to a good working arrangement with the Bristol Education Office, but there were still no Instrument or Articles of Government. During the next three years there were periodic discussions about what these documents should contain and the conclusions were referred to the Minister. They were sealed in February, 1953. The Local Authority had not yielded on several key issues, including holidays.

The Foundation Governors felt aggrieved. The controversy over the religious status of the School did not end there. It was prolonged by the Ministry. A new Scheme was being prepared for the Colston's Hospital Trust and in October 1953 the legal department of the Ministry offered to change the clause describing religious instruction back to its original 1875 form. At the next Governors' meeting the thirteen Foundation Governors present voted to accept this change and the five Local Authority Governors voted against it. When the new Scheme was published the change had not been made, on the grounds that the Governors already had the power to offer parents the choice of Anglican religious instruction. The argument as to how this choice should be presented continued until 1957 when a document almost identical to that drawn up by Miss Sparks was accepted by both sides.

The School was content to leave the selection of pupils at eleven to the Local Education Authority; wisely, for competition for places was intense and any entrance examination run by the School would have presented the staff with an immense task. The Eleven Plus was a complicated procedure in the early years. Every child took Part I of the examination and a smaller number proceeded to Part II. Primary school records and the opinions of primary school head teachers were consulted. At one stage all potential grammar school candidates were interviewed in their own schools by representative head and assistant teachers working in grammar schools. Later only those children who were borderline for admission to a grammar school were interviewed and as so called intelligence testing became more sophisticated and better understood the whole process was streamlined. Although there were changes in detail one feature remained the same: from 1946 to 1965 the eleven year old pupils were chosen by the Local Authorities and not by the School. Their first year in School was probationary. If they had not reached an acceptable standard by the end of it, their probation was extended for a further year. If they were still unsuccessful at the end of the second year, they would be removed to a secondary modern school or, mercifully, their parents would be encouraged to request a transfer. In theory, this was a two way traffic, and secondary modern pupils who had made exceptional progress could be transferred at the end of their second year to a grammar school. No such transfers were ever made to Colston's, although very occasionally a girl who had completed her course at a secondary modern school successfully spent two years in the senior school, preparing for admission to a training college.

The probationary first year may have been one of the causes of the problems the teaching staff had with the eleven year old new girls. Knowing that they could be asked to leave may have made some of them feel less than full members of the School, but what the staff complained of was that they were arrogant and noisy. Miss Green thought many of them had been overtaught in their last years in the primary school and were unready for the more complicated demands made by secondary work. The School doctor, still Dr Richard Clarke, considered their health and physique less good than the girls he had examined before and during the war. Whatever the reasons, there was some mismatch between the School and its new pupils. When the different years in all secondary schools were renamed and the old Third became Form One, the fact was emphasised that Colston's Girls' School now began with eleven year olds. No longer was there a core of girls in every class who had been in the Junior School for several years and knew all about Colston and Commemoration Day and Sports Day in the summer. There was talk at the time of first generation grammar school pupils, those whose parents had not had the educational opportunities now offered to their children. This can not have been an important disadvantage in the case of Colston girls. The School had always taken a number of pupils whose parents wished them to have a better education than they had had themselves and successive Head Mistresses had seen part of their task as ensuring that all parents knew as much as possible about the nature and the aims of the education their daughters were receiving. One of the ways Miss Green achieved this was by holding Open Evenings when parents could visit the School and examine displays of work. It is, of course, possible to exaggerate the change made by the selection procedure which started in 1946. A great many girls came to the School who would have come even if it had not become Aided; every class had members who were the daughters, nieces, cousins and even granddaughters of Old Girls and who thereby had the right of membership of a particular House.

The school leaving age was raised in 1947 to fifteen, but the grammar school course leading to the first public examination, School Certificate and later Ordinary level, took five years and it was expected that children for whom parents accepted a grammar school place would stay at school until they were at least sixteen. They did not all do so, and the problem of early leaving from grammar schools was so widespread that a Commission was set up by the Central Advisory Council for Education to enquire into its causes and possible remedies. The only effective remedy came in 1972 when the school leaving age was raised to sixteen for everyone, but the Report published in 1954 was enlightening as to its causes. Mistaken selection at eleven turned out to be less important than parental attitudes and the pupil's own motivation. In Bristol there was ample employment for fifteen year old girls from a well known school and Miss Green waged constant battle to dissuade girls from leaving before they had taken even the first School Certificate. That she was largely successful in this made possible the subsequent growth of the Sixth form.

In 1947 there were just over a hundred girls in the Sixth. There were three special forms: 17 girls in the Clerical, doing commercial subjects; 16 in the one year Prenursing course; and 16 doing the Domestic Science course. In the first year of the two year academic course there were 24 girls, and 28 in the second. These girls were aiming at the Higher School Certificate. 26 of the second year sat the examination and 18 passed. The remaining two probably joined the first year: 26 of them took it in the next year and 18 passed, several of them very well. These figures seem small to us now, but they were already an improvement on, for instance, 1944 when there were only two candidates. As had for long been the case, the high fliers were distinguishing themselves but by modern standards there were not many of them. In 1949 there were two State Scholars and seven other girls had County Senior awards which could be held at Universities. Girls who wished to take entrance examinations to the Oxford, Cambridge and London colleges usually stayed in the Sixth for a third year.

With the coming of the General Certificate of Education in 1951 the two year sixth form course was made accessible to more pupils. Neither at Ordinary level, the equivalent of the credit pass in School Certificate, nor at Advanced level, the equivalent of a Higher School Certificate pass, was it necessary to pass in a range of subjects at a single sitting to secure a Certificate. Many educationalists deplored this change, pointing out that unless the school ensured that each pupil pursued a balanced course of study it was possible for a successful candidate to have given up the subjects she found difficult or unattractive. Miss Green and her staff put a great deal of thought in to planning the curriculum so that this early specialisation was avoided.

They decided that seven subjects at Ordinary level should be the most that any girl should take at the end of the fifth year. It would have been possible for girls who were going to take a subject at Advanced level to bypass the Ordinary level examination in that subject and take examinations only in the subjects she was not continuing in the Sixth form. The staff rejected this plan, which would have reduced the number of external examinations candidates took, because they thought the girls needed the stimulus and the encouragement of examination success at sixteen. They were right in this, and more girls did go on after Ordinary level to take Advanced level subjects in the Sixth.

With hindsight it seems that the School was less successful in deciding how many girls were capable of taking the full range of academic subjects to the age of sixteen. Of the hundred or so girls in each year it was at first estimated that sixty could profitably pursue a course of study involving mathematics, languages and science, and the remaining forty should take less demanding subjects. Later, in the light of experience, more girls were given the opportunity to continue the 'hard' subjects and all were expected to pass the Ordinary level examinations they sat.

It could be expected that when the girls who from 1946 onwards had been so rigorously selected by the Local Education Authorities at eleven took external examinations at sixteen and then eighteen there would be a sudden increase in the number of successful candidates. This was not the case. Instead, there was a steady rise in the achievement of the girls already in the School which merely continued and accelerated as time went on. One of the outstanding years at Advanced level was the one which for the last time contained girls who had entered Colston's as members of the Junior School. What was happening now was that the girls themselves, their parents and the teaching staff were raising their expectations of what the girls could achieve.

The number of pupils in School increased. This was partly because the Local Education Authorities sent 102 girls each September. The Ministry of Education permitted classes of 34 pupils because of the shortage of grammar school places, and Miss Green redivided the hundred or so girls into four forms in the fourth and fifth years. More girls were staying for two years in the sixth form. Soon there were fifty more girls in the building than there were when the last of the Junior School departed for Cotham Grove. Even while the debate about the move to the Bishop's Palace site still continued, the Inspectors' Report recommending the improvement of the present building encouraged the Governors to do what they could. Mr Edwards drew up plans and made representations to the War Damage Commission. Such was the shortage at the time of both labour and building materials that a Regional Priority Officer was appointed to decide the order in which bombed buildings could be rebuilt. It may have been providential that in 1948 the corrugated iron in the Hall roof began to show signs of disintegration and Mr Edwards obtained permission to rebuild the roof. This was done during the Autumn Term of 1948, which meant that necessary library books had to be removed from the bookcases in the Hall, and the Hall itself could not be used at all after the first fortnight of term. The opportunity was taken to improve the Hall lighting and to light the shelves of the bookcases. At the same time the City Engineer found it necessary to repair the Cutler's Mills culvert which ran under the Library wing and had been damaged by the same bombs. The result was that both in the building and in the playground there was for a while even less space than there had been before. The School carried on amid the dust and the noise with good humour, as it did when the Cheltenham Road front of number 182 was rebuilt and when two years later the Studio and the classrooms which had adjoined the old Library wing had to be repaired. When Advanced level examinations were moved to an earlier date in June, they were held at the field in the Nissen huts given to the School by the Royal Air Force Balloon crew at the end of the war. Some lessons were given in the wooden structure which had been built for the Kindergarten in the Pleasaunce. The small rooms in the two houses at either end of the building were used for teaching. The Governors and Mr Edwards continued to do everything they could to get permission to rebuild the Library wing.

The postwar years were drab in many ways, in the appearance of roads and buildings, the state of furniture and decoration and even in the clothes people wore. It was extremely difficult to keep school uniform looking smart when coupons as well as money had to be surrendered for every garment. The Clark's sandals which were part of the summer uniform could be worn for a few more months if the front of the upper were cut and toes allowed to peep out. The end of clothes rationing in 1949 was celebrated by the introduction of a new school uniform, notably a new winter hat for senior girls, a navy felt bowler with an enamelled brooch badge at the front. When properly worn it had a certain distinction: less elegant headgear has been worn by air hostesses.

The cooperation between schools which had been so evident during the war continued, although in a less formal way. After school dancing classes to which boys from Cotham Grammar School or Colston's Boys' School were invited led to enjoyable parties and there were musical and dramatic activities in which several schools joined. When travel restrictions were lifted, holidays abroad were again possible. A School party went to the Austrian Tyrol in 1949 but in 1952 came the first Bristol Bordeaux exchange visits. At Easter 220 Bristol school children spent a month in France and their French hosts and hostesses returned the visit in the summer. On the way they had two nights in Paris and the whole party travelled by public service surface transport. Miss Stoneley took a party of more than thirty girls on that first expedition. Nowadays the travellers go by plane from Lulsgate airport and the duties of the accompanying staff, while still quite onerous, are not so alarming. A much smaller party exchanged with school children from Hanover. The Colston girls were from the fourth year and the lower sixth forms. They gained a great deal from the experience.

In 1953 Miss Green was offered and accepted the headship of Kidbrooke School, a large multilateral school in a new building, which was being formed by the amalgamation of five existing schools in south east London. The new name 'comprehensive' was beginning to be used of schools which offered secondary education to the whole range of ability, and there was much pioneer work to be done to develop the curriculum and organisation of a School which had few precedents. At Colston's, like Miss Sparks before her, she had had to supervise the introduction of a new examination and reorganise the form structure of the senior school. She had also had to work much more closely than her predecessors with a number of officials outside school and had shown a remarkable talent for establishing good working relationships with them, to the great advantage of the School.

In the New Year Honours list of 1968 she was made a Dame of the British Empire and she retired from Kidbrooke in 1973. Her work outside the School has included membership of the Donovan Commission on Trades Unions and Employers' Associations and Governorships of both the London School of Economics and the B.B.C.

MISS DUNN

The post of Head Mistress was advertised in the *Times Educational Supplement* and the *Times* in July 1953. This is not a good time of year for recruitment advertisements, but as the new Head Mistress was required in January 1954, no time could be wasted. Thirty-nine applications were received and six were selected for interview. One candidate withdrew and after the interviews the Governors had a discussion and ballot and unanimously offered the post to Miss A M S Dunn.

Amy Margaret Sarah Dunn, born in 1921, was the daughter of a mechanical engineer who was the designer of Alvis Cars and, during the second world war, of various military vehicles. Educated at Barr's Hill School, Coventry, Sarah Dunn went on to read English at St Hugh's College, Oxford; and Social Sciences at the University of Leeds. She was Second Mistress at the City of Worcester Grammar School for Girls and took up the Headship of Colston's Girls' School a few days before her thirty-third birthday. She was to become the longest serving Head Mistress the School has had, retiring twenty-seven years later at the end of 1980.

What sort of woman was to stamp her character so firmly on the School for more than a quarter of its existence? She was to be known for her calm and disarmingly modest public image; a reflective personality, perhaps a little remote. In relaxed and informal gatherings a good conversationalist and excellent company, Sarah Dunn could surprise her young pupils. At an experimental drama evening at which she met some sixth formers she 'actually sat on the floor!'.

Her reports, meticulously prepared for Governors' meetings – there are eighty-one in all – reveal a Head Mistress who was a keen observer of human nature. Girls might have been surprised with what warmth, wit and insight into the human condition she regularly documented the outstanding achievements, the poignant problems and, let it be admitted, the sheer hopelessness of some girls. Miss Dunn knew her pupils.

Girls who gained the highest academic honours were mentioned with pride. Take as an example Priscilla Jenkins, who won a *Spectator* Competition in July 1954. The subject set was a review of a book by Osbert Sitwell within a fortnight of its publication. During the first week Priscilla was appearing in the School Play and had no time for writing, but she borrowed the book from the School Library and read it and wrote her review in the last few days of term. She beat professional journalists and reviewers and the judges commented on the maturity of her critical principles. Macmillan, the publishers, approached her to know whether she had a novel ready for publication. Miss Dunn wrote,

'She is starting her Oxford Entrance Examination today, so she must postpone writing her novel until she has a place there. She is seventeen.' Contrast this with girls whose sad and depressing home lives attracted Miss Dunn's sympathy and whose every small success filled her with delight. She had no time for girls who squandered their potential and, incidentally, their places at the School. Like Miss Green before her she deplored parents who attempted to make their daughters leave to seek employment before they had taken any public examinations. Her greater wrath was saved for the employers, particularly public bodies. When the Post Office employed a girl without reference to the School, Miss Dunn was very displeased. 'Public money is being spent on girls in this school and one of the aims of such spending is that they should qualify themselves by taking public examinations. It seems illogical that government departments should actually encourage girls to leave without fulfilling their obligations.' Miss Dunn wrote to the Civil Service Commissioners and the Post Master. We are left in little doubt as to the tone of her letters.

Miss Dunn was very concerned with the health and consequently the attendance of the girls. Epidemics of Asian Flu and even of heavy colds are reported, and the frustrations of poor attendance are documented. 'The difficulties of class teaching in epidemics is not that so many girls are away, but that so many different girls are away each week and the same work has to be done two or three times over to the intense boredom of the healthy minority.' The School had always had a Matron Housekeeper and a School Doctor. Dr Richard Clarke retired in 1956 after 36 years as the School's Medical Officer. He had advised early bedtimes to generations of girls and as time progressed found he was examining the daughters of girls he had advised twenty years before. The brother of C Cyril Clarke, the Chairman of the Governors, he exemplified once again the close knit family ethos of Colston's Girls' School. He was succeeded by Dr Kathleen Faulkner, an Old Girl!

Miss Dunn returns on several occasions to the problems relating to allowances for responsibility and seniority amongst teachers. In 1956 she explains at some length the difficulties envisaged under the new scheme for allowances. Although creating a career path to the higher scales, it could also discourage teachers of minority subjects who would never be likely to reach the most attractive promoted posts that might await graduates in, for instance, English. Miss Dunn remarks, somewhat caustically, 'The exceptionally gifted young teacher of Geography who wishes to rise in his profession must either be content with a smaller allowance when he rises to become Head of Department or begin to teach English in which he is not specially qualified. Or, of course, he can become a Headmaster and do very little teaching at all.'

Her use of the masculine pronoun is intriguing. Her staff was almost wholly female and her concern for them always evident. It was still some years before women teachers were to receive pay equal to that of their male counterparts.

In the Inspectors' report of 1964 surprise was expressed that no second chemistry mistress had been employed. Miss Dunn had tried unsuccessfully for eight years to find a suitably qualified teacher and finally succeeded in the summer of 1965. The problem outlined here was not unique; it was often difficult to find well-qualified and experienced staff and to retain them, particularly as there was still the possibility in the Fifties that a woman would resign her post if she married and virtually no chance of her retaining it if she became pregnant.

The academic standards of the School were high. Every year many girls gained entry to University and Training College, often with three or four winning open Scholarships or Exhibitions. A marked concern during these years was that Training College places were scarce and girls who had a strong vocation to be teachers were not always fortunate enough to gain places. In 1958 three girls failed to gain entry. They were amongst the two thousand five hundred candidates nationally who were not allocated places. There was already a grave shortage of teachers; no-one could understand why the number of places was not increased.

Relief was on the horizon with the expansion of Higher Education that came about in the 1960's with the Robbins Report, but it was no comfort to the disappointed candidates of 1958.

Every girl who has been a pupil in the School will remember that the Autumn Term was a busy one. Prize Day came first, held in the afternoon with only the Seniors present and the parents of prize-winners and Sixth Formers, owing to lack of space. There was a sense of occasion about this and the fact that the proceedings always followed the same pattern did not detract from it. The staff wore gowns, the only occasion in the School Year when they did. Some of the Governors were present. The Head Mistress gave her report, the prizes were presented and the guest speaker gave his or her address. At Miss Dunn's first Prize Giving the speaker was Sir Ian Jacob, Director-General of the BBC. After this there was music provided usually first by the Senior Choir and then by the whole School. A happy innovation of Miss Dunn's was to have prizes won by girls who were at university and unable to return to Bristol taken by the girl's mother or father.

November is the month in Bristol when Edward Colston is commemorated. By now the School held its Commemoration Service on the first Friday of the month, in the Cathedral. Bronze chrysanthemums were worn by everyone: the Cathedral and School were decorated too. Any passers-by would have seen the whole School gathering at their appointed places, ready to lead into the Cathedral in order: in the nave they joined the former members of staff, Old Girls and parents of present pupils, waiting in silence for the music to begin. A member of the school in 1954, returning to Bristol in 1991 would find the hymns, the anthems and the readings reassuringly familiar.

In the afternoon, after the bronze chrysanthemums had been laid at the foot of Colston's statue on the Centre, the more light-hearted side of Commemoration was observed in the plays performed by the Sixth Form (at first the whole Sixth Form, then only the second year Sixth) and the staff. What enjoyment when the different members of staff were recognised!

Later, on November 10, some of the Sixth Form attended the Charter Day service when the Merchant Venturers remember the granting of their Charter: and the Fourth Form prefects attended the Service at All Saint's Church on November 13, which was kept as Colston's birthday by the Anchor, the Dolphin and the Grateful Societies. The Head Girl always laid a wreath on Colston's Tomb.

December saw Christmas music at School Association meetings, services in School at end of term, and in various other out-of-school events.

After this exciting Autumn Term, the Spring Term was comparatively calm, beginning with examinations for some and ending with hockey and netball matches. The Summer Term included examinations for everyone, cricket and swimming activities, Sports Day, the Swimming Gala and the Fete. This yearly round formed a framework in which many activities occurred.

The success of any school depends very largely on the good relations between parents and staff. The School Association continued to play a lively part in School affairs and meetings were always well attended. Parents increasingly during these years encouraged their daughters to stay into the Sixth Form. There was in 1954 a wide range of subjects at Advanced level – English Literature, History, Geography, Latin, Greek, French, German, Physics, Chemistry, Biology, Botany, Zoology, Pure Mathematics, Pure and Applied Mathematics, Applied Mathematics, Art, Music, Domestic Science and Needlework. Some of these subjects later changed their names and new ones were added – Classical Civilisation, Economics, Pure Mathematics with Statistics.

In spite of probable difficulties with staffing, Miss Dunn introduced Spanish in the Sixth Form in 1957 and two years later she remarks, somewhat laconically, 'Although at present I have neither candidates nor teacher, I should like to introduce Russian, probably for scientists, at some time.' Within months she had engaged Miss Maria Pienkovska to teach the language. This marked the beginning of the great interest in Modern Languages that has persisted in the School and which has determined the career paths of so many girls. Records suggest that the first girl to win a University place to read Spanish was Leona Watkins; she is now, as Leona Nickless, the School's Spanish teacher.

In 1954 Molly Bryant went to Somerville College, Oxford, with an exhibition in Chemistry and in the next year Priscilla Jenkins gained the Mary Ewart Scholarship for English at the same college. Both were academically distinguished and Molly Bryant as Dr Molly Scopes became a School Governor, a position she still holds. Teaching and nursing were popular careers at this time. Other girls aimed at secretarial work and were able to gain a full training in this field. The numbers of girls going on to University grew, especially as financial support became more easily available.

As Higher Education expanded, the systems that supported it were changing. In 1963 Miss Dunn complained that the new University clearing system (now known universally as UCCA) was very slow and inefficient; by March exactly half as many girls as in the year before had received offers of University places.

Even earlier, in 1956, it was clear that the money that was set aside to help University candidates, such as the Proctor Baker, Openshaw and Gamble Scholarships, might be better diverted elsewhere. Whereas University Scholars were once so hard-pressed to find the money for tuition fees, maintenance and books, they were now becoming quite well provided for by State Scholarship or Education Authority Awards. As the value of these awards was likely to be decreased by that of any other Scholarship held, Miss Dunn felt it was time to consider how the funds could be used to encourage girls to stay on in the Sixth Form.

By 1957, the Edith Openshaw Scholarship was awarded to girls wishing to take a course of professional training, the first such award helping a girl to train as an occupational therapist. By 1958 the terms of the other Scholarship funds had been amended so that they could be used for those who 'are about to attend, are now attending or for not less than two years have attended' the School. The money could now be used for girls in real need.

The reconstruction of the Library wing was already under discussion when Miss Dunn was appointed. By March 1955 permission to include the rebuilding in the Local Authority's 1955–56 estimates was received from the Ministry of Education. At the Governors' meeting Mr Ralph Edwards, the School Architect, explained that proposed plans would have to be approved by the Governors, the Education Committee and the Ministry of Education. He emphasised that the destroyed building was sited immediately on top of Cutlers Mills Brook Culvert and that any reinstatement would require special foundations and substructure. The floor levels in the ruined Library wing did not coincide with those of the main building. Mr Edwards drew up the necessary plans and presented them within a month to the Governors. In the meantime the War Damage Commission offered £22,000 towards the reconstruction. This would leave the Foundation Governors to find £5,000 to meet the probable cost. It must have been a shock when in February 1956 the lowest tender for the work was £35,688. Early in 1957 the Society of Merchant Venturers agreed to a loan of £3,000 to help finance the work, which by now was almost complete. The final cost of the building was £37,334–19s–9d. of which the War Damage Commission paid £30,781–2s–2d.

Fortunately the books were saved and housed in shelves in the Hall – not the most convenient place for study and, furthermore, the Hall was often needed for other purposes than as a library. Space was short as several form rooms had been lost. The Studio and the rooms below were boarded off from the bombed out part. Now in the school year 1955–56, work on the re-building began. Noise was considerable and it was necessary to remember that it was in a good cause.

At last the building was finished and in use for the September term 1957. Some Old Girls were disappointed with the Library, but it is doubtful whether it could ever have been rebuilt as it was. The Governors had gone to considerable trouble to remove the Delft tiles, the memorial stained glass window and other items and a fireplace was included in the new design. It had at least two advantages over the old Library: it had one more storey and the extra space offered cloakrooms and a bookstore; and the three upper floors were on the same level as the main building, whereas in the demolished building there had been stairs at every level.

The official opening took place on September 24 by the Bishop of Bristol. He first addressed some of the School and some parents in the Hall and reminded everyone that the dedication was not an empty formality. The building was to be dedicated to the service of God, for it was wrong that education and religion should be separated. Miss Dunn said that, as the Hall was a symbol of the corporate life of the School, so the Library symbolised the individual study which was essential to each girl in her own search for truth. Then the company moved to the new wing along corridors lined by girls and a short ceremony was performed in the Library. 'Except the Lord build the house, they labour in vain that build it'. The School had acquired a handsome modern wing and especially a library which was a delight to work in and a fitting setting for the original books left by Charles Julius Ryland and the ever increasing additions.

In 1956 the Classics department went to Italy during the Easter holidays, visiting Florence, Naples and Rome. This became a regular event occurring every two or three years. Two years later the Fifth and Sixth Forms went on a geographical week in North Wales and this too became a regular, yearly event, though the venue varied from year to year. Emphasis on practical work of this nature has received increasing attention as the years have gone by.

In addition to those who went on the Bordeaux and Hanover exchanges 1963 saw some Sixth Form girls who took Spanish go to Barcelona and more went the following year. All the girls who took part in these expeditions undoubtedly gained from them, not only in connection with the subjects concerned but in a more general way by having their horizons widened by seeing other ways of life.

The year 1960–61 saw three girls going on an expedition of a much longer nature. They went to the United States of America for a year, under the American Field Scholarship Scheme, one to Lawrenceville in Illinois, one to

Birdville, Texas and the third to Phoenix, Arizona. They had much to tell about their experiences, some of it being a corrective to the mental pictures formed from the cinema!

In School, plays provided an opportunity for not only budding actresses, but for many others to help with costumes, lighting, scenery and work behind the scenes. In the summer of 1954 two short plays were performed – W B Yeats' '*Deirdre*' and Christopher Fry's '*Boy with a Cart*'. Individual girls took part in school productions with Colston's School, Bristol Grammar School and Bristol Cathedral School. After many other productions with all female casts, '*The Trojan Women*' was staged in 1965 with some boys from the Cathedral School taking part.

Music played an important part in school life and during these years increased its scope considerably as opportunities occurred. The Senior Choir every year sang at Prize Day, Commemoration, Parents' evenings, the Carol Service for Bristol Secondary Schools in the Cathedral and out of doors near the Christmas tree on the Centre. In 1954 they took part in the Combined Schools' Concert at the Colston Hall. The School Orchestra was again formed during the following year and went on increasing in numbers and expertise. This was possible because Bristol employed peripatetic instrumental music teachers and many girls learnt to play an instrument in School, very cheaply. All the parents had to do was provide an instrument and they could do this by paying in small weekly instalments of one shilling. There was quite a bit of resistance. The girls initially thought tuning the instruments was funny. The staff were reluctant for girls to leave lessons for their music lesson, and Miss Lewellen had to make elaborate rotas so that the girls did not miss the same lesson each week. The orchestra played regularly at the Christmas meetings of the School Association. In 1958 the House Festival of the Arts was inaugurated and before the day devoted to the music section a great deal of work had been done by the music staff selecting the individual finalists. In addition to these, each House had to produce a choir trained, conducted and accompanied by a girl. An outside adjudicator came on the day and at the first festival this was Mr Vaughan Davies, Director of Music for Bristol. The Junior Choir was revived in the following year.

From 1961 onwards, Colston's joined with Bristol Grammar School in Choral performances – in that year Mendelssohn's '*Elijah*', followed later by Haydn's '*The Creation*' and Bach's '*St Matthew Passion*'. In 1965 the School Orchestra appeared with that of the Grammar School to perform four rather more ambitious works: and was complimented on its performance at the area music festival by Vaughan Davies. That year, Colston's had seven girls in the Bristol Schools Orchestra. Many people had the opportunity of hearing the orchestra as they played at the School Fete in 1965 and 1966.

Games, including swimming, formed a part of every girl's weekly timetable. First Formers swam throughout the year while for those higher up this activity took place in the summer only. Everyone played hockey or netball during winter and tennis or cricket in the summer. The field was admirable when reached but many girls must have mixed memories of walking uphill to it. The day when everyone was at the field was Sports Day, which in the Fifties still retained a fun element, having sack races, egg and spoon races, a slow bicycle race and an obstacle race. An innovation for the serious competitors in 1954 was that each winner was timed! Also a new loudspeaker had been installed and a sandpit for the long jump. A cricket match with the Fathers took place in the early evening. Later in the Fifties, new events were introduced at Sports Day – javelin throwing, discus throwing, 220 and 440 yards sprint, and later, the 880 yards race.

In 1954–5 a team entered the Inter-School Athletic Championships for the first time and did very well. Seven girls were chosen to take part in the Gloucestershire Schools' Championships and from these one girl from Colston's took part in the hurdles races at the All-England Schools' Championships at Manchester.

Colston's has always been strong in swimming. The annual Gala allowed everyone to see the prowess of the School's good swimmers and divers. In 1955 in the Bristol Schools' Swimming Association Gala they regained the Senior Trophy and won the Medley Relay Cup. An exciting event for several Third Formers occurred in June when they acted as ballgirls at the West of England Tennis Tournament at Redland Green. This became an annual event and was much enjoyed by the girls concerned. Each year, too, parties have been to see hockey matches at Wembley and tennis at Wimbledon.

During these years a good number of clubs or societies flourished, some of them purely in School and others belonging to wider organisations. All of them had meetings with outside speakers and discussions at different times. The School's Christian Movement was well supported, as was our branch of the Council for Education in World Citizenship. In 1956 a District Council was formed which held a one-day conference at the Royal Fort in that year and annually thereafter. To it schools sent pupils from over a wide area and over the years it attracted distinguished speakers who dealt with important themes in the post-war world. The Geographical Society held meetings in school and the summer meeting always took the form of an expedition.

The Reading Club met regularly and its Christmas meeting was a very special one to which Old Girls and former members of staff came. This meeting was held in the decorated Library where the chairs were arranged so that all could see the splendid fire especially lit for the occasion. Readings, both spiritual and secular, were all connected with Christmas and carols were sung. A Writing Club was formed as an offshoot of the Reading Club. Other clubs included a Debating Society, an Art Club, a Gymnastics Club, Senior and Junior Science Clubs, a Classical Music Society, a Sixth Form Religious Discussion Group, a Political Club and Red Cross Cadets group.

During the course of the year various competitions were held. In School, there was the Verse Speaking competition with an outside adjudicator, and with the Music competition this formed the Festival of the Arts which was competed for by the seven Houses. There were inter-school competitions, mostly arranged by the University, in which there was a most commendable success over the years. There were reading competitions in English, Classics, French and German.

In September 1960, some Fourth Formers were the first girls in School to enter the Duke of Edinburgh's Award Scheme. Since then, many girls have followed the courses which may be taken to gain bronze, silver and gold awards. The emphasis is on individual endeavour and through this for the girl to gain an interest and purpose in life. The Scheme requires considerable time and energy not only from the girls but from all those concerned with organizing the courses.

Edward Colston was a High Church Tory and his School was originally limited to members of the Church of England: and church teaching was given. Although no such limitations on admission applied to Colston's Girls' School, much emphasis was placed on Christian values and Church of England teaching was given to those who wished for it. A small number of girls were prepared for Confirmation who could not for one reason or another do so in their own parish. The numbers varied from year to year, but, for instance, there were 30 candidates the first year and regularly between 10 and 20. Sometimes it was a joint confirmation with another School – Clifton High School or Colston's Boys.

There was a corporate communion every term in the Cathedral at 8 a.m. one morning, and breakfast in School afterwards (cold ham, very delicious). Later the Cathedral had found this 8 a.m. celebration inconvenient, as the Cathedral School held Morning Assembly there. Then it was held several times in School, which worked well. When the Rev Ray Brazier came to do some teaching the corporate communion, and once or twice the Confirmation Service, was held in his church, St Nathaniel's in Redland Road.

A school owes a tremendous amount to its governors and the end of an era came in 1957 when Mr Cyril Clarke retired from the governing body. He had been a governor for forty-one years and Chairman for thirty-three.

Miss Dunn wrote of him:

> His conception of education was wide. He recognised that women were, through the home, the major influence on the future generation, and was concerned that that influence should be deeply and actively Christian. He rated intellectual

> achievement very highly and was always pleased to hear of those unusually capable and gifted. His own scholarly and literary interests are a continual pleasure to him and he found it natural to associate learning with delight, so that however tiresome the practical details of running a large school became, he knew that the learning itself must be joyous.

Cyril Clarke had served the School with great distinction as Chairman of the Governors. He had overseen the appointment of three exceptionally able Head Mistresses and had guided the School through a long period of immense change. His generosity to the School was seen in the gifts of books and prints, especially the sets of Jane Austen's works given as the C Cyril Clarke Prize, endowed in perpetuity, although no longer marked in that particular way. He also gave the School a large painting which was rather sombre and dark. It was hung at the back of the gallery. It was not until 1990 that the painting was 'discovered' by David Cross, who had visited the School at the invitation of Mrs Chard, the Librarian. He declared it to be a Newlyn School work by Thomas Cooper Gotch, '*A Night in June*'. Its provenance was certified by Francis Greenacre of the City Art Gallery and, duly restored and cleaned, it was moved to a better position near Colston's statue in the entrance hall. There, subtly lit, the complex tones and delicate detail of the painting are revealed, probably for the first time. Cyril Clarke's son, Charles, visited the School to view it in Centenary year. He wrote a letter to the Governors explaining his family's links with Gotch and congratulating them on the excellent new setting for his parents' gift.

At the meeting when Mr Clarke gave up his Chairmanship, the Governors were also sad to learn of the death of Miss G M Morgan, former Head Mistress and still a Governor of the School.

The shattering blow to the stability of the School when it lost its Direct Grant status had overshadowed Miss Green's arrival as Head Mistress in 1946. By 1953, when Miss Dunn was appointed the new Voluntary Aided status was well-established and the School's relationships with the Bristol Education Authority fairly amicable. Never quite enough money was available for improvements to buildings, better provision of books or equipment, or for the appointment of additional staff, but that was accepted with the stoicism that marks the School's response to hardship through its history. The first hints that the continuous provision of able girls to fill the hundred or so places every year could not be guaranteed came in 1955 when Somerset County Council opened a Grammar School in Keynsham, followed by another in Nailsea in 1959. The unilateral decision of Somerset County Council to limit their pupils' choice by directing them to specific schools was called 'very menacing', by Miss Dunn.

Within four years the Bristol Education Authority Development Plan was published. In its draft form it proposed to abolish selection at 11+ and to admit girls at 14+ without selection and from a restricted catchment area.

To a School which had been used to drawing pupils from all parts of the City as well as from parts of Gloucestershire and Somerset, this posed a very serious threat indeed. The Governors, who considered these proposals at their meeting in November 1963, were divided in their response. The Chairman reported that he had already told the Education Development Plan Sub-Committee that the Governors could not accept the proposals and he was supported by the Foundation Governors, who deeply regretted the loss of parents' right of choice and the inevitable change in the character of the School. The Representative Governors urged further consideration of the proposals which were still in their draft form.

It seemed that the stage for conflict was set, with the Foundation Governors only being asked to vote on the motion

> . . . that whereas the raising of the age of entry would not be opposed, all restriction of the catchment area or abolition of the entrance test would be opposed.

One Foundation Governor opposed the motion; the Representative Governors were not consulted.

A month later an extra-ordinary meeting of the Governors was called. A General Inspection was in progress and the Governors were called to meet the four Inspectors. Although a full and detailed report would be issued to the Minister, with a copy to the Governors, in due course, the Senior Inspector revealed that he had been pleased with the School. 'The girls were nice and unspoilt; the staff were a strong, well-qualified team led unobtrusively by the Head Mistress.' The current uncertainty over the School's future led Councillor Berrill to ask if the production of the Inspectors' report, which would obviously be complimentary, could be expedited.

The Inspectors were undoubtedly anxious about the adequacy of the buildings, the provision of textbooks and the level of staffing. Applications for additions to the estimates were made in the spring of 1964, but the question mark over the School's future led to delaying tactics by the Bristol Education Authority; similar behaviour was detected over the next two years as wiring and redecoration were delayed, furniture not replaced and stage lighting deferred. To their credit they did allow the appointment of an extra member of staff.

During the early months of 1964 there were meetings of parents and of Old Girls. In both cases there was enthusiastic support for the School's continuing in its existing form and petitions of protest against the proposed change in status. The Old Girls' signatures totalled 609.

In July the Governors discussed the proposals for the re-organisation of Secondary Education in Bristol, outlined in a letter from the Chief Education Officer, Mr Sylvester. He was anxious to negotiate with the Governors over the reduction of the School's catchment area. Whether at this stage any other future for the School was envisaged by the Education Department is not clear, but the Governors were advised forcefully by the Chairman to reject all compromise.

It was clear that if the School continued to take selected pupils from the proposed, restricted catchment area it could rely, at most, on 20 girls a year. It seemed that the School could not survive even if it were permitted to retain selection.

If it were to become a non-selective neighbourhood school with entry at 14+, the result would be a smaller school with a much wider ability range. Colston's Girls' School would no longer be able to offer the education it so carefully tailored to meet the needs of able girls. In the opinion of a small minority of Governors, traditions could change, staff could adapt and all would be for the best. The majority, however, could see nothing in the new plans that pleased them.

Immediate attempts to avoid the fate that awaited the School were undertaken. Questions as to the legality of the unilateral setting-aside of the Instruments of Government were raised; the contravention of the 1944 Education Act was hinted at. It was Mr C N Clarke who seems to have been the first to bring up the possibility of independence.

In the meantime, a bullish letter was drawn up by the Chairman in reply to that received from Mr Sylvester.

> At present parents residing in any part of Bristol have the right to choose to send their daughters to this School. If the children reach the required standard they are admitted.
>
> We are aware that it is now proposed to divide the City into areas and to prevent children from a primary school in one area proceeding to a secondary school in another. We deplore this restriction of the right of choice enjoyed under Section 76 of the Education Act of 1944.
>
> We understand from your letter that it is now proposed to allocate a catchment area to this School. We are not greatly concerned with this since we oppose the entire restriction proposal on principle.

Eleven Governors voted for this letter to be sent; three opposed it. The Hon W R S Bathurst signed it with his indecipherable flourish.

Earlier that year at the June Standing Committee of the Society of Merchant Venturers the Chairman had explained the difficulties his School faced. The Society was to spend a year considering whether the School would have a viable future if it were to become an independent fee-paying institution. If it were to become independent it would need considerable financial resources and if the Society were to back it, then it might find itself financially involved for an unknown amount. If it decided not to support the School and it were to close, the Society might be accused of betraying the School and its position as Trustees of Colston's Hospital Trust. The Society certainly did not wish to withdraw from another educational venture since it had abandoned the

Merchant Venturers' Technical College in 1949 and would have only the Boys' School left out of its numerous educational enterprises.

The School's case was pressed with great determination and it is said 'with excessive enthusiasm' by the Chairman and he did not lack support at the Hall. Monica Britton had been a Governor since 1954. Her husband, J H Britton, a Merchant Venturer and a great philanthropist, moved by his wife's great affection for and devotion to the School, added his voice to that of the Chairman. On 23 June 1965, by 31 votes to 8, after some inspired and impressive addresses by the School's supporters, the Society made a grant of £6,000 a year for 7 years to establish a new Independent School for Girls in Bristol.

The Governors, after their refusal to co-operate with Bristol Education Authority, thought it prudent to have professional legal advice. Messrs Osborne, Ward, Vassall, Abbott and Co were instructed to act on the Governors' behalf and on the second meeting of the Governors with their new legal advisors they encountered Mr Simon Awdry who was to become Clerk to the Governors after the School's independence.

The Governors had by now approached the Secretary of State for Education who expressed the opinion that he had no power to determine the dispute between the Governors and the Education Authority. He did, however, offer to meet the Governors if it would be helpful. In the discussions with his representatives Governors were encouraged to think that the Department of Education and Science would not oppose their seeking Independence for the School and the Governors, knowing that time was not on their side, were ready to give notice to determine the School's Voluntary Aided status. Two years should elapse before this took effect, but it would obviously be more convenient if the intake in September 1965 were the last to be financed by Bristol Education Authority.

It was suggested that two forms chosen by a selection test, and one form chosen on the basis of school reports, should enter the School in September 1965. This third form would be drawn from the whole City and Gloucestershire. The other two would be selected from the new catchment area, called North Central. This 'once and for all operation' drew in many applicants and the School had to employ extra secretarial help to deal with those who had to be offered places on the basis of reports rather than selection tests.

It was felt that if the School were to become independent it should, in return for its co-operation over the 1965 entry, seek some reciprocal help from Bristol. The retention of the Playing Field was a major issue. It had been bought by the Society in 1910 but it had been sold to the Corporation in 1952 for £6,500 as part of the Voluntary Aid Settlement. Now the land was needed; would the Corporation be generous? The position of girls already in the School and paid for by the Education Authority also needed protection. It

29. Mr Cyril Clarke, Chairman of Governors 1924–1957.

30. Small garden plots were made on top of the air raid shelters.

31. Commemoration Day, 1956.

32. Miss Sarah Dunn, Head Mistress 1954–1980.

33. *Miss Kathleen Murphy with a Sixth Form physics group in 1956.*

34. *Colston's Birthday, 1956.*

35. A typical staircase and stained glass window.

36. Opening of the new Ryland Library in 1957 by the Bishop of Bristol watched by Miss Dunn and Mr Cyril Clarke.

37. Charter Day, 1956. Fourth Year girls receive the Colston shilling.

38. Junior String Group, 1962.

39. Language laboratory with Miss Jeanne Stoneley in the 1960s.

40. Swimming Gala at Bristol North Baths, 1960s.

41. The Dolphin Block, 1971.

42. *The impressive Cheltenham Road entrance.*

43. The laying of the Sixth Form Block foundation stone by Mr T Lloyd Robinson in 1978. Mr John Gordon, Chairman of the Governors 1974–1984 is standing behind Miss Dunn.

44. An English lesson with Miss Marea Morgan in the new Sixth Form Block, 1980.

45. Ninetieth Birthday Celebrations, July 8 1981. The staff versus sixth form croquet teams.

46. Miss Ann Parkin, Head Mistress 1981–1989.

47. The new Gym nears completion, 1983.

48. Hockey players outside the Pavilion, 1983.

49. School choir with Miss Anne Hughes and Mrs Sheila Linfield at the Llangollen International Eisteddfod.

50. Germany: a school holiday in 1986.

51. Mrs Judith Franklin, Head Mistress 1989–.

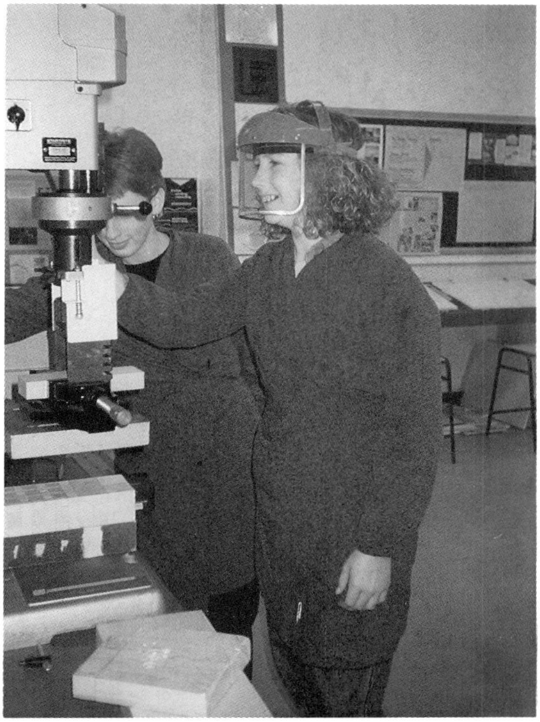

52. The pupils at work in the Design and Technology workshop opened in 1988.

53. The Information Technology room. The Apple Macintosh network was installed in 1990.

54 & 55. Dr George Carey, Bishop of Bath and Wells (Archbishop of Canterbury Elect) at the Centenary Assembly, January 18 1991.

was hoped that their education would continue to be funded by Bristol until it reached its normal conclusion. These proposals were put to the Education Authority and, with minor alterations, they were accepted. Mr Sylvester, the Chief Education Officer, and the Deputy Town Clerk, Mr Tomlinson, seem to have tried hard to make the severing of connections as amicable as possible. A letter, delivered by hand on 18 May 1965, agrees to all the assurances sought by the Governors. The School was to move towards Independence. A brief paragraph at the end of Mr Tomlinson's long letter is a salutory reminder of what the fate of the School might have been.

> If the Governors decide not to seek Independent Status for the School the Corporation would wish it to continue for at least two further years after the school year 1965-66, and would be willing to maintain it, but no pupils will be admitted to the School after the entry in September 1965.

The die was cast; at this stage the Society of Merchant Venturers had not held its historic vote in the School's favour.

The School has always been fortunate in its benefactors, but never has this been more evident than at the time of its independence. Generous donations were made to ensure that places could be offered to intelligent girls whose parents could not otherwise afford to send them to a fee-paying school. Scholarships and Bursaries were endowed by the gifts of John James, the Hon W R S Bathurst, Mr & Mrs J H Britton, Mrs Robert Bernays and Mr R R S Harvey.

There is little one can do at this distance to recreate the tensions and anxieties that must have plagued Miss Dunn through those uncertain months. On the face of things few people will have realised what difficulties she encountered. School events continued untouched by the deliberations of the Governors. Certainly Miss Dunn had other concerns which could not be neglected, and the welfare of pupils and the maintenance of staff morale must have had high priority at that time.

On 6 July 1965 the Governors formally passed the five Resolutions which would set the School on its road to independence. A draft scheme was published, made by the Secretary of State for Education and Science under Section 18 of the Charities Act 1960, in which the new Instruments of Government were set out and, after its acceptance by the Government, was sealed on 15 February 1966.

The Chairman, the Hon W R S Bathurst, having successfully campaigned for the School's independence, resigned. His service to the School was unique and the gratitude owed to him inestimable. He remained a Governor until his death in a road accident in 1970, a few days before the opening of the Dolphin Block. He was an aristocrat; an old Etonian with two Oxford degrees: one in History, the other in Chemistry, and a member of the Athenaeum.

Before the School became Independent in September 1966, a new Governing Body was created to prepare for the momentous change. It met for the first time on April 1, 1966 at Merchants' Hall.

The majority of Governors was still drawn from the Society of Merchant Venturers or its nominees, but the University and the City of Bristol still had their members. The Hon W R S Bathurst remained Chairman of the 'old' board, overseeing the day to day running of the School through the final year of its Voluntary Aided status, while Mr R S W Clarke was appointed as Chairman of the new board. The Clerk to the Governors was now a Solicitor, rather than the Head Mistress's Secretary. This change alone signalled the more onerous responsibilities of this body of men and women.

The duties of this new Governing body were substantially related to finance. The fees to be charged to parents of the first intake were set; they were to be £50 a term. The generous settlement by Bristol Corporation for the fees of existing girls enabled the Governors to feel optimistic for the first few years of Independence. Unlike the flat rate school fee, the Corporation would pay an enhanced amount for girls over sixteen which was to be very much to the advantage of a school with an academic intake and a well-established sixth form.

Although the school buildings had never been owned by Bristol Corporation, all equipment they had purchased still belonged to them. Again the Corporation behaved most generously, writing-off the value of any equipment over three years old and charging reduced values for the remainder. The entire cost to the Governors was £1,448. The Governors were now wholly responsible for the Income and Expenditure of the School and it became necessary to produce budgetary estimates. This new aspect of their work was the responsibility of the Finance Sub-Committee. This Committee was empowered to appoint an Accounts Assistant; the School's accountant was of the opinion that no Bursar was necessary.

The Head Mistress prepared a School prospectus. By today's standards it was modest; it contained one photograph (of the Ryland Library), a list of teaching staff and of governors and four pages of text. It was obviously intended to be used for several years as the fees were recorded on a separate sheet.

The prospectus briefly outlines the School's debt to Edward Colston and the Merchant Venturers. It goes on to state the ethos of the School:

> Care is taken that in the case of each individual girl the timetable contains a balance of arts and science subjects, so that no final choice of course, and hence ultimately of career, need be taken before the sixth form.

Somewhat briefer than the National Curriculum Council documents, this statement embodies much of what they sought to establish over twenty years later.

Acknowledging the generosity of the benefactors, the prospectus indicates the existence of bursaries. The social emphasis of the School would inevitably change as fee-paying pupils gradually outnumbered Scholarship girls, but the establishment of a means of entry to girls whose parents could otherwise not afford fees went a long way towards protecting its essential character.

The Bursary Fund would become the focus of much generosity in future years; the estate of Miss Eveline Jenner, a pupil in the school from 1907 to 1920, who became Head Mistress of St Margaret's School, Henleaze, funded the Jenner Scholarships in 1985; the Wolfson Foundation's £30,000 in 1985, as well as lesser but no less valuable gifts, would be directed towards the provision of assistance to girls with good academic potential.

The School began the year in September 1966 as an independent, fee-paying grammar school and has retained that status. It was the first school in England to take this adventurous step from Voluntary Aided status to independence. The new entrants were fee-payers; gradually, as the years went by, they progressed through the School until there were no scholarship girls left.

Exchanges and expeditions continued to flourish. The Bordeaux and Hanover exchanges retained their popularity and school received the French and German visitors with interest. In the autumn of 1966, a group of Sixth Formers went for the first time to a ten days' conference, on 'Social and Cultural Relations between East and West' in Sonnenberg. It was a new experience for most of the girls to join a group whose other members were Germans and Swedes. From 1967 onwards, the Sixth Form Biologists went on a week's course for Field Work to one of the study centres. In 1975, Classical Civilisation was taken for the first time as a subject at Advanced level standard and earlier in the year the group had been to Greece. From that time there was an expedition to Italy or Greece in alternate years, so that every candidate had been to one of the countries during her 'A' level course. This was an excellent opportunity to see in the present what remains of the glory of the past.

Nearer home, field work played an integral part in the geography syllabus. The First Forms did a simple land use study of the school locality and a walk round the old city. The Third Forms visited South Wales to see changes in the iron and steel industries: and later in the year made a study of Cotswold villages. The Fourth Form began the year with a survey of the business district of Broadmead, later investigated the River Trym and in the summer visited the coast to carry out a beach study and observe the effect of tourism on a coastal area. The Fifth Form visited Cwmbran New Town in the spring. The Advanced level groups continued their week's field trips until 1977, after which economic pressure replaced these by day expeditions.

In the spring of 1976, the first energetic school skiing holiday took place in Fieberbrunn in Austria, and was such a success that others followed to Leysin in Switzerland in 1977 and to the Italian Dolomites in 1978.

The idea of going to the United States of America for a whole year, necessarily involving a third year in the Sixth Form before Advanced level could be taken, began to be less attractive. A new scheme, introduced in 1976, allowed eighteen girls to go to America for a month in the spring and their hostesses to return in July. They spent a short time in New York and then went to families and to school in Philadelphia for the rest of the month. They were able to make comparisons of the two ways of life that were very illuminating.

Drama continued to be a very important part of school life. Plays were performed at School and girls took part in productions at various boys' schools. It would be impossible to give a detailed account of all dramatic activity, but there were a great many productions in the Seventies. There was usually a Third Form play, a full production with very disciplined rehearsals; a school play; a house drama Festival, in which the four Houses produced and acted one act plays after Advanced level. The School produced an endless supply of actresses for the boys' schools; because they had had so much more acting experience than the boys they were conspicuously good.

All these productions gave great opportunities to many girls, not only to those acting but also to those concerned with costume, scenery, lighting and many activities behind the scenes. Girls regularly paid visits to theatres in Bristol, Bath, Stratford-on-Avon and London, often to see productions of plays they were studying.

Music played a more and more important part in school life during these years. Every year, for the Senior Choir, there were the staple engagements in the Autumn Term concerned with Prize Day, a variety of Commemoration activities and the Association evenings. The Spring Term usually saw joint musical productions with one of the boys' schools; '*The Messiah*' was sung with the Grammar School in 1967, Carl Orff's '*Carmina Burana*' were sung with Colston's School in 1968.

A more unusual event occurred in 1969 when fifteen of the choir sang a grace before the annual banquet of the Society of Merchant Venturers at Merchants' Hall. In 1972 they sang for the first time in the Colston Hall, with the Grammar School and Queen Elizabeth's Hospital. That year they were on radio in a service from Horfield Baptist Church. In 1977 they sang '*Carmina Burana*' in the School Hall with Queen Elizabeth's Hospital. This was later made into a record and the profits went to the School building fund. In a 'Sunday Half Hour' programme from Cotham Parish Church the choir took part in the massed hymn singing and sang alone the spiritual '*Steal Away*'. In 1979 Senior Choir members joined senior pupils from other Avon schools in the First Night concert of the Bristol Proms at the Colston Hall. Four hundred and four voices sang '*Carmina Burana*'; the third performance of this popular work in eleven years!

The orchestra increased in size and provided a good number of girls for the Bristol Secondary Schools' Orchestras, including, in 1970, the leader of the

Senior Orchestra; one girl secured a place in the National Youth Orchestra. Recorder and guitar groups were also formed in school. Many girls can look back with gratitude to the good grounding and enjoyment they had in making music.

The main games of hockey and netball in winter and tennis, cricket, athletics and swimming in summer continued, the teams meeting varied success in different years. In swimming, the School has always done remarkably well and in the year of independence in the Bristol Schools' Swimming Association's Final Gala Colston's girls won five trophies. Four girls represented the School in the Final of the English Schools' Swimming Association Championship and were placed second. Four girls received Woodcock Trust Awards for outstanding work in Life Saving and/or Swimming.

From September 1971 the seven Houses were reduced to four, renamed Cabot/Canynge, Chatterton/Drake, Trelawney/Grenville, and Tyndale/ Brunel, and this made the assembling of teams for inter-house competitions much easier, as captains had a greater choice. In the early 70s, the Sixth Form, and then the Fifths, were allowed a choice of activity on Games afternoons. Some hardy spirits went sailing, many went to the ice rink and more played badminton as alternatives to team games at the field. Gymnastics had always been popular with many girls. In 1973–4 it was possible to enter for tests for awards of the British Amateur Gymnastics Association and there were many successful entrants and enthusiasm was high.

During those years new clubs and activities began. In 1966 the Social Service Unit was initiated. Members of the Sixth Form took part in many kinds of social work: with old people, by shopping, gardening, hospital visiting: with youth clubs and junior play groups in areas where there might otherwise have been none: with handicapped children, both in term time and during the holidays.

In 1968 the Science Club began to publicise the many careers in science open to women. There were presentations on engineering, medical, veterinary, pharmaceutical and dental careers and on chemical and radio-nuclear research. Two Science Society meetings were held that year: one was to show the performance of the new film projector, at the other, a member of staff, the only woman member of the team which discovered and explored a new cave in the Mendips, talked on the proper use of caving equipment and showed slides of underground rock formations.

In 1967 some Sixth Formers entered for the first time the Hispanic Council Prize Examinations. Three girls who began Spanish ab initio in the Sixth Form were gratified to be commended in the Late Beginners' section and in the Latin-American section. Two years later, the Rotary Club of Bristol began its Public Speaking Competitions. We were delighted to win both the Senior and Junior Cups in that year and the next.

In School, a dinner hour Chess Club was started in 1967 – and two years later a Political Club. A team took part in a Top of the Form competition on television in 1966. This was exciting for the contestants and it was remarkable that such a lot of cables were necessary. The School won in the first round but was beaten in the second.

The General Election of 1974 was mirrored in School. Four parties were represented – Conservative, Liberal, Labour and Communist. Each candidate spoke to the whole School in Assembly and addressed individual classes in form time, known at this time as Period 8. The election was carried out with all proper procedures. The result was, against the national trend, a win for the Conservatives, though the Liberal candidate gained a large number of votes.

The School magazine, which had not changed in appearance since 1952, received a new format in 1967–8. The cover was different every year, usually designed by one of the girls. Photographs could now be included as could reproductions of design and craft work. In that year there took place the first of many annual 'write ins'. A theme was given and girls came to the Hall and wrote down their own thoughts anonymously. A selection of this work was then included in the magazine and it was marked by freshness and spontaneity. The theme for this first 'write in' was 'Love'.

Each form decided its own charity and girls have been very generous over the years and ingenious in devising ways to persuade others to give to their particular choice. In 1966 however the Sixth Form felt that it would be a good idea to 'adopt' a child whose care and upbringing could be helped by the united efforts of the School. The deputy Head Girl heard about a Home in Hong Kong started by three English girls in 1964 for handicapped children – the House of Loving Faithfulness. The Home takes in children who would not have much chance in life otherwise. The girl whom Colston's adopted, Fung Tai, was epileptic and spastic and could not walk, but she was full of energy, loved the younger children in the Home and was delighted to receive presents. As the years have gone by, Fung Tai has naturally become an adult, but she will never be fit to leave the Home. Several people from Colston's have visited the Home and seen her, so that a personal link has been maintained.

Within a year of Independence Miss Dunn and the Governors were addressing the School's accommodation problems. Setting aside the threat of a new overhead road system 'encircling' the School, the restricted inner city site offered few opportunities for building expansion. Throughout 1967 various options for development were examined and rejected; the blessed disappearance of the overhead road scheme focussed the Governors' minds on using the car park site, more usually known as Pugsley's Yard. This site was expensive to build on as the levels between Cheltenham Lane and Station Road rose rapidly and it concealed an underground culvert so that piling alone was likely to cost £9,000 of the £100,000 the Governors felt able to assign to the project. However, it did offer the School the opportunity to acquire a building which would meet its curricular needs for some years to come, so the decision to proceed was taken in 1968.

When term began in September 1969 the only visible sign of what was to be a long process was an enormous muddy hole! Soon, however, more encouraging signs appeared and by July 1970 an obvious building emerged at Station Road level, with a staff car park beneath on piers, connected to the original School by a walkway at first floor level. It was strange to see a room disappear and be replaced by a wide staircase and the Domestic Science room lose a third of its width to the walkway.

The new building, named the Dolphin block, contained art studios and a photographic dark room at first floor level. At second floor level there were music rooms, a recording room and a Home Economics department where each girl worked in a simulated kitchen. There was also a dining area where entertaining could be practised. On the same floor there was a large assembly room which could be used for choir and orchestra practices and large meetings. This could be converted into two large classrooms by the use of double sliding partitions which formed a central corridor. The whole structure was modern in outline, the building being of reinforced concrete with brick cladding.

It had been hoped that the Dolphin building would be ready for use by the beginning of the September term 1970, but the difficulties in construction meant that it was not ready until November 23, 1970 when the rooms on the walkway level were used for the first time: and the whole building by January 1, 1971. With the Dolphin block, the School had accommodation and equipment suitable for modern teaching methods. The stark new lines of the building did not please everyone but nearly everyone liked the interior. The Magazine for 1971 records the reactions.

> 'The Dolphin Block consists of teaching rooms and pleasure places'
> 'There is also a very extensive music department, with wasteful and extravagant carpet'
> 'I wish there were lifts'
> 'A rather embarrassing name'
> '. . . from the outside it looks very superior and expensive'
> '. . . it is modern, clean and ugly'

It was sad that Mr Bathurst, who had fought so hard and with such success for the School's independence, was killed in a road accident on September 10 1970, before the Dolphin block was occupied.

Another change, though on a much smaller scale, concerned the Hall. It is a fine room but the noise from the traffic outside used sometimes to drown the words of a speaker on the platform. What is more, some small pieces of the stained glass had fallen out of the windows during war-time bombing. The repair of the windows and the fitting of double glazing was a great improvement. The School Association raised funds for this work and the absence of outside noise in the Hall was a great benefit to everyone.

The main building facing Cheltenham Road, with its 'streaky bacon' brick effects, has been held in affection by many of its occupants, but often with a certain amount of ridicule too. Now, early in 1977, the School was placed on the list of buildings of Special Architectural or Historical Interest by the Secretary of State for the Environment. Victorian architecture was back in fashion!

As early as 1975 the Governors were considering the implications of Boys' Independent Schools admitting girls, predominantly to their sixth forms. The decision made by Bristol Grammar School to become co-educational was discussed in detail in 1979 and the Governors explored, albeit tentatively, the possibility of a co-educational rôle for Colston's Girls' School. The Colston's Hospital Trust would not limit its freedom to pursue this, nor to consider full amalgamation with a boys' school. It is pleasing to note the Governors' scepticism about nominal co-education based on limited quotas and their predisposition to retain and protect the School's single-sex status.

However, it was clear that it was necessary to make the sixth form an attractive option for girls and parents and it was no doubt a source of confidence to Miss Dunn that the newly-commissioned Sixth Form block was nearing its completion. As early as 1973, two years after the opening of the Dolphin block, the School's needs were once again being identified and costed. At this stage, new kitchens, dining facilities and showers in the gymnasium were seen as priorities; by the time an Appeal was launched in 1977, the preference was for sixth form accommodation.

The proceeds from the School Fete that year, a most encouraging £2,500, went towards the Appeal, and also £2,000 from the 1978 Fete. A year later, over £90,000 had been raised. Work on the new building began in the Summer Term of 1978. A tremendous amount of enterprise and hard work went into raising the money, apart from generous donations and covenants. A book of recipes was compiled, typed and illustrated by Sixth Formers. It was aptly titled 'Colston's Appealing Recipes'. Other very successful events were an auction, an 'As New' sale and a jumble sale. T-shirts, badges, note paper and sherry glasses, all bearing the dolphin symbol, were on sale; sponsored walks, a sponsored slim, concerts and dances were organised throughout the 1978–9 school year and by the summer only £10,000 was still to be found. The Appeal was in the hands of Mrs Sheila Rawcliffe who through her energy, guidance and persuasion finally managed to exceed the target of £125,000.

The foundation stone of the Sixth Form block was laid by the Master of the Society of Merchant Venturers, Mr T Lloyd Robinson, after the Prize Giving in 1978. In his address, the Chairman of the Governors, Mr John Gordon, had been able to announce that the basic costs of the new building could be met from funds either in hand or promised. The opening of the building took place on January 16, 1980 when the Lord Lieutenant of Gloucestershire performed the ceremony.

The plaque records the School's debt of gratitude to Jack and Monica Britton who had been such generous benefactors and after whom the building is named. Two of the rooms are named; one in memory of Roger Clarke and the other as a mark of gratitude to Miss Dunn, whose decision to retire at the end of 1980 had already been conveyed to the Governors.

The first Chairman of the Governors of the School after independence was Mr R S W Clarke, who had been a Governor since 1948, as had both his father and mother before him. When the pre-1966 Board of Governors went out of office, it was a sign of his skill and the trust he inspired that so many of the old Governing body literally signed on again for the task of leading the newly-independent school. A man of broad and liberal education and astute judgement, it was said that his observations on a balance sheet or on a performance in the theatre were equally penetrating, and delivered with a critical acuity as unyielding as his courtesy. Chairman until 1974, he died in 1980.

The Vice-Chairman after 1966 was Monica Britton. Once committed to the project of independence she was a doughty protagonist as she recognised the difficulties of the situation as clearly as she saw the advantages. She saw the School flourish after 1966 and it played an important part in her full life and she loved it. In her last illness the news of school life brought to her by John Gordon, the then Chairman, gave her joy; she always called it 'our 'School'.

John Gordon, who was to retire from the Board as late as 1990, was a Governor from 1966 and Chairman from 1974 to 1984. His loyalty and affection for the School knew no bounds and he is remembered as much for his good-humoured acceptance of face-paint at a School Fete as for his great wisdom and balanced judgement in Governors' meetings. An accountant by profession, John Gordon betrayed none of the pedantry traditionally associated with that calling; he spoke with measured eloquence and wrote exquisite prose, as many tributes composed by him for the School magazine will testify.

The School has always been fortunate in the quality and loyalty of its staff. Many women made their entire teaching career at Colston's Girls' School, retiring as the head of the department to which they had been appointed as a junior teacher thirty five or forty years before. As the pattern of professional development changes it is unlikely that the School will see careers like theirs again. It must be recorded how many of these splendid and devoted women reached their retirement during Miss Dunn's headship, itself notable for its length.

At the end of the Summer Term 1954, Miss Gibbon and Miss Rashley retired. Miss Gibbon had been Senior French Mistress for 30 years and had joined the School in 1917. She had been director of countless school productions and most memorably, the star of many Commemoration staff plays. Miss Rashley had been Miss Openshaw's assistant and so was a link with the very early days of the School. She had been at the School for 29 years and Clerk to the Governors since 1928. Miss Gillard, the Senior Mathematician, retired after 35 years; Miss Boughton left to become Head Mistress of a large girls' school in North Borneo. Miss Jenkins left her post as French Mistress after 23 years. Miss Page left in 1962 after 41 years' service in the Biology department. Miss Goaman left in 1966, after twenty years in the Craft department.

Miss Murphy, Senior Science teacher, left after 22 years in 1968. Miss Tuson left in 1969 after 19 years' service. A member of the Society of Scribes, Miss Tuson designed the School Crest which appears on the dustwrapper of this history and was the illuminator of several works, including a Book of Collects, in the Head Mistress's collection. Miss Pick left, to be married, after 26 years in the Domestic Science department. Miss Bowell, an Old Girl, left the Mathematics department after 19 years' service; Mrs Harding, Senior Chemistry Mistress and Head of Science, after 27 years. Miss Agostini, an Old Girl, who taught French part time from 1949 to 1976, felt it was time to give up at the age of 73! In 1978 Miss Stoneley retired after 31 years, 24 as Head of Modern Languages. In the same year Mrs Austen retired after 23 years, latterly as Head of the Home Economics department.

The level of staff commitment to the School and particularly to the well-being of the girls, is illustrated most aptly by one example which must serve to stand for many. In 1975 the Houghton Committee recommended a substantial salary increase for teachers. The award was backdated. At that time many members of staff donated part or all of their retrospective award towards bursaries for girls in the fifth and sixth forms to ensure the continuance of their education. Forty pupils were enabled to stay at school, in spite of the sharp increase of fees brought about by the Houghton Award.

Miss Sarah Dunn's retirement in December 1980 brought to an end an era exemplified by startling change and extraordinary stability. The confidence of the School was hardly shaken in those eventful years; much of this must be attributed to the strength and inner certainty of its Head Mistress. This inspired others to champion and defend the School of which she was the calm centre. The presentations to her from the School, the parents, the staff and the Governors showed the regard and affection in which she was held. Her care for the School as an institution and for its individual members never wavered. After independence, her administrative and financial skills were used to the full and her decisions were of great importance. The School that Miss Parkin was to inherit combined a reverence for the past with a readiness to adopt new ways for the future.

MISS PARKIN

Ann Parkin took up the headship of Colston's Girls' in January 1981. A fortnight later, on February 3, the old gymnasium burnt down. A more sensational beginning to her career as Head Mistress could scarcely have been imagined.

Ann Cecilia Parkin was a very different personality from Sarah Dunn. Born in Portsmouth on 26th January 1940, she moved to Bradford in 1946 when her father, a civil servant and Inspector of Taxes, rose up the career ladder. She was the youngest by far of four children, and the two big brothers had a considerable influence upon her development, especially when the family was evacuated, without Mr Parkin, during the war years. There was also an older sister, who later became a deputy head. When Miss Parkin was 14 the family moved south again to Dover, where she completed her schooling at Dover Grammar School for Girls. In 1959 she went to the University of Hull to read a BSc Joint Honours degree in Chemistry and Pure Mathematics. For a girl whose earliest recalled ambition was to be a bus conductor, this represented a slightly more exacting aspiration. Like many another, she embarked upon a Post-Graduate Certificate of Education because she had no idea of what she wanted to do, and was startled to discover how rewarding teaching could be.

In 1963 she accepted a junior post at Croydon High, one of the largest schools in the Girls' Public Day School Trust. By the time she left, she had served under three headmistresses, and experienced a wide variety of responsibilities, including Head of Science, Third Mistress and Senior Mistress. She had worked for many years in a young, close-knit, harmonious team of staff, had a considerable sense of mischief and would have been the first to agree that action was her forte rather than cerebral analysis. She had an immensely practical approach to life.

All schools depend for their ethos upon the personality and convictions of the head teacher, girls' schools more so than boys'. Sarah Dunn had presided over CGS for virtually 27 years. Girls who had been at the School in her early years remembered her for the hushed quiet which floated along the corridors in her wake, and for the muted but inescapable insistence on high moral standards. She had seemed a remote and daunting figure, despite her accessibility. Those who knew her towards the end of her regime were aware of her striking wit, her dramatic flair, her incisive turns of phrase and the slight hesitancy of speech which came with her selection of the mot juste. She was always able to inspire silence with meaning.

Ann Parkin, on the other hand, had to train herself to walk rather than run up stairs. Her natural inclination was to roll up her sleeves, so to speak, and sort out difficulties by example rather than by explanation. If she hesitated, it was because she could not find the right word, whereas Miss Dunn would have been rifling through a mental thesaurus. Miss Parkin was characterised by great curiosity about human nature, considerable intuitive insight into human dilemmas, and a rare combination of idealism and decisiveness. All this was concealed beneath an unassuming demeanour.

What she found at Colston's in the first relatively tranquil days before the fire impressed her. Although the schools of the Girls' Public Day School Trust have a fine reputation for academic excellence, with what such standards imply for every kind of talent, Colston's seemed to possess a special quality. Its traditions were very strongly maintained. There was an enthusiasm and confidence in the pupils, and a strong sense of communal purpose in the staff and pupils which was new to her. Many of the staff had been in post for years and worked closely together. A number were ex-pupils of the School, and their own daughters in turn were added to the roll.

One of the more distinctive traditions – the 'Misrule' of Commemoration, in which the senior girls satirised the staff, and the staff accepted it – might explain some of the unusual rapport between staff and pupils. This had to be related to the family atmosphere prevalent where mothers, daughters, cousins and nieces all underwent the same educational experience, whether as staff or as pupils: an atmosphere compounded of high and exacting expectations, and profound commitment to the institution.

For example, when Frances Martin retired in July 1985, she had been a pupil, had been Head of Home Economics for fifteen years, and had just overseen her granddaughter's induction as a pupil. (She was succeeded by another old girl, Anne Gibbs.) Olive Hoskins retired in 1987, after 40 years association with the school, her daughter Jane having successfully completed her education at the school in 1982. All three daughters of Judy Chard, still a member of the English department and an old girl, were in the School at one point during the decade of the 1980s. Jill Clough, also a member of the English department for a while, had two daughters at School. Members of academic staff who, during the 1980s, brought their daughters with them to school in the mornings included: the Braziers, Jenny Geyl, Marian Hunt, Anne-Marie Keith-Smith, Ann Lewis, Jean Littler, Heather Kippin, Nicola Mortimer, Leona Nickless, Elizabeth Perry, Jenny Reese, and Rosemary Routledge. Mrs MacKay, a member of the kitchen staff, was one of the first to take advantage of the Government Assisted Places Scheme for her daughter; Brenda Allen, one of the office staff, saw her daughter through the School, also using the GAP Scheme and another old girl, Gillian Forward, not only joined the finance office but became a fee-paying parent. Another member of the administration to enrol her daughter was Brenda Singleton.

It was inevitable that in a school with so many long-standing members of staff, mothers and daughters were taught by the same generation of teachers; and ex-pupils became the colleagues of those who had taught them during their formative years. Apart from deepening the loyalty and affection in which the School was held, this characteristic also confirmed a social trend: the increasing desire and necessity for women to develop professional as well as domestic roles; the growing importance attached to a good education for girls, and a willingness to pay for it; and the success of the School over the years in educating women to work at a professional level.

Miss Parkin perceived in the staff a blend of the formal and the casual which other institutions would not have accepted. One might have met almost any Second Mistress of the time wearing jeans; Pat Jones, for 16 years Head of Art, exercised initiative by travelling across the Dolphin walkway to the art rooms on roller skates; Marea Morgan, Head of English, would wear dungarees if she felt in the mood. Jean Williams, who taught Chemistry, invariably inspired envy by making Marks and Spencer suits look as if purchased at Jaeger.

Miss Parkin recognised that she had inherited from Miss Dunn a style of leadership which had been liberating. Miss Dunn had been able to recruit and retain teachers of striking ability – most of them women; and she had allowed them to work in an environment which was at once secure and stimulating. She had been an outstanding example of a particular kind of charismatic head mistress, who ruled from a core of personal authority undoubtedly intensified across the 27 years of her reign.

In such circumstances, staff, pupils and parents form very clear expectations about what headmistresses should be like, and for a character less self-assured than Ann Parkin, the task would have been daunting. As it was, the culture shock for everyone was considerable, for although her ideals were in tune with what the School needed, her style was very different. Miss Dunn was self-evidently an exceptionally talented and intelligent person. She had an astonishingly wide range of aptitudes. Miss Parkin's most important quality was her ability to perceive talent and to harness it to the goal of developing the School. In the terminology of modern management systems, Miss Dunn's was a 'personal' culture, whereas Miss Parkin's was a 'task' culture. These differences of emphasis permeated the entire school. The fire which was obviously a disaster served as a line of demarcation between the past and the present.

It also coincided with some significant external social changes: anxieties about the relationship between schools and industry; the advent of GCSE; the Education Reform Act of 1988, and all the debate preceding it; deep unrest amongst teachers in the nation at large; and a revolution in management and marketing which reached every independent business and eventually the great national institutions – including the education system – the revolution which the generic term of Thatcherism will probably explain.

MISS PARKIN

Miss Parkin embarked upon her new post with some simple and clear ideals to sustain her: the desire to ensure that every girl attending the School should have breadth of opportunity, security and fulfilment; and that on leaving Colston's she should be able to look back upon her education with pride and satisfaction. In her first Prize Day speech in September 1981, Miss Parkin spoke of her belief that man 'is an active force in society and not a passive tool to be manipulated . . . We hope that our pupils will have the courage to carry through their convictions and become forces for good in their own fields . . . Each pupil is an individual and it is important that there should be scope for personal development.'

She had also formulated a conviction which reinforced what was inherent in the Colstonian tradition: a belief in the quality of education, for those able to benefit regardless of their social background; with emphasis on what girls in particular needed if they were to thrive. She was deeply affected by the School's history and the devotion evinced by successive generations. The vitality of the Old Girls' Association entertained and impressed her.

She was, in addition, committed to scientific and technological education. She saw no conflict between the need to bring new ideas into the curriculum and management of the School and the maintenance of its traditional values. Innovation of the appropriate kind would emphasise its importance as an educator of working women, and supplier of rôle models for success.

In the few weeks before the fire, Miss Parkin observed the considerable ingenuity expended by the staff in order to operate a complex timetable within a confined site. The old gym in doubling as a dining hall posed a number of problems: for the timetable, for the kitchen staff, for the staff who had to control behaviour during lunchtime; for hygiene; and most of all, for girls who had gym lessons after lunch, and had to hope that the floor was clean. This was just one symptom of the constraints under which the School was run – not only of space but of finance. What was most striking was that everyone was remarkably resilient. Superb facilities might make the Head Mistress's life easier in marketing the School, but did not ensure the quality of teaching or learning.

In such circumstances, the impact of the fire upon the School was far greater than just the loss of a facility; for that facility in itself represented a crux of problem and resolution.

Similar problems were to arise in later years: by 1983 the leaks in the roof of the Dolphin block could no longer be dealt with by simple repair. A new roof was needed. Instead of a new roof, a new storey was added, with new science laboratories and classrooms.

In Station Road, behind the School, British Rail had sold railway land to developers to raise capital. Miss Parkin realised that the only way for the School to develop further – for that supremely temporary building, the Annexe (now 73 years old) to be replaced – was for the School to purchase the land as soon as it became available, just as land had been bought along the Cheltenham Road, in the hope of improving the School's premises. By March 1989, when Miss Parkin left, negotiations were well in hand for the purchase of half the land, and provisional plans for buildings had been drawn up. Such possibilities created stress as well as relieving it, for they imposed the need to cope with changed perspectives. The very existence of the fresh opportunity implied a demand that it must be exploited.

The fire coincided with the introduction of the Government Assisted Places Scheme. This had been embraced with enthusiasm by the Governors, for it provided the chance of reuniting the School with its founding principles. Under the conditions of the Scheme, schools of a designated size and quality could apply for a number of places which would receive means-tested assistance from central Government towards the payment of fees. Instead of 'ability to pay' being the chief determinant of entry, ability itself could be rewarded. Once again, girls from impoverished homes could join the School, their fees being subsidised.

At the time of the fire, the staff had been preparing for the Entrance Examination, and were considering the criteria by which the new intake should be admitted. The new Head Mistress had expected that her chief priority in the first months of 1981 would be to interview candidates and review the curriculum to ensure that the new pupils would be properly provided for. Instead, she was precipitated into activity of an intensely practical nature. It was congenial to her, and useful in that it enabled her to get to know a lot of people very quickly. However, the need for practical decisions subsumed any ability to make other decisions.

In fact, the aims which presented themselves to Miss Parkin were potentially conflicting, but such was the pressure of time that there was none in which to agonize. The School's founders had settled its ethos. It was to provide for girls to earn their own living by selecting those academically able to benefit from such an education. Independence had made parental ability to pay equally important as a consideration, and those for whom the School was most beneficial were those most disadvantaged, who had most struggle with finding funds for fees. The new award schemes restored the original intentions; moreover, alongside the Government Assisted Places there were to be School Assisted Places from a fund set up by John James, a Bristol philanthropist. Whereas with the Government Assisted Places parental income was the criterion for the Award (with knowledge that the government would find whatever funds were necessary) School Assisted Places would require more complex calculations, since resources would be more obviously finite.

In conflict with this was the need to appeal for large sums of money; and money to build what many would have regarded as a luxury. There was no doubt that the gym would have to be replaced, in order to retain the School's attractiveness in the competitive market; and yet pupils were being admitted from the other end of the economic spectrum.

One of the advantages of emergency is that it focuses loyalty. The Appeal Committee was formed from representatives of staff, parents, girls, governors and old girls. Miss Dunn returned to help, with her experience of the previous Appeal. (In this she successfully over-rode the truism absorbed by all retiring head teachers: that you leave your successor a clear field. Only the scale of need compelled her to come back.) John Gordon took the chair, Mrs Rickards and Mrs White spoke for the staff, Mrs Pope and Mr Hamer represented the parents and Victoria Mortimer and Sian Williams were the girls' voices. Margaret Bond was the Old Girls' representative. Kay Clewett was the Head of PE with the task of recommending what would best fit the bill. The Committee was typical in its format. Kay Clewett had been Head Girl at the end of the Second World War, and Victoria Mortimer was the incumbent Head Girl. Her mother, Nicola, was a member of staff (the Art Department). Sheila White was an Old Girl who became a most distinguished Head of Classics, pioneering the Cambridge Latin Project, and becoming Chief Examiner in the subject after her retirement.

In the first days after the fire there were several meetings, amidst the filth of the ashes which seemed to spread everywhere. All visitors took to leaving their shoes outside the Head Mistress's room in order to spare the carpet. Outside the door would be an array of shoes belonging to the police, the insurance assessors, the legal adviser, the chairman of the Board of Governors, the Head Mistress herself – whilst inside they sat shoeless around the huge, gleaming table.

There was a horrifying gap between the insured value of the old building and the cost of comparable replacement, let alone what was desirable. Every kind of alternative was costed, from the ideal (which incorporated a swimming pool as well as sports hall) to the commonplace. Another dining room was also needed as a matter of urgency. Priorities were not easy to determine and were limited by financial constraints. At length it was decided that the Hall should be the size of 3 badminton courts, built to as high a standard as could be achieved. The swimming pool would have to remain a dream.

The Appeal was to be organised internally, since the previous Appeal had been so successful. This would reduce costs; and the costs would in any case be substantial.

Appeal costings:	Gym and caretaker's flat:	£300,000
	New dining room:	£32,000
	Fees:	£40,000
		£372,000

Sources of funds:	Under Governors' control:	£190,000
	Insurance settlement (est.):	£60,000
		£250,000
	Balance to be raised:	£122,000

Thus began a programme of fund-raising, with on average one event every ten days. Such events included a very successful Art Exhibition in September 1981, a Jumble Sale, a series of Tupperware parties, fetes . . .

By July 1981 the New Dining Room had been placed on the site of the burnt-out gym. The largest donations came from direct giving, and by September 1982, £40,000 had been raised. By February 17, 1983, £66,350 had been raised, with another £5,000 from the Sports Council. In April 1983, John James offered to match pound for pound what had been raised from that date; and this act of generosity, combined with a magnificent and unexpected bequest from an Old Girl, Evelyn Jenner, meant that when at length the Hall was open for use in the Summer of 1983, there was very little left of the money to be raised. The John James support was significant, since the costs had escalated from the original sum to £425,000.

There was a cheerful diversion from the purely monetary in the shape of the 90th Birthday celebrations. In June a Victorian school-day was recreated, to the intense amusement of city-dwellers who met on the trains and buses that day a gallery of Victorian stereotypes en route to school. The photographs in the magazine of 1981 hint at the enormous entertainment value of the day; and there are suggestions of cane-wielding on the part of the younger members of staff, perceived with relish by their pupils.

Building of the Sports Hall began on July 5, 1982, with a 38 week schedule. In fact, there were the inevitable delays and the Hall was not handed over until June 16, 1983. There were, for instance, problems with a tree which had a preservation order on it. In consequence, the building had to be set further back than was intended, and had to be supported by additional piles. The land was the site of the Cran Brook, and there was much infilling. The air raid shelter between the Annexe and the main school building had to be demolished when access to the back of the School was needed and it was found that the entire area was subsiding. Ironically, the preserved tree harboured honey fungus and had to be cut down.

Prize Day 1983 was held in the John Gordon Sports Hall, so that a large gathering of parents and guests could see the splendid new facility; and by December 1983, the next serious building problem was under discussion.

It would have been fatally easy to accept as the major preoccupation the maintenance of the fabric of the buildings – especially as staff and girls renewed their complaints about the chill factor. In 1982, Miss Parkin commissioned a survey from the Department of Energy, in the hope of acquiring good advice on how best to keep everyone warm. This was another dream. There were other more pressing needs to be met, and other priorities to assert in the teeth of material demands.

The magazine of 1982 provides a very good and clear example of where the strengths of the School lay. For instance, the reader may deduce something of the scope of staff initiative from the different activities reported in it: the Classical Reading competition, the visit to Bradfield College to see a Greek play, the two school productions (*Dr Faustus* and *A Midsummer Night's Dream*), the Public Speaking Competition (a clean sweep of prizes for CGS), the Concert with QEH, the Dance Festival, the House Music Competition, the usual array of school trips, exchanges with Washington DC, Bordeaux, Hannover, and Valladolid, and attendance at a Russian course. Girls leaving the Sixth form in 1982 went to study, on degree or similar courses, History, Geography, Spanish, Dutch, German, Russian, French, English, Law, Mathematics, Classics, Pharmacology, Business Studies, Surveying, Biochemistry, Accountancy, et al; and degree results from Old Girls were reported – in Geography, Nursing, Planning, French and Spanish, Music, German and Russian, History, Management Studies, Mathematics, Law, Hellenic and Roman Studies, Psychology, French and Drama . . .

Old Girls' professional activities were hinted at: young women embarking on research degrees in subjects as varied as German, Fishery, Music and Dentistry. One Old Girl was Mayor of Wandsworth, another was a commercial apprentice at British Aerospace, another was working for British Steel in France and yet another had just celebrated her 100th birthday and could recall being at the School when it opened in 1891. There was the Old Girl who was trying to get her Equity Card and another had been President of her University Law Society.

There were obituaries on two Old Girls who had also been members of Staff: Miss Marjorie Davis and Mrs Ware. Miss Davis had graduated in Mathematics from Westfield in 1933, had been Second Mistress from 1946–48, and had gone on to her own headship. Mrs Ware had graduated from Bristol as a botanist in 1920, had been a member of staff from 1947–1960, and after her retirement had gone to establish a library at a Methodist school in Rhodesia.

Eva Martin retired after 25 years as Head of German; she had been Second Mistress, Careers Advisor and Wardrobe Mistress. As a Sixth Form Mistress she was outstandingly supportive, being remembered with deep gratitude for the cheerful way in which she said to those approaching Advanced level examinations: 'We don't make an unseemly fuss about public examinations in this School. We just take them.'

Sylvia Beare retired after 31 part-time years in the Classics department, notable also for her teaching of Philosophy; and Anne Sloper retired after 22 years in charge of the Clerical department, amassing a reputation so impressive that prospective employers approached her personally when looking for recruits.

Such lists draw attention to the diversity of talent promoted in the School and its importance throughout the century in encouraging Bristol girls to use their talent and energy to the full.

In a school so busy and so evidently succeeding in its aims, what more could or should be done? Natural changes meant that the balance kept having to be redressed. For instance, at Christmas 1983, one of the School's most distinguished producers of plays took early retirement. Patricia Browne had acquired a formidable reputation for her productions, especially of Greek tragedy. In the summer of 1984, Barbara Lewellen retired after 33 years as Head of Music. When she had arrived at the School there had been no school orchestra. From almost nothing, she had built up a department which ran two orchestras, two choirs, and a large number of individual instrumental lessons.

Her successor was Anne Hughes. Within a year, Miss Hughes had introduced the School to the idea of a large-scale Carol Service in Clifton Cathedral, to five choirs, including the 150-strong Clangers (no audition necessary), to a string quartet, wind band, guitar and recorder groups, and an ambitious programme of performance. In 1985 she took a choir to the International Eisteddfod at Llangollen; it was placed 15th in a class of 37. The following year the choir was placed 4th, and in 1987 it went to Germany to take part in an international choir festival.

In 1986 Kay Clewett, former Head Girl and Head of PE for 20 years, retired, having seen her new Sports Hall used to capacity. Her place as Head of Department was filled by another Old Girl, Elizabeth Hunter. Miss Hunter, known to the girls as Witch Hunter, expanded the Dance Evening still further so that it became one of the most popular events of the year. She encouraged another member of the Department to work with the Dance Club until it was able to enter the Six Counties Dance Festival in 1989. An avid horsewoman, she also organised the first ever CGS Horse Show in 1987.

In fact, the opportunities provided to the pupils were very largely influenced by the skills and interests of the staff. Changes of staff meant changes of curriculum, whether formal or informal. Miss Parkin was proving to be as successful as Miss Dunn had been in recognising talent and encouraging able staff to use their skills. The corresponding knack was to preserve the balance between newcomers who developed the potential they found, and the already-serving staff who wished to continue with well-tried and successful activity.

That such newcomers were often Old Girls added a peculiar flavour to any discussion of plans for the future. The lively staff-room over which Miss Dunn had presided showed no signs of abating its energy or becoming complacent. Miss Parkin's respect for the traditions of the School encouraged rather than repressed innovation, since initiators felt confident that they were sustaining the essential spirit of the School's foundation.

Other factors made change unavoidable. External pressures were intensifying. The new Government Assisted Places had renewed interest in the country's independent schools; but they coincided with falling rolls. There were fewer children in need of schooling. Market forces began to operate. Schools had to be competitive. Parents were being taught to ask more demanding questions when selecting a school, and ever more time had to be spent in showing them around the School premises, introducing them to its facilities and demonstrating the skills of the staff and the successes of the pupils.

Related to this were large-scale mooted changes in the national educational system. By 1984, in her Prize Day speech, Miss Parkin was introducing the parents and pupils to some of the initiatives which were imminent: the General Certificate of Secondary Education, to be examined in 1988 for the first time; Records of Achievement, in which pupils might record their own judgements as well as their examination and other results; the absence of a centralised national curriculum, and hence the importance of the existing standards of examination, and the weaknesses of the system.

Her most significant statement was a quotation from Sir Alistair Pilkington's address to the British Association for the Advancement of Science: 'British education is designed neither to help the individual lead a full life, nor to help the nation to hold its own in a competitive world.' She was not endorsing his view, but drawing attention to the increased urgency with which government, industry and commerce were looking to schools to provide a better-educated workforce. At the end of 1983, when the first discussions about replacing the roof of the Dolphin block were taking place, Miss Parkin was stressing the need to improve laboratories. CGS had been in the forefront of science education earlier in the century, with what had been exceptionally well-equipped laboratories. They were now cramped and outmoded. In addition, she was pondering how Craft, Design and Technology might be made available to the girls. There was a dawning recognition that this was a subject of great importance denied to most girls, whether in single-sex or mixed schools. Just as girls' schools had been spectacularly successful in teaching the sciences and mathematics, so they must ensure that the technological world should be opened to their pupils.

Miss Parkin's growing emphasis on the importance of single-sex schools for girls was given bite by two factors: her membership of the national Council of the Girls' Schools Association, from 1984; and her awareness of the market forces which led boys' schools to admit girls, for largely economic reasons. They needed to boost falling rolls. Competition meant that for the School to remain strong it would have to justify both to the girls and their parents that girls remaining in the CGS sixth form would do better than if they went to one of the boys' schools or to a sixth form college for Advanced level courses. Examination results were to be increasingly scrutinised, especially in Mathematics and Science, and teaching staff would be asked to account for their results. There was talk of teacher appraisal. 'Good facilities' would have to be identified and advertised. A start was made with an Open Evening for members of the Fifth Form about opportunities in the Sixth Form; and the Evening was advertised in the local press. In 1987 one of the advertisements placed by the School was designed by a group of second form girls. It showed a leaping dolphin above the byline 'We're leaps and bounds above the rest'. Although some of the staff felt anxious about taking to the market place, the girls had no such qualms.

One of Miss Parkin's most frequently-asked questions became, 'How must we adapt to cope with change?'

New staff brought changes, and such changes were healthy and stimulating, if at times exhausting. At a time when large-scale examination and curriculum change was being developed, all staff had to consider where their priorities would lie. If more and more had to be taught, for example, what would have to be omitted if the School day were not to be intolerably lengthened? What could the School afford to omit if its standards were based on a curriculum already established? What was the importance of the extra-curricular, if normal teaching was to be disrupted by increasing numbers of academic field trips, or prolonged assessments?

In a school such as CGS, where girls regularly went out to be ball-girls for the West of England Tennis Tournament; where a day would be set aside for House Music or House Drama competitions; where Sixth Form Seminars became established, in order to bring into the School the most significant and stimulating of current issues; where the School Play, Sports Day, the Dance Evenings and other such events took time not so much from the daily curriculum but from hours which might otherwise have been spent in academic study – in such a school, where should emphasis be placed?

More pressing still was the matter of where staff were to find the time to continue with such activities if they were about to embark upon an entirely new and demanding examination system, with far more stress laid upon teacher-assessment. At the same time, they had to learn how to look upon the School as a business. Suddenly 'education' was becoming politically significant and sensitive as an issue.

Such matters had repercussions for pupils in very unexpected ways. For example, the old family service lunch sitting had to be abandoned in favour of an improved self-service cafeteria. This was not only by way of response to heightened expectations about the quality of food offered by the School, but also a way of finding more flexibility in the lunch hour for the number of activities which had to be operated. Girls were travelling in to the school from further afield, and therefore needed either to leave promptly at the end of the School day, or to use the coaches organised by the parents.

This too was a delicate issue. The area of the Cheltenham Road had been gradually degenerating. One of the reasons for the School's becoming independent in 1965 was that the catchment area it was offered under the scheme of city comprehensives would have distorted the intake beyond recognition. By the mid-1980s there were considerable problems in securing the School premises. Complex matters of racial tension, drugs on the streets, inner-city degradation and threats to young women's safety could no longer be ignored. Girls had to be taught how to deal with intruders. Glue-sniffers had to be chased away from the Dolphin car-park and the need for a good police community liaison officer became obvious. In due course, Avon police launched an initiative in which CGS swiftly participated, and the community policeman became a familiar figure not only in the staff room but in classrooms. His advice was sought on many matters, from those of personal safety for girls and women, to how to handle the case of a 16 year old pupil who had left home but was still at school. He brought transcripts of trials into class for girls to enact, so that they had a better understanding of their own vulnerability.

The School had three times to deal with other particularly trying episodes, which tested the security and good order of the institution to the utmost: there were outbreaks of fire, which – unlike the gymnasium fire – seemed to be malicious. No clear explanation was ever given, but the police were actively present, asking questions and probing to establish exactly where everyone was. On the second occasion, a member of the bursary staff was severely injured, and it was important in every way to be as exhaustive as possible in the investigation. The staff learned much from the police procedures at this time, which they were able to use in the future to ensure that the girls were fully accounted for, and that the buildings were carefully supervised at all times.

The School's success depended upon its providing a busy and secure environment, for a cross-section of society. The changes in its immediate local area were not resented, since they provided a vivid picture of daily reality – and in due course, there would be refurbishment and urban renewal. No girl could claim that her education left her in some way isolated from the real world; but if pupils were to retain any freedom of movement (for instance, in walking up the Cheltenham and Gloucester Roads to the swimming baths, or the field in Redland) they had to know exactly what was expected of them. The School's grasp of security had to be exceptionally strong.

All these matters figured in the need to use lunch time effectively. At one point the School appointed dinner ladies to take charge of lunchtime supervision both in the grounds and in the dining rooms. The intention was to relieve the academic staff of additional work, so that they could concentrate on the other increasing work-load. However, the staff themselves found that dependence on dinner ladies removed a vital area of contact with the girls. However hard-pressed the staff were, they needed to keep in touch with what happened, even in the pupil's leisure time, if the characteristic discipline of the School were to be maintained.

Early in 1984, plans were drawn up to replace the defective roof of the Dolphin block with an entirely new floor, holding new science laboratories, classrooms and music practice cells, together with a new music teaching room. There was some foresight in this, though no-one at that time could have known that the subject probably to undergo most radical change in GCSE was Music. From being a purely theoretical and historical study, it became intensely practical. Pupils would have to perform, to compose, to conduct. The noise level would rise dramatically. The new room atop the Dolphin block would help to seclude the musicians from the rest of the school – away, for example, from the Modern Linguists who desperately needed silence during GCSE listening examinations, so that candidates could hear the tapes being played to them. Innocent activities such as cutting the grass outside the Annexe windows at the height of the examination season could bring death-threats to a well-meaning caretaker.

In the meantime, staff and pupils had to contend with workmen rushing to meet a deadline in finishing the building before VAT was added to new building works. Astonishingly, it took little over eight months. The new floor was available for use in January 1985. During 1984 the staff maintained their usual demeanour: producing ever more initiatives even in the midst of a chaos of building paraphernalia.

For example, it was in 1983–84 that Sixth Form Seminars began, with whole days devoted to major issues: in the first year, Self-Presentation, The Law, and Human Rights. The first 'Challenge of Industry' two-day seminar, with QEH, took place at Colston's in March 1984. This was organised at first by the Industrial Society, but in due course the Head of Careers, Helen Hinksman, took over the administration, eventually setting up another two-day seminar called 'The Challenge of Management'. Career development took a step forward, with members of the Sixth Form being interviewed by members of the Bristol Junior Chamber of Commerce. A school bookshop had opened the previous year and was now operating through personal accounts. The usual vigorous programme of debates had been extended to include a House Debating Competition. In her final term at the School, Patricia Browne, who was then in considerable pain, took her production of 'Murder in the Cathedral' to Clifton Cathedral, of which she was a parishioner. It was an unforgettable experience.

A programme of General Studies for the Sixth Form was introduced, the brainchild of Jean Lord, who left the School in the summer of 1984 after 17 years on the staff, as a junior and as Head of Mathematics. For four years she had been the Second Mistress who saw out the old Head Mistress and saw in the new. Mrs Lord became Headmistress of Stroud Girls High School.

The School was feeling the same financial pressures as other independent schools, and numbers of pupils were dropping (they reached their lowest in 1985, with 601 girls on roll. By 1987 they had returned to 661 – the highest for many years). But there was good fortune in a number of guises. John James decided to contribute still further to the security and status of independent schools in the city. September 1984 saw the award of the first two John James Scholarships, for the girl leaving the School with the best record, and the girl entering the School with the highest mark in the Entrance Examination. These were given to Nicola Tickner and Rachael Gilmour respectively. He also provided a fund from which awards for travel or other initiatives could be made to girls who applied to the fund. The first such award went to Amanda Smith, who visited Khartoum.

In the same year (1984) died Evelyn Jenner, who had been enrolled at the School on September 5, 1907, aged 6 years and 6 months. She had reached the height of her career as Headmistress of St Margaret's School, Henleaze. At first, it was thought that her chief bequest to the School was in the form of books, some very beautiful. However, she also left the School half the residue of her estate; and by September 1985 the School was able to award substantial Sixth Form Scholarships – the Jenner Scholarships.

John Gordon had retired as Chairman of the Board of Governors in March 1984, after many years of outstanding service. He remained a member of the Board; and his successor as Chairman was Mr Andrew Burn, who quickly decided that the pace of educational change meant that Governors needed educating too. He requested the establishment of more regular meetings between Governors and members of staff. The first of such discussions was held later in 1984. The subject under scrutiny was the education of 16–18 year old girls who were not aiming at higher education. Within a year another formula was adopted: Heads of Department took it in turn to make formal presentations to the Governors of the work of their department. The first member of staff to tackle this task was Sheila Jones. Miss Jones had been leading a strong and forward-looking department for many years. She was a member of the Schools Council Geography Committee in the 1970s, until the project was disbanded, pioneered the 'Geography 14–18' Project, and enabled Colston's to be one of the first schools to move away from formal examination to a system of continuous assessment. In 1975 she had been the first woman President of the Geographical Association. Her authority, therefore, in embarking upon the task of demonstrating to the Governors the new complexities of the educational system, was immense. In the next couple of years, as staff began to prepare for GCSE, the experience of teachers like Sheila Jones was very influential and comforting.

The huge changes in the educational system nationally were beginning to affect morale in the teaching profession at large. In the mid-1980s, numbers of teachers (none at CGS, of course) decided that they must strike or withdraw from certain duties in order to express their sense of powerlessness and dissatisfaction. Children from other local schools were left roaming the area freely at lunchtimes. It was impossible not to know of the stresses and unhappinesses in other schools and staff-rooms.

At the time, Miss Parkin was involved in a pilot management training scheme for headteachers in maintained and independent schools. For 20 days in 1984–85, she was meeting other headteachers who were among the first nationally to receive training as managers of large and complex institutions. She learned at first hand how in some schools a wedge was being driven between staff and pupils, between staff and senior management teams, as the pressures of national educational change revealed weaknesses or differences of value-judgement in the structure of the teaching profession.

Knowing that the staff were already fully committed; knowing that yet more changes were to come; that 1984 was designated WISE – Women Into Science and Engineering – she reiterated the question: what must we do to adapt to the pace of change?

She now embarked on what proved to be the most radical changes the School had seen for a long time. These changes were not dramatic, as far as the pupils were concerned; but they had major implications for staff. She had been led to think about the way in which decisions were made as to the School's whole policy: the development of the curriculum, the identifying of the School's aims, the way in which the image of the School was projected to the outside world. Moreover, she wanted the School to take part in national initiatives such as WISE; but there was no obvious member of the staff to whom she could delegate so large a task, despite the fact that several of them had the talent to deal with it. She wanted to introduce Design Technology into the curriculum; she know that schemes such as Pupil Profiles would have to be assessed and considered; increasingly her own time was consumed by business administration, and yet she felt that it was vital for her to embark upon some form of staff appraisal.

In short, in this rapidly-changing environment, there was a need for more flexible leadership, with more members of staff not only prepared to take on increased authority, but recognised by others as having the right to do so. The result would be an increased range of opportunities offered to pupils, within a structured framework. The rate of change would be controlled and monitored. Girls would not be confused by having too many choices, but nothing essential would be overlooked and therefore denied to them.

The staff room of Colston's Girls' School had a characteristic which was shared with other schools having a similar system of management. The second most senior post in the School was that of Second Mistress, and this post was allocated on the basis of seniority, rotating every two years. A number of predictable consequences ensued.

Not all good teachers are good administrators, nor should they be. Therefore, the Second Mistress had occasionally been someone who had found the whole experience extremely stressful; so had her colleagues! Others, with organisational gifts, found that after two years, when they had just begun to understand the scope of the task, they had to relinquish it and to watch someone else struggle to grasp and control the organisation and discipline of the School. The value of the system was that very many long-standing members of staff had been Second Mistress in their turn and understood well how to deal with major events or crises. There was a substantial and important willingness to accept responsibility, to serve a common goal. The disadvantage was, that for all the appearance of authority in the staff room, true power remained with the Head Mistress, because there was no continuity of delegated authority. There was also a vast expenditure of energy on the part of each Second Mistress in turn, which was to some extent wasted, because every newcomer to the post used her own methods for sustaining it and discarded some of what her predecessor had done. From the girls' point of view, standards of expectation about discipline and behaviour could vary considerably. It certainly provided them with a wide range of rôle models for women in authority.

Another repercussion was that there was an innate resistance to change where so many changes occurred as a matter of course. Highly-experienced newcomers to the staff could find themselves treated as novices – there were so many ex-Second Mistresses around them. No one person any longer could act as the sole decision-maker about major matters. She could not have enough information at her disposal when so much was being promulgated at any time. Prize Day speeches give a clear picture of the changes.

In her first Prize Day speech in September 1981, Miss Parkin spoke of her belief that the value of an independent school was its standing for freedom, individual enterprise and a sense of responsibility. In 1982 she drew attention to an impending technological revolution and the need to assess both the balance of the curriculum and the means by which it was assessed. The 1983 audience heard her considering how the acquisition of learning can be balanced by the ways in which solutions are found to the moral problems presented by the new learning.

Sir Alistair Pilkington provided the motif for her speech in 1984; and in 1985 the theme was the maintenance of balance and perspective in time of change. Educational change should always have one aim in view: the provision of a system to satisfy every pupil's needs. 1986 – Industry Year – found her reviewing not only the effects of industrial disarray in the teaching profession but the new systems of teaching, examining and appraising which were just being established.

In 1987 she spoke of how society was changing from an industrial basis, with large-scale mass production, to an information society, depending on emerging technology, relying on small teams and individual effort. In this year schools were awaiting decisions about the national curriculum, city technology colleges, revisions to Advanced levels. In her final Prize Day speech, in 1988, Miss Parkin was talking of the demographic time-bomb which was by then daily alluded to in the press: the fact that by 1990 there would be one-third fewer school leavers. The position of women would be ever more important, and the education offered to girls would be crucial in determining their future freedom of choice.

In all of these addresses, Miss Parkin encapsulated the major preoccupations of those who made decisions about schools and education. She examined what was happening at Colston's in the light of the external pressures, and asked what were the characteristic features of a good school.

She had inherited a School which undoubtedly provided marvellous opportunities for its pupils, and had manifestly succeeded in generating loyalty, respect and affection. Change was inevitable, was sought as much as resisted and yet the School needed to be able to maintain the unique quality which sustained and strengthened its traditions.

Industry Year, in 1986, was marked for the School in a number of ways related both to the curriculum and to its management. In this year, the 'extra-curricular' became the 'informal curriculum', with activities which were obviously entertaining, had substantial elements of 'play' in them and yet were essential to learning. It had always been clear that the informal activity of a pupil might well denote her personal strengths and possible future career. Such indications were now to be systematically encouraged and recorded, in careers interviews, in work experience, and in the Records of Achievement which schools had to consider implementing.

Firstly, Miss Parkin spent the Christmas holidays in The Gambia with one of her brothers. She returned fired by the aim of encouraging the School to raise large sums of money for well-building. What had particularly drawn her attention was the rôle of women in a Third World country. The women were chiefly responsible for growing the food as well as for looking after the children. They were enslaved by the problems of carrying water to their crops; and aid in general was extremely slow in getting through to them because of the corrupt practices of the governing system. By direct liaison between the School, ActionAid, the relevant charity, and Mr Parkin, there was a chance that money could be channelled to where it was most needed. Young women in England could give positive help to women in a deprived country, and at the same time could be helped to understand more about the general economic and social conditions of women in the world at large. Within the next two years the School raised enough money for the building of two new wells.

Secondly, there was a dramatic new Industry Project, organised by Mrs Rickards, who had just spent three years as Second Mistress. In the Summer Term of 1986 the second and third form girls followed a completely separate curriculum for two weeks. They were split into eight groups. Members of staff were linked to eight employers who all assigned different problems to the groups. Girls were encouraged to work in small groups, resolving real problems, and finally presenting their solutions to the assembled employers. Tasks varied from setting up and running a new restaurant, establishing a service industry, marketing a computer software package which would give medical diagnosis to PC users, to devising a bulk-handling system for transporting heavy goods to South America, or determining the site of a new branch for a metal production company.

Their reflections included: 'Work is getting up on Monday morning'. 'Work is drinking tea from 9 till 5'. 'Work is like debt: it never goes away.' 'Work is like the bath: the longer you stay in it, the more wrinkled you become.' 'Work is like the washing-up: you don't want to do it, but you have to.' 'Work is a four-letter word for the three million workless.'

One group was completely sidetracked from its official task by the accidental discovery of how much it could really cost to establish and run an office. Within a few days they had learnt to knock on the doors of accountants, estate agents and bank managers on the Gloucester Road as they sought for instant answers to questions about cash-flow, bank loans, renting office space and negotiating for good business rates. The School's phone lines were jammed by girls trying to call a Consulate, the DHSS, the Fire Brigade (what were the most up-to-date fire regulations?). Propensities to tea-drinking, at first seized with relish, were rapidly disposed of as denoting the work-shy and irresponsible.

The staff probably derived their greatest amusement from the various trade union disputes which broke out, including one where the managing director of a firm walked out with all the accounts the night before the presentation, and stunningly presented an entirely new resolution to the problem the following morning. She had set up a rival concern.

There was also some stiff competition among the staff to be invited to the opening of the new restaurant.

The Sixth Form were not to be outdone, and one General Studies group decided to set up their own small business. Success was considerable when they embarked upon the making and decorating of cakes for Mothering Sunday, although they found their purchasers highly critical of the size of cake offered.

Other senior girls took part in work-shadowing schemes, set up for Industry Year in Avon. The whole programme of work experience took on new significance and complexity, and staff had to develop more direct understanding of commercial and industrial processes.

Behind the scenes, Miss Parkin started putting into practice what she had learnt on her own training course. Staff who were to work alongside local employers from business and commerce in the Industry Year projects became directly acquainted with some of the personal training techniques established in large commercial firms. Companies which were in due course especially helpful were Hewlett-Packard, British Aerospace and the West of England Management Centre.

The staff began the year by working together on a pilot scheme for 'whole staff appraisal' organised by the National Foundation for Educational Research. This involved the completion of a complex questionnaire about their views on the running of the School, the handling of paperwork and administration in general, their policy on marking and assessing pupils' work, the ways in which decisions were made, and their understanding of the aims of the School. The intention of the questionnaire was to reveal the areas where points of view diverged.

Later in the year the first Colston's Staff Study Day took place: staff embarked upon their own professional training. The results of their self-appraisal were available, and they were able to decide how next to proceed, in order to maintain stability in the midst of change.

Miss Parkin had previously tried to establish a discussion group for senior heads of department, in which major educational issues could be assessed. There was disquiet about what constituted 'senior'. Finally she established a staff working party, open to anyone who was interested, which would provide advice for her on how best to reorganise the management of the School.

The working party took several months to arrive at a satisfactory conclusion; and in 1987 Miss Parkin was able to appoint, from within the staff, three new senior posts: Head of Upper School, Head of Lower School, Director of Timetable and Curriculum. The decision to appoint a Head of Upper School was particularly astute, in that it made provision for 14–18 education to be considered as a whole, rather than with a natural break at 16. Shortly afterwards Miss Parkin decided to create a permanent Deputy Head instead of the rotating Second Mistress post; and the new appointment was fixed for September 1988.

Colston's now had a senior management team similar to those found in many other schools; and characteristically, the decision had been made after a great deal of consultation and self-appraisal. One of the benefits of the new arrangement was that there were now people who could take responsibility for investigating, for instance, what equipment would be most suitable for the new Design Technology room. Miss Parkin had already ensured that several staff had been on residential courses to introduce them to Technology, but she was well aware that more would be implied than simple additions to the timetable or alterations to facilities. The Computer room had already been substantially remodelled; but the relationship between Design and Information Technology needed to be defined.

In 1985 Miss Parkin had warned the Governors of the need to make substantial budgetary provision for the changes indicated by GCSE; and indeed the teaching style of GCSE had enormous implications at every level. The problems for Music and Modern Languages have already been mentioned. Other departments took to prowling the School, assessing classrooms, storage facilities, the juxtaposition of rooms, in order to see if they could persuade members of other departments to exchange rooms with them. The Science department was delighted with its new laboratories at the top of the Dolphin block but perplexed as to how the necessary expensive and sometimes dangerous equipment could be moved from one laboratory to another, across the Dolphin walkway and up several flights of stairs. Nearly everyone seemed to be involved in oral work, in practicals, in coursework. There was pitched battle beside the photocopier, around the photocopier, for the photocopier. Incantations of every hue went up over its recalcitrant body, and Mrs Allen was the High Priestess of the Mysteries. A single Modern Languages internal GCSE-type examination paper could consume 74 sheets of A4 paper.

It was a greedy beast, this new examination, dominating the landscape. The Brent Knoll of paper in the staff room began to assume Everest-like proportions. Moreover, Sin of varying kinds accompanied it. One concerned copyright; another concerned theft, which was less diverting. Coursework was stolen – as in every school in the country. One of the more ingenious hiding-places was in the holder for disposable towels. That the missing work was discovered indicates the ingenuity of the staff in locating it.

Records of Achievement were imminent – were to be mandatory, were to be voluntary . . . The Department of Education and Science seemed unable to decide, but schools had to be able to respond once clear directions were given to them.

Heads of department argued ever more persuasively for the resources they needed for their subjects to flourish. The new team learned to set aside departmental loyalties in the interests of seeing the whole picture. They could correlate cross-curricular work, could bring together groups of staff considering pastoral matters, could review the balance of the curriculum, or answer the increasing number of detailed parental enquiries about examination courses or travel problems. The possible educational and financial implications of introducing a national curriculum would be so great that Miss Parkin would need a team of people to assemble and assess the information as it became available.

Meanwhile, she laboured to raise money for bursaries. In the magazine of 1984 she had written 'The unwritten credo of Colston's Girls' School is that any girl who wants to be educated here, or to continue to be educated here, should have the opportunity to do so.' The donations from John James had been extremely helpful, especially those which enabled the awarding committee to give grants to girls wanting to try their wings in very varied activities. (Applications were made to go hot-air ballooning; to travel round Europe by Inter-rail; to cycle round France collecting recipes; to buy a trumpet; to take a course in cartoon drawing; to visit Hong Kong.) In 1985 she persuaded the Wolfson Foundation to make a substantial donation to the School for further Sixth Form scholarships. The first Wolfson Scholarships were awarded in September 1986.

In order to assess these potential Sixth Form Scholars – for the Bathurst, Jenner and Wolfson Scholarships, together with Sixth Form Government Assisted Places, presented excellent opportunities – a new and demanding test was used. Staff were enabled to identify and evaluate the different kinds of intelligence which might be developed in pupils.

This matched the School's plans to introduce Design Technology – the neglected factor in many pupils' education throughout the national system. Technological teaching was certainly practised at Colston's, but it went under other guises. With the advent of GCSE, the Home Economics department suddenly became one of the most innovative, discovering the joys of 'the design brief'. In this, they joined the geographers, who had also been teaching girls systematically how to assess a problem and design a solution. Other disciplines used similar techniques, but it was Design Technology which focused concentration on the process of thinking in shapes, rather than in words or numbers.

The Science department had already been organising visits to the recently opened 'Exploratory', which offered the public the chance of investigating scientific principles in action: the 'hands on' approach, where the relationship between an idea or concept was made not only visible but tactile – Design Technology in another of its disguises. The introduction of Double and Single Award Science (the first GCSE examinations being taken in 1989) further modified the balance of the curriculum.

However, the most visually striking innovation was in D1 where, after much consultation and planning, the new Design Technology room was opened in 1988, with a member of staff appointed to take charge of the Department. It was sited near the Art teaching rooms, Home Economics, and close to the new Science laboratories, in anticipation of the eventual development of an entire Design Technology wing.

The new girl entering the School in 1981 would have found in D1 a large and conventionally formal classroom, with a few shelves accommodating some books. By the mid-1980s it had become the fully fledged Junior Library, with ranks of shelves at one end of the room, a carpeted area, and a clear division between the library and the rest of the room, which still presented itself formally with rows of desks and chairs. Later, the books were moved to the centre of the School; and established next to the Computer Room as part of a Media Resource Room. The new girl of 1988 found that in D1 electricity was trunked around the walls, with power points suspended from the ceiling above the workbenches. Seating was limited, confined to the edges of the room where pupils could make their designs and calculations. She saw tool-kits, soldering irons, heated wires for cutting thermoplastics and polystyrene, fretsaws, a band-saw, a vacuum-forming mould; the entire room indicated that girls would be flexible in their approach and active, moving from one area to another and one kind of material to another.

In short, the staff continued to find ways in which the education of pupils was made relevant to contemporary needs. Their success may be charted from two sets of statistics. In 1988, the first girls to have completed their education with Government Assisted Places completed their Advanced level examinations and embarked on higher education. About a quarter of the total leavers' list comprised such GAP pupils. Girls went to courses as diverse as the following: Medicine (3), Law, Fashion, Rural Resources, Electrical and Electronic Engineering, Mechanical Engineering (2), Natural Environment Sciences, Chinese, Russian, Film and Literature, English, French, Statistics and Computing, Geography, Business and Finance . . . One of them achieved a Choral Scholarship to Oxford.

At the other end of the School, for the second year in succession the entire First Form was taken to France for a study visit. 'That afternoon we went to a hypermarket called an Intermarche . . . The group that I was in was really pleased with a French chocolate cake that we had bought between us – until we discovered on the coach that it was a "make-it-yourself" cake!'

The Old Girls' news continued to be remarkable: Mary Tanner (Fussell) had been appointed to the Archbishop of Canterbury's commission investigating the possible consequences of the ordination of women. She was the only woman member. Elizabeth Butcher had died at the age of 91, having in her time been the first woman lecturer in History at the University of Bristol. Claire Sisman had been acclaimed 'Avon Student of the Year' in her secretarial course, rivalling a hundred others, and was now taking her pick of the offers of jobs. Others were working or studying in France, Italy, Germany and Israel.

(In 1987, in fact, there had been a 'Fifty Years On' Reunion, for the class of '37. Open the main school door and you will find that the assembled company immediately "gells" into one very happy group who never stop talking. Miss Parkin had shortly beforehand received a letter from an Old Girl of 81, living in New Zealand. 'On arrival at school one rang the bell and the butler opened the door; does this still go on?')

Results in 1989, a term after Miss Parkin left, were even more impressive. About one third of the Sixth Form pupils progressing to higher or further education had been GAP pupils, and virtually all of them went to universities or polytechnics.

Although the results achieved by others were equally notable, the presence of the GAP pupils undoubtedly strengthened the School. These were girls from families where parents were prepared to make considerable sacrifices to give their daughters 'a good education'. Some were from ethnic minorities, or from areas of the city acknowledged as deprived. None of this was relevant to the girls' achievements, although each success was the more satisfying because so highly valued.

The list of courses followed by all leavers in 1989 included: Veterinary Science (2), Latin American Studies, Russian and Soviet Studies, Civil Engineering, European Business Administration, Mathematics, Applied Chemistry (2), Mechanical Engineering with sponsorship from British Aerospace, Spanish and French, History, Geography, English, Drama, Psychology, Nursing . . .

The School Miss Parkin inherited in 1981 had been thriving, wide-ranging in its appeal, with a strong sense of its own identity. In 1989 that sense of purpose was, if anything, more vigorous than ever. The presence of staff who were parents and past pupils, alongside other long-standing members of staff, created a commitment and sense of traditional value which was all-pervasive. Underlying everything was that faintly possessive pride which seemed natural in a School where so many were related to one another by bonds of family, work or continuity of association. The School had always been important to the City of Bristol in its educating of professional women, able to assume responsibility and expecting to do so.

In the Spring of 1988, Miss Parkin decided that she must prepare to leave the School. She had helped to bring about large-scale change, had drawn attention to the inescapable nature of that change, and to what was needed for an institution to remain abundantly healthy and prosperous. She believed that it was time for someone else to consolidate decisions, and to pilot the School through the shoals of changes yet to be announced.

Nonetheless, she had been so strongly affected by the Colstonian ethos, of service to the community and the need for women to be well-educated, responsible and professional, that she found it impossible to shift her allegiance to another school. She became instead the Secretary of The Girls' Schools Association, in March 1989, drawing on her experiences at Colston's in order to advise all girls' independent schools.

It was typical of Ann Parkin, and of the girls who emerged from CGS in her years, that the outgoing Head Girl, Lisa Bhopalsingh, felt able to request an interview with the Head Mistress and to publish the result in the School magazine.

Lisa wrote, 'Miss Parkin had noticed that pupils had become more confident over the years, showing a greater willingness to accept a higher level of personal responsibility. She agreed that pupils were capable of developing their own ideas and opinions of social and political issues at an earlier age, something she is thoroughly in favour of, and she thought this was exemplified by the successful song dedicated to Nelson Mandela, composed and performed by Amy Wadge at this year's music festival.

'Miss Parkin has been leader of the School through a number of important changes, in the education system with the instigation of the new GCSE, and also in the improvements of buildings and facilities like the gym, computer room and, most recently, the design and technology room.'

Lisa's account reveals almost as much about herself as about her subject. At the end of the decade, the typical CGS girl expected to be able to set her own targets, to be dealt with on an equal basis and to voice her judgements with confidence.

Anyone meeting one of the Old Girls at a reunion would rapidly come to the conclusion that nothing had changed, except the sheer range of choices now available. Then, as now, the young women leaving the School were ready to seize their opportunities; and were determined to use their talents as widely as possible.

MRS FRANKLIN

The Governors received thirty-one applications for the post of Head Mistress. Preliminary interviews of eight candidates narrowed the field to two, who were invited for interview and lunch at Merchants' Hall. The appointments committee offered the post to Mrs Judith Franklin.

Judith Penelope Franklin, née Owen, differed from her eight predecessors in several respects. Born in Cardiff, the daughter of a furniture manufacturer, she was educated at Howell's School, Llandaff and University College, Cardiff, where she took a First in English. Her career in teaching had been spent entirely in co-educational schools; at first in grammar schools in Nottinghamshire and Worcestershire, and then in comprehensive schools. She had been Head of Sixth Form at South Bromsgrove High School and Deputy Head at Evesham High School. These factors might have intrigued the staff but of greater interest to the girls was the fact that she had two teenage sons. The first married Head Mistress she was, at forty-six, the oldest on appointment to the post.

Judith Franklin was a natural communicator. Her lively and warm interest in all members of the school community was clear to everyone from the start. Even before she took up her appointment she impressed many staff by greeting them by name at a buffet lunch, subsequent discussion showing that she was au fait with their area of responsibility and interest. The girls who were used to a more formal relationship were initially surprised to find that their new Head Mistress's relaxed approach ensured that they often gave away more than they intended. Judith Franklin's belief in the individual was such that she demanded self discipline, with the needs of the School understood and striven for by each member of the community.

Education never stands still. The 1988 Education Reform Act had imposed a National Curriculum on Maintained Schools and discussion of the National testing was in the air. Independent Schools had to decide how to react to the changes. Should they ignore them with the lofty certainty that they were already offering all that was required? Should they embrace the precepts of educational reform uncritically and unhesitatingly? Clearly they had to decide. The bandwagon of the National Curriculum was gaining momentum, taking on board ten subjects plus cross-curricular themes; Standard Attainment Targets jostled with Key Stages and the Government even re-numbered the School years!

Colston's Girls' School had to respond to the changing climate, if only to ensure that it was still offering the pupils what they needed for their future education and careers. Parents were becoming far better informed on educational matters and were, rightly, asking incisive questions about what the School was going to do.

The decisions were too complex to be taken by the Head Mistress in isolation, or even by the Management Team alone. The staff had to be involved in what amounted to a full curriculum audit and the laying-down of curriculum policy for the next decade. The structure for such a policy-making group almost existed; four senior Heads of Department, English, Mathematics, Modern Languages and Science, were already in place. To reflect all aspects of the Curriculum two further appointments were needed. With the approval of the Governors two promotions created the Heads of the Faculties of Humanities and of Creative and Aesthetic subjects.

By the Summer of 1990 a statement of curriculum policy existed. The School was not to be limited by the National Curriculum. It could meet its demands for ten subjects and moreover offer additional courses. Latin and Classics would be protected, as would Religious Studies. English Literature would not be buried within the bland definition of English and a second Modern Language would be studied by all girls. Rightly suspicious of the reliability of Ministerial pronouncements made at conferences the School had defined its education aims in its own terms.

It was to continue in the tradition of independence which it cherished while respecting the real need for educational reforms. This had already been amply illustrated by the School's adoption of balanced science a few years before, an innovation pioneered by Miss Bridget Burton in the years before her retirement in 1991. It now became clear that a Dual Award Science GCSE should be offered to all, thereby increasing the overall number of GCSEs to nine for every girl. The demands of this new curriculum inevitably exceeded the time available. The next task was to consider a restructured day.

The new structure was to be presented to the staff at an extra-ordinary early morning staff meeting. The Head Mistress could not have guessed that there would be one of the heaviest snowfalls in Bristol for several years the night before. Up at 6 a.m. to check on the state of the roads she then telephoned the local radio to announce the School open for the day, though travel was not recommended. Amazingly, by 9 a.m. almost every member of staff was in school; there were only one hundred and fifty girls. About to launch the new Scheme, the Head Mistress was interrupted; one of the junior girls had been distressed to see a 'flasher'. The incongruity of such an incident in such appalling weather amused the staff, who proceeded to adopt the new plans, with a nine-period day and a corresponding increase in teaching time, with good grace. The benefit to off-set this was to be five days' additional holiday.

Changes in the Curriculum will always lead to increased demands on the buildings of a school. As classrooms are refurbished as specialist rooms, the available teaching space diminishes. For a long time the Governors had been trying to acquire the site at the top of the bank behind the School. This area, once Billy Ware's scrapyard, had been sold to a property developer to build factory units. After much negotiation, for the property developers were reluctant vendors, the School bought a triangular piece of land of less than half an acre, on which to build.

A staff working party had identified the greatest needs of the School; to replace the Annexe, now in its seventy-second temporary year; to re-locate the Music department with all its associated noise and exuberance; to provide more small sixth form tutorial rooms and a multi-purpose Hall for teaching, exhibition and performance.

The plans for what was optimistically known as the Centenary building were submitted to the local authority. The School knew that they were dealing with a sensitive site. Before the School bought the land the property developers had begun to fell the poplar trees, planted by the School eighty years before. Almost as soon as this work began local conservation groups moved onto the site, thus preventing further felling. They were soon joined by itinerant protesters and a 'green' camp sprang up on the land adjacent to the Dolphin block. To the fascination of the girls wigwams were constructed from branches and tarpaulin; fires were lit; a street theatre 'bus arrived; a wood carver began to create bizarre shapes from the fallen (and, it must be said, rotten) trunks of the poplars. It was several weeks before the site was cleared of its illegal but colourful occupants and the remaining trees felled or pollarded. The result was a row of distorted and ugly stumps which bore no resemblance to the elegant Black Poplar Grove which had shaded the bank for so many years.

As the School feared, there were objections to its plans for development. The School's Architect, Michael Axford, and the Deputy Head, Miss Anne Hughes, attended a stormy meeting of the local conservation group. The City Council delayed its consideration until July 1990, then rejected the plans. It insisted that the land was zoned for industrial purposes and would not compromise. The School's Appeal to the Department of the Environment was unsuccessful and the hopes of a building completed in Centenary year faded entirely.

This was a profound disappointment but it did little to affect the enthusiasm of staff and girls for the exciting opportunities of the decade. The themes were to be Technology, Enterprise and Europe.

Technology was playing a significant part in the life of the School. The first GCSE group started CDT in 1989; Rolls Royce took an almost paternal interest in the girls' progress and marked their approval of what the School was doing with a donation of the Technology trophy, first presented by Mr John Grimshaw at Prize Giving in 1990. New computers were installed in 1990, AppleMac machines which made Information Technology accessible to all; many staff took and passed RSA examinations in IT. In that year the School Magazine was typeset 'in-house' for the first time. It signalled a great technological advance to hear Miss Marea Morgan, Head of English and tireless campaigner for high standards and one in whom much school tradition was invested, discussing desk-top publishing, justification and choice of fonts with superb aplomb. The Centenary magazine which would be her last before retirement, was being enthusiastically planned long before the publication of its predecessor.

A Young Enterprise Scheme was launched in 1989 with two trading companies in the Sixth Form: Dolphin Enterprises and COGS and Co. Both won trophies in the Area Finals, showing how resourceful and skilled they were at presenting business plans and outlining marketing strategy. In 1991 Sarah Gay was in the last ten of 17,000 candidates who were considered for an American exchange through the Young Enterprise Scheme.

Europe cannot have been far from anyone's mind in the years leading to the Single European Market of 1992. The breakthrough in the Channel tunnel may have symbolised the end of our island status, but Colston's Girls had been European long before that. The School's ability to offer four modern foreign languages was a strength the new Head Mistress was keen to promote. To make her point, although being no polyglot herself, she carefully rehearsed the closing remarks of her first Prize Day address in four languages; French, German, Russian and Spanish. Her heart was glad when she heard the story of the second form girl who had been learning Russian for exactly a term and a half. A member of staff, bound for Moscow at half-term, asked the girl for some Russian phrases. She charmingly obliged, until asked to say 'I cannot speak Russian'. 'I cannot tell you that,' the girl remonstrated, 'because I can.'

On International Day the whole School enjoyed small group activities with boules in the Pleasaunce, computer games, quizzes, plays and board games in languages from all over the world. Before a European lunch there was a splendid fancy dress parade where bunches of green grapes jostled with a Red Dragon and the Mont Blanc.

The Governing Body was also responding to the changing expectations of the educational world.

As long ago as 1972 the Governors considered a proposal that a member of staff, other than the Head Mistress, should be invited to the meetings of the Governors. A letter was sent to the Second Mistress. Miss Bridget Burton, Second Mistress at the time, replied that confidence in the Governing Body had always been so high that the privilege of representation would not normally have been sought. Since the suggestion had now been put forward the staff would take it up with pleasure and thanks. The first staff representative was Miss Marea Morgan, whose period of office as Second Mistress began in the Autumn of 1972.

The linking of the duties of Second Mistress and Staff Representative continued until 1989. At that time the post of Deputy Head Mistress had been created and the expectation of automatic succession to the post of Second Mistress every two years had disappeared. It was agreed that a further staff representative should be appointed and Mrs Joyce Edwards was elected by the staff. In 1990 the question of a Parent Governor was raised. It was generally felt that the School Association should be represented but there were different views over the method of appointment. It was proposed that the vacant position of a co-optative governor should be offered to Professor Paul Dieppe who had two daughters in the School. His acceptance was coincident with his being taken hostage in the Kuwait crisis of August 1990 and it was not until March 1991 that he was able to attend his first meeting of Governors.

From the moment of her appointment as Head Mistress, Judith Franklin had been aware of the imminence of the School's Centenary. It probably arrived far more quickly than she would have wished. Lacking a proud new building on which to focus effort and hope, the School needed other less tangible proofs of its celebration of a hundred years on the Cheltenham Road site. It was also important that the Centenary should be not only a time for nostalgia but a time of optimism for the future.

Events were planned: the Centenary year would end with Commemoration on November 1, 1991. Before that would be a grand Prize Giving in the Great Hall of the University at which Baroness Young had agreed to present the prizes. The months of high summer were to be marked by a Centenary Dinner in a marquee in the School gardens, at which all four living Head Mistresses of the School would be present. This was to be preceded by a Centenary Fashion Show and Soirée of costume and music. An Old Girls' May Ball, a splendid concert at St George's, Brandon Hill, a sparkling School musical production 'Bombshells' filled the springtime, together with a packed Old Girls' Evening of Nostalgia, and a 'birthday party' complete with school photograph, cake, a present of a silver Dolphin stickpin and fancy dress.

The great event which marked the end of one century and the birth of the next was the Centenary Assembly. Planned to coincide as nearly as possible with the day a hundred years before when Clara Guest's name was the first to be entered in the School Register, it took place on January 18. A distinguished friend of the School, a former parent, had agreed to preach at the Assembly some eighteen months before it took place. In the middle of August 1990 it became clear to the School that it was to welcome the Archbishop of Canterbury-elect to its Assembly in January the following year.

It did not rain on Centenary Day, but the caretaker was ready with his green and gold centenary umbrella in case it did. Dr George Carey and his wife, Eileen, arrived in a School polished and gleaming and decked with flowers as it always is on such occasions. The entire School, pupils, staff and governors, was packed into the Hall, revealing the inadequacy of its size but the grandeur of its aspirations for such an event. The television cameras were there; they had not been expected but the announcement of the opening of hostilities in the Gulf War the previous day had lured the press and television journalists to seek a comment from Dr Carey. He was, however, very careful to ensure that the day belonged to the School. He spoke words of comfort and encouragement to the girls who feared the consequences of the war that was about to begin; he reassured them all that celebration could still take place in the midst of international disturbance. There were garlands in the Hall; there was music. The service encompassed traditional hymns, chamber music and the haunting setting of the Prayer of Saint Francis, commissioned to mark the Centenary. After the prayers and the blessings there were the buns, specially baked with a large 'C' encircling them by John Williams the neighbouring baker. The School was glowing both inwardly and outwardly.

There was a degree of bathos in the fact that after lunch the Head Mistress was invited to Merchants' Hall. Accompanied by Mr J A S Burn, the Chairman of the Governors, and Lady Merrison, the Vice-Chairman, she attended a meeting to hear that Colston's School was to become co-educational, merging with the Collegiate School. If she had thought (which she had not) that the Centenary celebrations marked a fulfilment, the completion of work to be done, she would have been wrong. This news, not dismaying in itself, reminded her that Colston's Girls' School had survived for one hundred years by responding willingly to opportunities and stubbornly to obstacles that came its way.

Earlier that day she had addressed the School with words that expressed the confidence she felt in its future:

> Earlier this week someone who should have known better asked me if we had any famous old girls. I replied, 'None that is a household name but . . .' I was interrupted. 'No pop singers?' he asked. To my knowledge no pop singers, but women distinguished in their field who have made significant contributions to society as doctors, lawyers, scientists, technologists, artists, nurses, teachers and writers. They may not be famous in the popular sense but certainly respected, valued and held in high esteem when they were here.
>
> Today we are celebrating what they have been and to anticipate what you and your successors will become. Girls who joined the School in 1891 knew nothing of radium and penicillin. They were born in 1880 and left school twenty years before women gained the vote. They were to live through two world wars, to see the popularisation of radio and television, on which some who lived long enough might have witnessed the first moon landing.
>
> Who knows what you will experience in your lifetimes? I hope that the excitement of discovery will far outweigh the grief of destruction and aggression. It is certain that you will never cease to be surprised and I hope never fail to meet the challenges of the twenty-first century in which you will spend the major part of your lives.
>
> I hope that you will never forget nor lose touch with this proud School which will mean much to you in the future and in whose future you will play an important part. Today we look back but we must also look forward as today we begin our second century. We will fulfill all that is demanded of us and, never forgetting our charitable origins, seek ways to repay the help we have received in the past by working for those who need our help in the future.
>
> I am sure Edward Colston and the Merchant Venturers who presided over our foundation would feel proud of us today.

HEAD MISTRESSES

Miss G A Smith	January 1891 – December 1900
Miss E M Hughes	January 1901 – July 1913
Miss B M Sparks	January 1914 – November 1922
Miss H Drew	January 1923 – April 1927
Miss G M Morgan	September 1927 – December 1945
Miss M G Green	January 1946– December 1953
Miss A M S Dunn	January 1954 – December 1980
Miss A C Parkin	January 1981 – April 1989
Mrs J P Franklin	April 1989 –

CHAIRMEN OF THE GOVERNORS

Mr William Proctor Baker	1891-1907
Mr William Wilberforce Jose	1907-1916
Mr Mervyn King	1916-1924
Mr Cyril Clarke	1924-1957
The Hon W R S Bathurst	1957-1966
Mr Roger Clarke	1966-1974
Mr John A Gordon	1974-1984
Mr J Andrew Burn	1984-

GOVERNING BODY 1990-91

Chairman: J A S Burn MC
Vice-Chairman: Lady Merrison BA

R E J Bernays
Judge Hazel Counsell LLB
Miss Angela Dixon, BSc, MEd, MIBiol.
Mrs E J Evans BSc
Mrs G Hebblethwaite
T J Hood
P H Lucas
J J D McArthur
D M Parkes
Mrs P M Phillips BA
A L Robinson
Miss Joan Sadler BA
Dr P M Scopes MA, BSc, DPhil. (Oxon)
Mrs V Tidmarsh
Mrs J M Woolley
Clerk to the Governors: S J Awdry MA

STAFF ON CENTENARY DAY, 1991

Head Mistress	Mrs Judith Franklin BA Hons (Wales)
Deputy Head Mistress	Miss Anne Hughes BA Hons (Dunelm)
School Chaplain	Rev Ray Brazier

Faculty of Creative and Aesthetic subjects

Head of Faculty	Miss M Viney BA Hons (Wales)
	Miss N Bradley BEd Hons (Bedford Coll of HE)
	Mrs A Chauhan Dip AD ATD (Cardiff)
	Mrs V Ford Cert PE (Bedford)
	Miss J Hunt BA Hons (Reading)
	Mrs M Hunt BEd Hons (Bath Coll of HE)
	Miss E J Hunter Cert PE (Chelsea Coll of PE)
	Mrs S Johnson Dip PE (Dublin Coll of PE)
	Mrs S Keep Dip PE (Anstey Coll of PE)
	Mrs K Kigwana Dip AD (Bath Academy of Art)
	Mrs L M A Nunn Dip Art & Science of Movement (Nonnington Coll)
	Mrs S Overend GRSM, LRAM, ARCM
	Mrs J Rogers BEd Hons (Bristol)
	Mrs J E Rossiter BSc Hons (Surrey)
	Mrs B Sudworth Dip AD (Kingston Coll of Art)
	Miss J T Wood BEd Hons (Sussex)

Faculty of English

Head of Faculty	Miss M Morgan BA Hons (London)
	Mrs A J Boyce BA Hons (Wales)
	Mrs J C Chard BA Hons (Leeds)
Director of Studies	Mrs J J Geyl BA (University of New South Wales)
	Mrs J Hook BA Hons (Bristol)
	Mrs R A Russell BA Hons (London)
Head of Lower School	Mrs J C Taylor BA Hons (Salford)

Faculty of Humanities

Head of Faculty	Mrs J Edwards BA Hons (London)
	Miss D M Ace BA Hons (Wales)
	Mr P G Barker BSc Hons (Bristol)

	Mrs Y Barrett BA Hons (Bristol)
	Mr G B Butcher MA (Oxon)
	Mrs A Greenslade BSc Econ Hons (London)
	Miss B M Outhwaite BA Hons (Keele)
	Mrs R A Robinson BEd Hons (Bristol)
	Mrs R J Routledge BSc Hons (Sheffield)
Head of Upper School	Mrs G M Weatherhogg BA Hons (Reading)
	Mr R J Wilkinson MA (Cantab)

Faculty of Mathematics

Head of Faculty	Mrs H A Kippin BSc Hons (Southampton)
	Mrs J J Duncan BA (OU)
	Mr D T McAll BSc Hons (Bristol) MBA (Brunel)
	Mrs M Parsons BSc Hons (Bristol)
	Mrs J M Reese BSc Hons (Exeter)
	Miss C Wadsworth BEd Hons (St. Paul's & St Mary's, Cheltenham)
	Mrs K M Wallace BSc Hons (Leeds)

Faculty of Modern Languages

Head of Faculty	Miss V M Kies BA Hons (Warwick) L ès L, M ès L, DEA (France)
	Mrs S Cattle BA Hons (Birmingham)
	Mrs C Durrant BA Hons (Liverpool)
Head of Careers	Miss H Hinksman BA Hons (Birmingham)
	Mrs A-M Keith-Smith L ès L, DES, Capes, Agrégée
	Mrs G Mander BA (Witwatersrand)
	Mrs L A Nickless BA Hons M Litt (Bristol)
	Mrs G Opstad MA (Oxon)
Head of Sixth Form	Mrs M Smith BA Hons (Bristol)
	Mrs M M Thomas BA (Southampton)

Faculty of Science

Head of Faculty	Miss B K Burton BSc (Nottingham)
	Mrs M J Bell BSc Hons (Bristol)
	Mrs B Davies BSc (Manchester)
	Mrs J Littler MA (Oxon)
	Mr W P B Moggridge BSc Hons (Hull)
	Mrs E P Perry BSc (London)

Mrs G K Ramsay BSc Hons (London)
Mrs J Watkins BSc Hons (Bristol)
Mrs J Williams BSc Hons (Wales)

Visiting Music Staff

Mrs R Amos
Mr P Ansley
Mrs J Francis GRSM ARCM
Mrs C Garland ATCL
Miss E Palmer ARCM
Mr S Preston
Miss T Staniak MGR (Warsaw Music Academy)
Mr M Thomas LGSM, LLCM
Mr R Walker LGSM

Teaching Support Staff

Mr P Britten
Mrs G Miller HD (Tech) (Wolverhampton)
Mrs P Prewett
Mrs C Saunderson BA Hons (OU)

Administrative Staff

Head Mistress' Secretary & Registrar — Mrs L Harrison
School Secretary — Mrs B Allen
Mrs S Sheppard
Bursar — Mr R A White FCII
Assistant Bursar — Mrs G Forward
Mrs B Singleton
School Nurse — Mrs J Beazer SRN, RSCN, HVCert

Kitchen

School Catering Manager — Mrs M McGrath
Staff Catering Manager — Mrs A Lupton
Mrs M Holden
Mrs G Mackay
Mrs A Rice
Mrs P Slade
Mrs C Wills

Caretaking & Grounds Staff

Mr P Jefferies
Mrs C Jefferies
Mr J Johnson
Mr J Workman

Head Girl Teams

1990–91		1991–92
Rachel Morris	*Head Girl*	Kate Day
Kirsty Hazell Jennifer Singleton	*Deputy Head Girls*	Clare Dieppe Vanessa Taylor
Lucy Wadge Kharis Wilkins Kim Garland Maria Norley Holly Wicks	*Senior Prefects*	Lucy Morris Victoria Lamb Zoe Dod Clair Alden Naomi Wilkinson

COLSTON'S GIRLS' SCHOOL

Centenary Year 1991

THE CONTRIBUTORS

SARAH DUNN, Head Mistress of the School 1954–1980, researched and wrote the majority of the History. Educated at Barr's Hill School, Coventry, St Hugh's College, Oxford and Leeds University she has, since her retirement, been a member of the Bristol Bench and a prime mover in the University of the Third Age.

MARGARET SWINDALE contributed much of the History 1954–80. She joined the teaching staff of the School in 1946 and retired as Head of History in 1981. She was educated at the Mary Datchelor Girls' School, Camberwell, and Bedford College, University of London. In her retirement she attends University lectures and art classes and took a history group for U3A.

JILL CLOUGH contributed the section 1981–89. An Old Girl of the School, she took her degree at Queen Mary College, University of London, and her PhD at the University of Hull. She returned to teach in the English department from 1981 to 1987, leaving to take up the headship of the Royal Naval School, Haslemere, Surrey.

Additional material was contributed by JUDITH FRANKLIN, ANNE HUGHES and VIVIEN KIES, all current members of the Colston's Girls' School staff.

ACKNOWLEDGEMENTS

I am indebted to the Society of Merchant Venturers of Bristol for allowing me to study their archives; to the Governors of Colston's Girls' School for access to minute books, ledgers and papers kept in School; and to the Public Record Office in Kew, the Central Reference Library in Bristol and the Education Library of the University of Bristol. I received helpful advice and encouragements from Dr David Allsobrook, lecturer in the History of Education at University College, Cardiff, and from Miss Elizabeth Ralph, lately Bristol City Archivist.

A.M.S.D.

Thanks must go to Anne Doran and Pat Jorgensen without whose work on the manuscripts and proofs this publication would not have been possible. Particular thanks must go to Lesley Harrison who has lived for two years with nine head mistresses, innumerable bishops, chairmen and Merchants and who has coaxed and chivvied an ever-increasing number of words into a coherent whole.

J.P.F.

INDEX

Abbot, Mrs. H.M., 28, 36, 45, 68, 71, 101
Abyssinia
invasion by Italy, 137
Academic results, 119-120
Academic standards
Miss Dunn, and, 172
Accommodation problems, 188-189
Adams, Dr. Barfield, 65
Address
Miss Hughes, and, 50
Administrative work
increase in, 58-59
Advanced Courses, 99-100, 173
Redland High School, 100-101
Agostini, Miss, 192
"Aided" School, proposal for
effect, 150-151
Aided status
Application for, 150, 152, 156
grant of, 164
Alford, Rev. G.J., 28, 29, 53, 68, 85
Allen, Mrs. Brenda, 194, 212
Allsobrook, Dr. David, 223
American Field Scholarship Scheme, 175
Anchor Society, 173
Andrews, Miss, 31
Annexe, 105, 219
Anroux, Mlle Renée, 121
Anstruther, Miss Edith, 62
Art Room, 60, 62
Art Union, 63
Assembly Hall - see Hall
Assistant mistresses
appointment, 30, 37
duties, 31
quality, 31
Athletic Sports, 67, 86
Athletics, 48, 177
Attendance Prizes, 37
Attorney General
action against Society of Merchant Venturers, 3
Audio-visual teaching aids, 136
Awdry, Mr. Simon, 182
Axford, Mr. Michael, 219
Baker, Mr. Arthur, 27, 62, 65
Bangor, Dean of, 80
Bathurst, Hon. W.R.S., Chairman of Governors, 181, 183, 184, 198
resignation, 183
Batten, Lily, 56, 96
Bazaar Working Parties, 117-118
Beacall, Miss, 113
Beare, Miss Sylvia, 200
Bernays, Mrs. Robert, 183
Berrill, Councillor, 180
Berry, Miss H.M., 144, 145
Bhopalsingh, Lisa, 215
Bicycle factory, 71
Birch, Marjorie, 88
Birthday celebrations, 1981, 199
1991, 221
Bishop, Miss, 158
Black, Miss, 120
Blake, Miss, 46
Board of Education
numbers of pupils, and, 61
pamphlet dealing with grants and recognition, 45
recognition of School, 54
Boarding
fee, 112
Bodleian Villa, 74
Bombshells - School Play, 221
Bond, Margaret, 198
Books
unsuitable, 74
Boughton, Miss, 192
Bowell, Barbara, 132, 192
Brandon Hill School, 11
Brazier, Rev. Ray, 178
Brierley, Miss Edith, 31, 32, 38
Bristol Bordeaux Exchange visits, 168
Bristol Cathedral, 143, 172
Bristol Cathedral School, 176
Bristol City Council, 219
Bristol Corporation
transfer of equipment from, 184
Bristol Development Plan, 157
Bristol Education Authority Development Plan, 179-180

INDEX

refusal of School to co-operate with, 179-182
Bristol Education Committee, 77
Bristol Grammar School, 10, 24
Bristol Municipal Charities, 10
Bristol Trade School, 1, 13, 14, 17, 18, 19, 20
Bristol Youth Group, 145
British Empire Exhibition, 118-119
Britton, Mr. Jack, 182, 183, 191
Britton, Mrs Monica, 182, 183, 191
Brock, Dame Dorothy, 158
Brown, Mr. Arthur, 45
Browne, G.F., Bishop of Bristol, 57, 76, 107
books, on, 77
speaker, as, 77, 81
Browne, Miss Patricia, 201, 205
Bryant, Molly, 173
Building regulations, 157, 161
Bunce, Mrs. Alice Mary Wensley, 36, 37, 53, 56, 78, 111
Bunce, Miss G.W., 57
Burn, Mr. J.A.S., Chairman of Governors, 206, 222
Burnett, Miss, 152
Burnham Committee, 84
foundation of, 103
Bursaries
fund-raising efforts of Miss Parkin, 212-213
Bursary Fund, 185
Burton, Miss Bridget, 218, 220
Burton, Miss A.L., 120, 137
Butcher, Elizabeth, 214
Butcombe organ, 96-97
Butler, R.A., 147
Byrt, Alderman, 142
Byrt, Kathleen, 142
Byrt, Mary, 142

Careers education, 205
Caretaker
appointment, 33
Carey, Dr. George, Bishop of Bath and Wells, Archbishop of Canterbury Elect, 221
Centenary building
plans for, 219
Centenary Day, 221-222
address by Mrs Franklin, 222
Assembly, 221-2
Chadwick, Miss
90, 107
Chard, Mrs. Judy, 179, 194
Charity, 66, 118, 209
Charity Commission, 15, 18, 19, 20, 23, 25
raising school fee, and, 39
Charter Day service, 173
Cheltenham Ladies' College, 113
Cheltenham Road
degeneration of area, 204
purchase of 180d, 132
Cheltenham Road site, 20-21
cost of developing, 24
delay in building on, 23-24
development of, 20-22
noise, 60
Choral performances, 176
Chown, F., 73
Christmas parties, 53
Church of England, 11, 70-71, 163, 164
Church School Proposal, 161-162
Churches
expeditions to, 75
City Architect
survey 1948, 160
Civics and Current Affairs
talks by Miss Morgan, 131
Clarendon, Lord, 5
Clark, Miss Elspeth, 120, 121
Clarke, Mr. Charles, 121, 179, 181
Clarke, Mr. Cyril C, Chairman of Governors, 109, 110, 117, 135, 142, 160, 161, 162, 171, 178, 179
bowl, presentation of, 110
loans, on, 128
opening of pavilion, 109
relationship with Church, 162
retirement, 178-179
Clarke, Olga, 110
Clarke, Dr. Richard, 110, 142, 165, 171
Clarke, Mr. R.S.W., Chairman of Governors, 184, 191
Class singing, 36
Classics Department
visit to Italy 1956, 175
Clewett, Miss Kay, 198, 201
Clifton College, 10
Clifton High School, 18, 32
Closure of school, proposed, 151
Clothes rationing, 168
Clough, Dr. Jill, 194, 229
Clubs and societies, 177-178, 187-188
Clutterbuck, Miss, 137
Clutton, Miss, 113, 114, 116, 137, 140
Cockin, Rt. Revd. 162
Co-education, 190, 222
Coldthurst, Mr. Arthur Bendon, 95, 96

INDEX

Collegiate School, 222
Collins, Mr., 84, 88, 90
Colston Cottage, 61
Colston Cupboard, 67
Colston, Edward, 1, 2, 3, 11, 14, 39, 51, 54, 70, 95, 163, 172, 173, 178, 184, 222
Colston Nominees, 12
Colston Settlement, 1. *See also* Scheme
Colston Hospital Trust, 15, 150
  income 1906, 69-70
Colston Trustees, 10, 19, 20, 24, 154
Colston's Boarding School, 22, 222
  creation of, 16
  Governors, 16-17
Colston's Girls' School, 1, 3, 6, 14, 17-20
  building - design of, 21-22
  Governing Board
  establishment of, 26
  first meeting, 27
  postponement of establishment, 18
  opening of, 26, 35
  public examinations
  adoption of, 38
  School examination, 38
  site, 21, 24, 25-26, 218
  Society of Merchant Venturers as Trustees, 2
Colston's Hospital, 1, 2, 6, 10, 11, 12-13, 16
Commemoration Plays, 173, 192
  'Misrule', 194
Commemoration Day, 53, 78
Commemoration Service, 1, 143, 172
Commercial subjects, 57
Committee of Inquiry into Charities, 3-5, 11, 13, 15, 17-21, 23, 25, 39, 44
Community policeman, 204
Confirmation, 178
Cookson, Mr. (His Majesty's Inspector), 76
Cornish, Rev. Charles E., 28, 68
Cosh, Joyce, 96
Cot Secretary, 66-67
Cricket club, 48
Cross, Mr. David, 179
Culverwell, Mrs. 112
Curriculum, 28, 46, 48-49
  changes during 1980s, 201, 203
  courses 1989, 215
  statement of policy 1990, 218

Dahl, Miss, 65
Dale, Miss, 47
Dame schools, 4
Davies, Miss Emily (Founder of Girton College, Cambridge), 6, 9
Davies, Hilda, 132
Davies, Mr. Vaughan, 176
Davis, Miss Marjorie, 200
Design Technology, 211, 213
Desks
  design of, 32
Dieppe, Professor Paul, 221
Dining room
  overcrowding, 85
Diocesan Education Committee, 162-163
Direct Grant List
  removal of School, from, 147-148, 151
Direct Grant Schools, 146
Direct Grant status
  transition to Aided status, 158
Doctor, 65-66
  examinations by, 65-66
Dolphin block, 139, 189
  additional floor, 205
Dolphin Society, 173
Domestic science, 73
Door monitor, 64
Doran, Miss Anne, 230
Drains, 94
Drama, 186
  development of, 111
Drawing
  external examinations, 87
Drawing room, 63
Drew, Miss Helen, Head Mistress, 115, 116, 117, 118, 119, 120, 122, 123, 125, 127, 133
  appointment, 115
  background, 115
  death of, 121
  leave of absence, 120
Drill Room, 83
Duke of Edinburgh's Award Scheme, 178
Dunkirk, 140
Dunn, Miss A.M.S., Head Mistress, 170, 171, 172, 173, 174, 175, 178, 179, 183, 188, 190, 191, 192, 193, 194, 198, 201, 229
  background, 170
  retirement, 192

Eberle, Mr. Victor (Master of the Society of Merchant Venturers), 120
Economic depression, 116, 130
Economic independence
  Miss Hughes, and, 56

INDEX

Edith Openshaw Scholarship Fund, 125, 126, 174
Education
  political significance during 1980's, 203
Education Act 1918, 101-102
Education Act 1944, 146, 153
Education Reform Act 1988, 217
Edwards, Miss, 51, 52, 64, 74, 75, 77, 78, 79, 81, 82, 83, 86, 96, 113
Edwards, Mrs. Greville, 103
Edwards, Mrs. Joyce, 221
Edwards, Mr. Ralph, 147, 159, 167, 174
Elementary Education Act 1870, 4
Eleven Plus, 154, 164
Eleven year olds
  complaints as to, 165
Empire League, 49
Endowed schools, 4, 5-6
Endowed Schools Commission, 1, 6, 10, 12, 15
  negotiations with Society of Merchant Venturers, 12-13
  transfer of powers to Charity Commission, 15
Entrance Examination, 35
  fee for, 91
Etiquette, 52
Examinations
  half-termly and termly, 67
Exchanges, 168, 175, 185-186
Exhibitions, 37-38, 40
External examinations
  results 1927, 124

Fairfield Higher Grade School, 40
Fancourt, Mrs. Mary, 33, 34, 35
Fancourt, Mr. Walter, 33, 34, 35
Farrow, Miss, 96
Fathers
  livelihood, 35
Faulkner, Dr. Kathleen, 142, 171
Field Club, 49
Field work, 185
'Fifty Years On' Reunion 1987, 214
Fire
  outbreaks, 204
Fire 1981, 193, 196-198
  Appeal, and, 198
  effect, 198
  fund-raising, 199
  insurance, 198
  rebuilding after, 199
Fisher, Rt. Hon. H.A.L., 113
Fitch, Mr. Joshua (Inspector), 6, 10, 11, 12, 14, 15, 17, 21, 23, 24, 29, 35, 69, 107
  criticism of, 11
  criticisms made by, 6-7
  first grade schools, on, 7
  second grade schools, on, 7-8
  third grade schools, on, 8-9, 10
Flower Clubs, 52
Flower Show, 67
  abolition by Miss Sparks, 87
Food rationing, 152-153
Foreign travel, 131
Form committees, 111
Form Magazine, 50
Form 18 Schools, 156, 162
Forms
  promotion to, 35
Forward, Mrs. Gillian, 194
Foundationers, 16, 17
Foundation Scholarships, 68
Foundations, 72-73
  'soft spots', and, 72-73
Fowler, Miss, 155
Franklin, Mrs. Judith Penelope, Head Mistress, 217, 221, 229
  background, 217
French
  development of teaching, 48
Froebel Institute, 64, 144
Froebel training department, 155
Furniture, 30, 32

Gadd, Barbara, 132
Gamble, Rev. John, 126
Gamble Scholarships, 132, 174
Games, 187
  importance of, 177
Games Club, 48
Gatcliff, Captain Geoffrey, 79, 80
Gatcliff Memorial, 96, 125
Gay, Sarah, 220
Geddes, Sir Eric, 116
General Certificate of Education, 166
  Advanced Level, 166
  Ordinary Level, 166
G.C.S.E.
  implications, 211-212
  introduction of, 202
General Election 1974, 188
General Inspection, 1914, 86-87
  Report on, 86-87

INDEX

General Inspection
  1922, 111
  1947, 160
  1963, 180
General Strike, 120
General Studies, 205
George, Mr.Charles William, 73, 74
George V., King
  death of, 134
German
  introduction of, 48
Geyl, Mrs. Jenny, 194
Gibbon, Miss Enid, 111, 112, 113, 116, 122, 137, 191
  retirement, 191-192
Gibbs, Mrs. Ann, 194
Gillard, Miss, 113, 192
Gilmour, Rachael, 206
Ginger, Mr., 117
Girls' Schools Association, 213
Gloucestershire County Council, 159
Goaman, Miss, 192
Golden Hill
  loss of playing field, 108-109
Golding, Madge, 92
Gordon, Mr. John, Chairman of Governors, 190, 191, 198
Gotch, Thomas Cooper, 179
Gough, W.V., 23, 25, 26, 44, 46, 61, 62
Governing Body
  first meeting, 27-29
  new, 1966, 184
  separation of, 55, 69
  setting up of, 26
Government Assisted Places Scheme, 197, 202, 214
Government money
  first acceptance, 45
Governors
  Foundation, 149, 156, 164, 180
  Representation, 149, 180
  relationship with staff, 206, 220
Graduated system of schools, 7-10
Grateful Society, 173
Great Pornography Scandal, 40-41
Green, Miss (now Dame) Mary, 51, 147, 150, 153, 154, 155, 158, 159, 160, 163, 165, 166, 167, 168, 171, 179
  background, 150
  resignation, 168-169
Greenacre, Mr. Francis, 179
Griffiths, Dr., 145
Griffiths, Mr. James, 57
Grimshaw, Mr. John, 219
Guest, Clara, 221
Gulf War, 221
Gymnasium
  destruction by fire, 198
  erection of, 117
  need for, 83, 115
  plans for, 116-117
  separate, proposal for, 84
Gymnastics, 48, 84

Hall
  extension, plans for, 128
  improvements 1971, 189-190
  rebuilding of roof 1948, 167-168
Hamer, Mr., 198
Harding, Mrs., 192
Harrison, Mrs. Lesley, 230
Harvey, Mr. R.R.S., 183
Hayes, C.A., 46
Head Mistress
  advertisement for, 28-29, 43, 80-81, 115, 122, 170
  need for appointment by Governors, 158
  salary of, 79
Health
  Miss Dunn, and, 171
Heating, 49
  advice from Department of Energy, 199-200
Helen Drew Loan Fund, 125
Hiatt Baker, Mrs., 129
Higher School Certificate, 99
Hill, Eva Saint (pupil teacher), 36
Hinksman, Miss Helen, 205
Hobhouse, Mr Arthur, 6
Hobhouse, Mr Henry, 57
Hockey, Club, 47
Holidays
  postwar, 168
Honour Day, 52, 119
Horne, Miss, 137
Hoskins, Mrs. Olive, 194
Hospital
  meaning, 1
Hospital Schools, 6, 10
Houghton, Minnie, 67
'House Beautiful', 52
House Captains, 106
House system, 105-106
Houses
  reduction to four, 187

INDEX

Housekeeper
  appointment, 33
Hughes, Miss Anne, 201, 219, 229
Hughes, Miss Evangeline (Head Mistress), 43-56, 58-61, 63-79, 80, 81, 85, 87, 92, 94, 96, 97, 98, 105, 106, 111, 115, 118, 123, 126, 149, 155
Hughes, Williams Rev., 43
Hunt, Mr. Hubert, 97
Hunt, Mrs. Marion, 194
Hunter, Miss Elizabeth, 201

Independent status, 182, 183, 204, 218
  Parents consulted on, 151
Industry Project, 209-210
Industry Year, 209
Industry Year in Avon, 210-211
Information Technology, 211, 219
Instrument and Articles of Government
  proposed, 156
International Day, 220
International League, Association of, 120
Ison, Miss, 46, 49
Italy
  invasion of Abyssinia, 137

Jacob, Sir Ian, 172
James, Mr. R.C., 72, 84, 88, 103, 104, 117, 129, 133, 141
James, Mrs. Edith, 94, 112
James, Mr. John, 183, 197, 199
James, Miss, 46
James-Nix, Kitty, 88
Jenkins, Priscilla, 170, 173, 192
Jenner, Miss Eveline, 185, 199, 206
John Gordon Sports Hall, 198, 199
John James Scholarships, 206
Jones, Miss Pat, 195
Jones, Miss Sheila, 206
Jorgensen, Mrs. Pat, 230
Jose, William Wilberforce (Chairman of Governors), 27, 40, 45, 48, 60, 68, 71, 73, 78, 95, 96
Jubilee Year, 140-141
Junior School
  number of pupils, 154
  Prizegiving for, 131
  problems, 154-156
Junior School Management Committee, 155

Kies, Miss Vivien, 229
Kindergarten, 62, 63, 64, 128
King, Mr. Mervyn Kersteman (Chairman of Governors), 27, 48, 68, 95, 108, 117, 120, 135
Kippin, Mrs. Heather, 194
Kitchen
  new 1931, 129
Kohler, Elsie, 88

Laboratories, 44, 45, 46
  need to improve, 202
  new 1935, 134
Latin
  choice of, 87
  re-introduction, 48
  removal from curriculum, 39
  School Certificate results, 119
League of Nations Union, 131
Lewis, Mrs. Ann, 194
Lewellen, Miss Barbara, 176, 201
Library, 49
  new accommodation 1907, 62
Library Committee, 64
Library President, 65
Littler, Mrs. Jean, 194
Littleton, Marjorie, 111
Local education authorities
  grants 1919-1922, 102
  role of, 69
London
  visit 1946, 153
Lord, Mrs. Jean, 205
Loveday, Dr. Thomas, 134
Lunches, 63, 85-86, 203, 204-205
Lyttleton, Lord, 6

McElderry, Miss A.L., 73
Mackay, Mrs., 194
Management training scheme
  headteachers, for, 207
Marketing, 203
Martin, Mrs. Eva, 200
Martin, Mr., 193
Mathematics
  size of classes, 123
Mellor, Beatrice, 75
Merchant Venturers, Society of, 2, 15
  action by Attorney General against, 3
  alterations to Scheme, and, 14
  appointment of Beadle, 2
  gift of pavilion, 109
Navigation School, 13
Merchant Venturers Technical College, 13-14
Meredith, Mr., 141

INDEX

Merriman, Miss Anne, 49, 78, 113, 120
Merrison, Lady, 222
Middleton, Mrs., 153
Modern Languages
  interest in, 173, 220
Morale of teaching profession, 206-207
Morgan, Miss Gladys Mary, Head Mistress, 122-130, 132, 134-143, 147, 150, 152, 155, 157, 163, 179
  achievements during first four years, 130
  first impressions, 122
  formal complaint in relation to builders, 134
  resignation, 147
Morgan, Miss Marea, 195, 219, 220
Mortimer, Mrs. Nicola, 194
Mortimer, Victoria, 198
Mottoes, 50
Murphy, Miss, 192
Music
  importance of, 176, 186, 201
Musical Society, 49

National Curriculum, 217-218
National Foundation for Educational Research
  whole staff appraisal, 211
New building 1902, 46-47
New building 1914
  proposals for, 88, 89
New building 1919
  proposal, 104
New Zealand
  visit of Prime Minister, 101
Nickless, Mrs. Leona, 173, 194
Norwood, Dr. Cyril, 77

Oatley, Sir George, 125
O'Brien, Nora, 91
Old Girls - Professions of, 200
Old Girls' Society, 53
  Annual General Meeting and Dance, 54
  May Ball 1991, 221
  support for school, 149, 201
Openshaw, Miss Edith Mary, 32, 37, 41, 43, 57, 58, 59, 61, 64, 68, 74, 80, 88, 89, 90, 93, 94, 95, 96, 97, 102, 103, 105, 118, 120, 122, 123, 124, 125, 126
Openshaw, Grace, 125
Openshaw, Rev. Thomas W., 32
Ord, Mrs. E.M., 57, 78
Osborne House
  acquisition of, 144
Osborne, Jere, 21, 25
Outdoor games
  fees, 108-109
Oxford University
  admission of women, 107

Page, Miss, 113, 135, 137, 192
Palin, Miss, 78, 85, 90, 111, 112, 113, 137
Parkin, Miss Ann (Head Mistress), 192, 193, 194, 195, 196, 197, 199, 202, 203, 207, 208, 209, 210, 211, 214, 215, 216
Parents, 218
Parents' Association, 144
  support for school, 149
Parsons, Marion, 137
  background, 193
Pavilion
  opening 1921, 109
Pearce, Mr., 71
Pedley, Mrs., 152
Pension scheme
  proposed introduction of, 59
Percival, Rev. Dr. John, 10
Perry, Mrs. Elizabeth, 194
Phillips, Miss, 136
Pick, Miss, 192
Pienkorska, Miss Maria, 173
Pilkington, Sir Alistair, 202, 208
Playing field
  developments during thirties, 135
Pleasaunce, 61-62, 110, 128
  weaknesses in retaining wall, 134
Poisson, M., 48
Pope, John Noble Coleman, 27
Pope, Mr. George Henry, 20, 21, 28, 59
Pope, Mrs. George Henry, 28, 68, 198
Poplar Grove, 72, 219
Potts, Miss, 51, 54
Powell, Mr. A.C., 75, 96, 97, 125, 126, 128, 130
Prefectorial system, 51
Preparatory School, 63
Prize Giving, 67, 172
  Junior School, for, 131
  1901, 55
  1912, 77
  1991, 221
Proctor Baker, Mr. William, Chairman of Governors, 20, 21, 27, 28, 33, 40, 41, 55, 68, 126
Public examinations, 38
Public functions
  reduction of, 87
Public Schools, 4, 5, 98

INDEX

Pugsley's Yard, 139
Punishments, 37
Pupils, number of, 60-61
  1890, 34
  1898, 40
  1903, 58
  1913, 78, 83
  1914, 89
  1918, 103
  1922, 111, 123
  increase 1948, 167
Pupils
  livelihood of fathers, 35

Queen Elizabeth's Hospital, 10, 12
'Quiet work'
  Miss Sparks, and, 111

Railway company
  negotiations with, 71
Ralph, Miss Elizabeth, 230
Rashley, Miss Evelyn, 122, 123, 125, 126, 137, 142, 150, 155, 158, 191, 192
Rawcliffe, Mrs. Sheila, 190
Reading Club, 49
Recitations, 116
Red Maids' School, 10, 11, 12, 19
Redland Court Estate
  acquisition of, 108
Redland High School, 18
  proposal to integrate Advanced Courses, 100-101
  removal from Direct Grant List, 151
Reese, Mrs. Jenny, 194
Rennison's Baths, 110
Richards, Mrs., 198, 209
Richardson, Mrs. Yda, 129
Robbins Report, 172
Robertson, Mr. Samuel, 20, 21, 61
Robinson, Canon Hugh, 6, 15
Robinson, Mr. T. Lloyd, 190
Roby, Henry, 6
Rogers, Miss, 136
Rolls Royce, 219
Routledge, Mrs. Rosemary, 194
Russian, introduction of, 173
Ryland, Mr. Charles Julius (Schools Auditor), 59, 64, 65, 68, 73, 74, 76, 77, 175
Ryland bequest, 68, 73-74
Ryland library, 75
  inventory, 75
  bombing of, 76, 141
  demolition of, 142
  formal opening, 76
  furniture, 75-76
  new, proposals for, 72
  reconstruction of, 174
  re-opening of, 175
  unsuitable books, 74

Salaries, 24-25
Salmon, Muriel, 95
Scheme 1875
  revision, need for, 54
Scheme 1910, 68
  proposed amendment, 93
Scheme 1936, 135
School administration, 94-95
  improvement, 98
  Miss Sparks, and, 94-95
School Association, 173
School Auditor, 59
School Bazaars, 129
School Captain, 51
School Certificate, 99
School Council, 111
School day
  reshaping of, 87, 218
School Examination, 38
School fees, 24, 30, 39
  increase 1913, 85
  increase proposed, 152
  level 1966, 184
  Miss Hughes, and, 70
  raising, 44
School finances, 38, 39
  improvement in situation 1934, 133
  loans, 62, 84, 104, 133
  Miss Drew, and, 118
  money raising 1930/31, 129
  outgoings, scrutiny, 127
  situation 1927, 124
  sources 1914-1916, 92-93
School leaving age
  raising of, 165
School magazine, 48, 51, 116, 188, 219, 220
  purpose of, 51
School magazine 1982, 200
School Museum, 49-50
School newspaper, 50
School orchestra, 186-187
School plays, 176
School prospectus, 184-185
School Sub-Captain, 51

INDEX

Science Club, 187
Science teaching, 45, 46, 213, 218
  improvement in accommodation, 133
Scott, Dr., 101
Second Mistress
  allocation of post, 207-208
  appointment, 51
  duties of, 220-221
Security
  problems during 1980's, 204
Selection of pupils
  Local Education Authority, by, 164
  power of, 159
Senior management team, 211
'Setting'
  introduction by Miss Sparks, 88
Shell
  introduction of, 58
Short, Hilda, 132
Shorthand and typewriting
  introduction of, 56
Singing
  development of, 111
Single European Market 1992, 220
Single-sex schools
  importance of, 202-203
Singleton, Mrs. Brenda, 194
Sisman, Claire, 214
Sixth Form
  number of pupils 1947, 166
Sixth Form Block, 190-191
Sixth Form Government Assisted Places, 213, 214-215
Sixth Form Play, 131
Sixth Form Room
  new accommodation 1907, 62
  1981, 190-191
Sixth Form Seminars, 205
Six-lesson day
  experimentation with, 145
Skeet, Miss, 128, 136
Sloper, Miss Ann, 200
Smith, Miss Annie, 36, 41
  appointment, 36
Smith, Miss Georgina Amy, Head Mistress, 29, 30, 31, 34, 36, 37, 38, 40, 41, 44, 46, 47, 48, 53, 54, 55, 65, 66, 94, 137
  appointment, 28, 29
resignation, 41
Smith-Keith, Mrs. Anne-Marie, 194
Social education
  Miss Hughes, and, 52
Somerset Education Committee, 69, 159, 179
Social status
  Miss Hughes, and, 56
Spanish - introduction of, 173
Spanish Civil War, 137
Sparks, Miss Beatrice Margaret, Head Mistress, 81, 83, 84, 85, 86, 87, 88, 89-94, 95-98, 100-103, 105-109, 111-115, 118, 119, 122, 123, 131, 137, 150, 164, 168
  background, 83
  death of, 114
  improvement, attempts at, 93
  printed letters from, 91
  resignation, 113
Specialist teaching
  introduction of, 13
Sports Day
  1924, 119
  1954, 177
Spraggett, Miss, 137
Staff
  commitment to School, 191-192, 194-195
  health of, 136
  length of time teachers staying on, 112-113
  rapid turnover, 136
  representation on Governing Body, 220
  study day, 211
Staff salaries, 37
  cuts, 116
  dissatisfaction with, 78-79
  inadequacy 1919, 102-103
  increase, 1917/1918, 98
  Miss Dunn, and, 171
  Miss Sparks' proposal, 84
  scale, introduction of, 84-85
  scales, proposal as to, 59
  war bonus, 102
Stafford, Miss, 114, 115, 116
State Scholarships, 174
Stockwood, Rev. Mervyn, 161
Stokes, Mr., 44
Stokes, Mrs., 44
Stoneley, Miss Jeanne, 168, 192
Stoodley, Miss, 113, 120, 121
Street, Mrs., 113
Stress
  staff, of, 136
Strong, Sir Vezey, 81
Studio, 62
Swedish drill, 48, 65
Swimming, 48, 177
Swindale, Miss Margaret, 229

Sykes, Mr., 57
Sylvester, Mr. George H., 147, 159, 160, 180, 181, 183

Tai, Fung, 188
Tanner, Mrs. Mary, 214
Tanner, William, 25
'Tapering', 151-152
Taunton Commission, 5
Taylor, Miss 'Fish', 113
Taylor, Miss C.I., 136
Technology
  significance, 219-220
Tennis
  introduction of, 48
Terms, 30
Tests, weekly, 67
Thatcherism, 195
Thomas, Mr. Josiah, 20
Tickner, Nicola, 206
Timetable skills, 127
Training College, places in, 172
'Transitionally-aided' status, 158
Travel to school, 112
Tuckey, G.F., 25
Tuson, Miss, 192
Typewriters
  introduction of, 56

UCCA, 174
Unity Street premises, 19-20
Universities
  numbers of girls entering, 77-78, 132, 166, 214, 215
Upton Lodge, 141-142, 143

Votes for women, 82, 107

Wadge, Amy, 215
Wait, Miss M.E., 28, 60, 68, 96
Walters, Miss E.L., 46, 47
Ward, Mr. W.W., 110
Ware, Mrs., 200
Wathen, Lady, 28
Welfare State, 146
  effect of, 153
Whitaker, Doris, 110
Whitaker, Gwen, 110
White, Dorothy, 55, 198
White, Mrs. Sheila, 198
Wilkins, Mr. Frank, 129
Wilkinson, Ellen, 147
Williams, Alderman F.C., 148
Williams, Essylt, 43
Williams, Mrs. Jean, 195
Williams, Mr. John, 222
Williams, Sian, 198
Wills, Mr. Melville W., 128
Wilson, Miss L.E., 136
Wing, Miss Eileen, 94
Wolfson Foundation, 213
Women
  unsuitability of speaking in public, 55
Women into Science and Engineering, 207
Women teacher's
  marriage, effect of, 113
Woodward, Colonel John Henry, 27, 68, 71
World War I, 80
  Armistice, 107-108
  Circular 903, 89
  deaths, 95
  declaration, 88
  effect, 97-98, 105
  effect on loan interest, 89
  effect on School, 90-91
  film shows, 106
  food shortages, 97
  holidays, 105
  Lighting Regulations, 93-94
  public lectures, 106
  response to declaration, 90
  Roll of Honour, 91
  women, effect on, 92
World War II
  air raid precautions, 137-139
  air raids, 141-141
  March 16, 1941, 141-142
  BBC radio news, 145
  evacuation, 142-143
  normality of School life, and, 143
  outbreak, 138
  'phoney war', 140
  'summer school', 140

Young Enterprise Scheme, 220
Young, Baroness, 221